D0655127

Elizabeth Jenkins
The MYSTERY OF KING ARThUR

Michael Joseph Limited, London

First published in Great Britain by
Michael Joseph Limited
52 Bedford Square, London WC1B 3EF
1975

All rights reserved. No part of this
publication may be reproduced or
transmitted in any form or by any means
including photocopy, recording, or any
information storage and retrieval system
now known or to be invented, without
permission in writing from the publisher
except by a reviewer who wishes to quote
brief passages in connection with a review
written for inclusion in a magazine, newspaper
or broadcast.

© Elizabeth Jenkins 1975

ISBN 0 7181 1171 0

This book was designed and produced by
George Rainbird Limited
Marble Arch House
44 Edgware Road
London W2 2EH

House editor: Yorke Crompton
Picture research: Victoria Nicolson, John Henderson,
  Andrea Stern
Design: Margaret Thomas
Index: Ellen Crampton

Printed and bound by Jarrold & Sons Limited, Norwich
Colour plates and jacket originated and printed
by Westerham Press Limited, Kent

REVERSE OF FRONTISPIECE From a
fourteenth-century French MS.: Arthur in
combat with the Emperor of Rome, and
BELOW the wedding night of Arthur and
Guinevere

FRONTISPIECE 'The Achieving of the
Sangreal'. The final quest that broke up the
Companionship of the Round Table:
Aubrey Beardsley's frontispiece to Malory's
Morte D'Arthur

To A. L. Rowse
great historian and *cher maitre*

Colour Plates

Throughout the book,
a number in **bold** type refers to
the page facing a colour plate

Contents

In the text and picture-captions, words like
Grail and Igraine sometimes appear with a
variant spelling taken from the source concerned.
Any question of identity can be settled by
reference to the index.

The sea at Tintagel, above which, in the
castle of the Duke of Cornwall, Arthur is
said to have been conceived

1 Britain before Arthur

All life began in water; this land was once under water; the story of Arthur, the
hero of its longest-lived and most potent legend, is seen against water. He was said
to have been conceived at Tintagel, therefore in the sound of terrific seas; to have
reclaimed Britain from its barbarian invaders in twelve great battles, five of which
were fought on the shores of rivers; to have been mortally wounded during civil
war in a battle fought, again, on a river; to have resigned his sword Excalibur to a
water spirit, whose arm rose out of a lake to take it back, and to have been borne
away across water, dying but never to die.

This story has maintained an extraordinary power over the minds of the varied
races of our ancestors for more than fourteen hundred years, and it enthralled them
before it had been written down. They saw Arthur on the earth, where hillsides,
caves, boulders and streams bore his name; they saw him in the sky, where they
called the glittering Great Bear 'Arthur's Wain', and Arcturus, the fastest-moving
of all the brighter stars, they saw as another symbol of his name; they heard him in
the air, naming the wind after him:

> Arthur o'Bower has broken his band
> And he comes roaring up the land;

and they replaced Odin with him as leader of the Ride of the Dead, who collects
the souls and rides with them through the air at night, an idea that probably
originated in the high flight of the wild geese, the 'Gabriel Hounds', who utter
weird cries as they stream across the sky at twilight. They projected his image
into the Other World. A legend from the Book of Taliesin, the Welsh bard of the
mid-sixth century, is called *The Spoils of Annwyn*, and relates that Arthur and his
companions, carried in his boat Prydwen, sailed to Annwyn, the Other World, to
bring away a magic cauldron 'blue at the rim with pearls'; clearly it was imagined
as a superb piece of enamel and jewel-work, arts at which the Celts excelled at a
surprisingly early date. The Fortress of the Other World is seen as one of glass
battlements, manned by mute defenders who will not answer the besiegers.

To assess our favourite myth, to decide how much is historical truth, how the
legend developed and why it has had such a hold on our imagination, it is right to
look at some of the remote past which contributed to its colouring.

When the tropical climate in which the dinosaurs, the 'terrible lizards', had
lived, became temperate, men came from what is now the continent of Europe.

They came on foot, for, except a narrow stream, the English Channel was dry ground, and the Irish Sea a small edition of its present self. The stories in the collection of Welsh tales called the Mabinogion were not written down till the tenth century, but one of them, *Branwen, Daughter of Llyr*, contains a trace of indescribable antiquity: 'We sailed towards Ireland and in those days the deep water was not wide.' The fourth and last ice age destroyed the invaders and the reindeer, hyenas, bears and wild horses which had migrated with them. Ice, hundreds of feet thick, moving down from Scandinavia, covered the land with its annihilating weight; when it dissolved, the land revealed was one of dense forests, inland lakes and overgrown marsh threaded with watercourses.

It was now entered by a new series of invaders, which, continuing as it did for the next twenty-five thousand years, makes one wonder how we acquired a reputation for insularity. The most gifted Celts from the Continent were the Gauls, who brought with them the art of making bronze weapons when they settled here in 2000 B.C. Their remains, excavated on Salisbury Plain, show that they traded widely, importing Italian wine and oil, Irish gold, Baltic amber and Egyptian blue glass beads. They left other traces of their mysterious contact with the East. Without mechanical aids, they erected on Salisbury Plain, between 1800 and 1400 B.C., the vast structure of Stonehenge, not only an astounding architectural feat, but an instrument for abstruse astronomical calculation. The final rebuilding consisted of a circle of eighty-one sarsen stones, some of them weighing thirty tons each; inside this a circle of blue stones from the Prescelly Mountains in Wales; inside this again, a horseshoe of pairs of stones with lintels laid across their tops; and inside this another horseshoe of upright blue stones, all joined by lintels. At the sight of these horizontal masses, so amazingly placed, the medieval historian Henry of Huntingdon described them as 'stones, as it were, hanging in the air'.

It is assumed that the structure was a temple of the sun. Professor Hawkins[1] has demonstrated that the great circular grove of massive stones provided a means of marking midsummer and midwinter and of exactly foretelling eclipses of the sun and moon. The vast, starry sky, the height and silence, must have made Stonehenge impressive beyond words; and that, through the pillars of one of the tri-lithons and above the Hele Stone, the movements of 'the great rulers of the day and night' could be predicted, invests it with an awe that holds us still.

After the decline of the unknown religion to whose gods Stonehenge had been raised, the Druids, who held a strong position in Gaul, proselytized the Celts in Britain and made a stronghold of Anglesey. They were called the Oak-knowers; they had established a mysterious relationship with trees and their temples were sacred groves. They had developed clairvoyant powers, and had so strong a belief in immortality, that life in this world and in the world to come were matters of equal conviction to them. They believed that life after death was sometimes lived on this earth still, in caves, or inside a hill, or across a wide water. These symbols of the afterlife were adopted as part of their beliefs by most Celtic peoples.

The development of supernatural faculties among the Celts seems to have some affinity with feats they achieved which, without evidence to the contrary, we should have said were impossible to a primitive people. Not only was Stonehenge erected; beyond it, in England, Wales, Scotland and Ireland, rise from their remains nearly three hundred stone circles; while, on the hillside above the Vale of Uffington in Berkshire, flies along the Uffington White Horse, a Celtic creation, cut out of the green hillside to expose the underlying chalk, a creature 360 feet long, evoked in seven lines: head, neck, back and four legs. Anyone who suggests that this is not a horse, but a dragon, can never have seen a racehorse in action. This creature is an inspiring sight to those who remember the importance of horses to the Britons, and the part played by horses in the victories of Arthur.

Some of the Celts whose ancestors had raised the gigantic stone circles, built for themselves great circular hill forts of earthwork, to shelter them against foreign invaders or hostile neighbours; in this way a local stability making civilized life possible was established. Those in marshy districts took refuge in a lake-village way of life, of which the remains at Glastonbury have been preserved by the action of peat. The sea of the Bristol Channel then came over the level ground between the Quantocks and the Mendip Hills. Around the base of Glastonbury Tor, the abrupt end of a ridge of hills at right angles to the southern end of the Mendip range, was a fresh-water marsh deepening to a lagoon. The inhabitants here raised an island of four acres, based on stones, faggots, rushes and peat and cased in logs.

Glastonbury, the legendary Glass Island,
rising from the moors of Somerset

Their skills in making objects for use and decoration were of a very high order. The Celtic idea of design was non-representational; they used a curve like the neck of a rolling wave. This idiom remained for centuries in the illumination of manuscripts, but it disappeared from other forms of art until it was resurrected in the late nineteenth century as *art nouveau*. Their imaginative quality was shown in their use of glass, a substance vulgarized by us, but in its early forms possessing for men a magical beauty. Its manufacture was known in Asia Minor in 4000 B.C. and it was being imported into Britain by 1800 B.C., but their kilns with the dregs remaining in them show that, of the glass beads for necklaces among the relics of the Glastonbury lake-dwellers, some at least, red, yellow and white, were made by themselves. The very early Celtic visions of the Other World are seen in terms of glass and air. Glastonbury itself was called Ynis Gutrin, the Glass Island, by 1130, but Loomis[2] says that the tradition of the Other World as a glass island is very much older. The association of Arthur's carrying away to another world was consistent with Glastonbury's name, the Glass Island.

The use of the name was a natural one. The Tor rose from, then, undrained marshes whose sheets of water reflected the sky. Water, mist and marsh-light create an ambience of unreality. The elements that make up a scene as an abode of the dead were there: a hill, an island, a ring of water, a defence, apparently, of glass. The Celtic population of the south-west of Britain had been formed chiefly by waves of invaders from Italy and Gaul, but their ideas, beliefs and folklore seem to have gained their magical, haunting quality from the atmosphere of Britain, where the air was often misty and the light had an uncertain radiance, rather than the perpetual clarity of Italy and France.

By 50 B.C. a fresh set of invaders from northern Gaul and western Germany, the rapacious, merciless Belgae, had worked their way through the Thames Valley and reached Somerset. Here they fell upon and destroyed the lake villages, whose remains are visible to us only from their preservation in waterlogged peat. Four years later occurred one of the most momentous events in the history of Britain, establishing the civilization which Arthur himself was heir to: Julius Caesar decided that the island must be brought within the Roman grasp.

At his initial reconnaissance, the sea played its first recorded part in the history of Britain. The fierce, offshore summer gales drove back the cavalry transports and wrecked many of the supply-ships. Used to the tideless Mediterranean, the Romans were dismayed by the powerful seas around Britain. Tacitus, writing a hundred years later under the governorship of Agricola, said of the northern parts of the island: 'Nowhere does the sea hold wider sway . . . in its ebb and flow it does not stop at the coast but penetrates deep inland and winds about, pushing its way among highlands and mountains.' In spite of the sea the Romans made good their footing, effecting a second landing with larger forces the following year. As a military commander of wide experience, Caesar was greatly impressed by the Britons' skill as drivers and managers of horses. He said: 'The British charioteers combine the mobility of cavalry with the staying power of infantry

A Roman highway running 'straight to the
horizon' over Blackstone Edge, Yorkshire

. . . even on a steep incline they are able to control their horses at full gallop, and
to check and turn them in a moment.' These were the people whose ancestors
had carved the White Horse above the Vale of Uffington.

Caesar's commitments had prevented him from establishing a thorough control
over Britain. This was achieved in A.D. 43 by the Emperor Claudius. His forces
disembarked at Richborough on the coast of Kent, where a massive marble
monument was erected to commemorate the Roman conquest. Its remains are
still standing, and it strikes a thrilling chord when the Anglo-Saxon Chronicle
writing of A.D. 450 says that a battle was fought 'near the inscribed stone by the
Gallic sea'. The implementation of Caesar's invasion of ninety years before was
now carried out with extreme thoroughness, securing the submission of Britain
from the south coast to a line between the Mersey and the Humber. The instrument
by which this was accomplished was the army of the Roman legions; it had made
Caesar master of the Roman world; its traditions were inherited by Arthur.

The soldier's armour was a bronze helmet and a bronze breastplate, worn over
a skirt of leather strips; their weapons were a short 'stabbing' sword and a throwing-
spear. As they were also engineers, they carried, as well as their martial equipment,
a saw, an axe, an entrenching tool and a wicker basket for transferring the soil
thrown up in their enormous operations of road-making, ditch-digging and the
erection of fortifications. Unlike the Celtic trackways, winding about and following
the configuration of the land, the Roman roads went straight to the horizon. They
were 25 feet wide, paved with stone or flint or gravel; over uncertain ground they
were carried on a causeway. These superb highways lasted the Britons for fifteen
hundred years. In 1670, Bunyan wrote a graphic description of villagers trying to
fill up the Slough of Despond, by tipping cartloads of rubble into it: allegorical in
intention, but based on the efforts of people attempting to carry out repairs to a
Roman road that had foundered at last.

It is easy to admire the Romans for their roads, their heating systems and
running water, and the beauty of their architecture, furniture and interior decoration that was the inspiration of the late eighteenth-century English houses, chairs,
chimneypieces, the loveliest this nation has ever produced. But the Romans, so
gifted, so practical, so self-controlled, maintained their supremacy by a merciless
cruelty. One of the most dreadful stories of the ancient world is the putting down
by Crassus of the rebellion of Spartacus in 73 B.C., when six thousand crosses with
their moaning burdens lined the Appian Way, to teach the lesson of a failed revolt.

The appearance of the legion on the march epitomized the qualities of Roman
civilization, maintaining the Pax Romana to the general benefit by a ruthless
authority. Preceded by archers and foot-soldiers, surveyors and pioneers, the
general and his staff rode with mounted escort, followed by the cavalry and by
mules carrying siege towers. Beside lances and swords, the Romans used arrows,
lead bullets thrown from slings and showers of stone balls shot from catapults.
Their traces were found in the skeletons of the defenders of Maiden Castle in
Dorset, reduced by Vespasian: bones cut by sword-blades, holes in skulls made by

throwing-spears, a bullet lodged in a spinal column. That anklets and toe-rings were clasping the foot-bones of the conquered shows that two civilizations had met on this formidable scene.

The resistance to Rome was not only of a martial kind. The Druids' settlement in Anglesey was recognized as a centre of disaffection, inspiring the dissident Welsh tribes with malevolence and hatred. So serious was the threat they posed, that in A.D. 59 the governor, Suetonius Paulinus, determined to crush the Druids before proceeding against the Welsh; he had barely done this, massacring the priests and felling the sacred groves, when he was recalled by a series of events which demonstrated the Celtic spirit that Arthur was heir to, as he was heir to the discipline of Rome.

Boadicea, the widow of the very wealthy Prasutagus, King of the Iceni, had been outraged by the Roman officials who came to collect the part of the dead King's wealth that was due to the Emperor. Meeting no doubt with aggression, they had flogged the Queen, raped her daughters and looted her palace. The neighbouring

16

tribe, the Trinovantes, were also seething with discontent. The rush of Boadicea's army to join the forces of the Trinovantes was the beginning of a conflagration. Colchester was levelled to the ground and its Roman inhabitants butchered with hideous savagery. The Ninth Legion, advancing from Lincoln, was routed and the victorious army set out for London. Suetonius received the alarm and came by forced marches from Anglesey; he brought the cavalry of the Fourteenth and Twentieth Legions; he could not wait for the infantry. *En route*, he sent to the Second Legion at Gloucester with orders to join him immediately, but their general was not there and his deputy, from caution or cowardice, refused to come.

When Suetonius reached London he was obliged to leave the panic-stricken inhabitants to their fate, so that he could consolidate his forces. Boadicea, in ferocious triumph, burned London to the ground, then turned north and attacked St Albans, where she called down a similar destruction. Suetonius now justified his policy of leaving the cities to their fate; a pitched battle was fought in a narrow valley, a site chosen by himself. Before the forces engaged, Boadicea, in a chariot with her two daughters, drove up and down the lines, exhorting and raving. The British had brought their families with them to witness the defeat of the tyrants, and the onlookers and loaded baggage wains formed a barrier at their back; the havoc wreaked by the Roman soldiers was complete because the enemy had no escape route. The frightful slaughter of the Britons culminated in the suicide of Boadicea; the prefect of the Second Legion who had refused to obey Suetonius's summons also killed himself. This episode, with its passionate hatred roused by intolerable wrongs, its terrific energy, bringing about a success that astounds the enemy, until the controlled forces of the opposite side inevitably defeat it at last, is characteristic of the Celtic temperament. Described as it is by two Roman historians, it is in sharp focus, brilliantly lit. Arthur's resistance to a foreign invader, four hundred years nearer to our own time, looms larger than life for being shrouded in mists.

The perpetual injury to Roman supremacy in Britain came, not from the native tribes, but from the Picts, who inhabited the north, and the Scots, a race who came from Ireland and eventually gave their name to the northern region. Forts to repel them were built between the estuaries of the Clyde and the Forth, and in the reign of the Emperor Hadrian, between A.D. 117 and 138, a tremendous feat of construction was accomplished. Hadrian's Wall, built of stone, stretched from the Solway to the Tyne; it was 76 Roman miles long, 10 feet wide and 15 feet high. Its remains are still a most stirring sight. Camden, who saw it in Queen Elizabeth's reign, wrote of it: 'Verily, I have seen the track of it over the high pitches and steep descents, wonderfully rising and falling.' This masterpiece of military architecture and the line of forts along the Cumberland shore enabled the Roman government to keep the northern marauders at bay, and a string of ten forts from the Norfolk coast down to Southampton was erected against the sporadic plunderers from Germany: the Angles, Saxons and Jutes.

The Roman conquest had introduced the Roman pantheon into Britain, and the

18

worship of these gods coexisted with the Celtic worship of immemorial ones, many of them tutelary deities of woods and streams. On the Antonine Wall, the great turf rampart built beyond Hadrian's Wall by the Emperor Antoninus Pius and completed in A.D. 142, there have been found remains of altars to gods and goddesses, not only of the Roman soldiers, but of foreign members of the legions; Baal and Astarte were worshipped in the bleak air of Scotland, and one altar was raised, with beautiful sympathy, to the Spirit of Britain. There was one, erected no doubt by cavalry men, to Epona, the goddess of grooms.

The Christian religion had been brought to Britain at some time during the second century A.D. A tradition says that Joseph of Arimathea landed in Somerset

with twelve companions about A.D. 60, and that it was they who built the little wattle-and-daub church, the *vetus ecclesia*, unquestionably one of the earliest Christian shrines in the country, which was afterwards enclosed in part of the original buildings of Glastonbury, all of which perished in the fire of 1186. At all events the establishment of Christianity in Britain was well authenticated by A.D. 200. The great advancer of the Christian faith in Britain was Constantine III, elected as Emperor by the Roman army in Britain, and famous as Constantine the Great. He determined to march on Rome and seize the imperial crown, for which there were several contenders. He took with him the legions that were garrisoning Britain and made a victorious expedition, inspired, it was said, by a vision in the sky of the monogram of the first three letters of the word 'Christ'. His edict of

Milan, of A.D. 313, granted toleration to Christianity in the Roman Empire. He moved his capital to Byzantium, which he renamed Constantinople.

Constantine's famous advance on Rome had been made on horseback, using the horse merely as a means of transport, as the Romans had used it for centuries. When the cavalry had been employed for fighting, mounted soldiers had acted as mere projectiles, charging through the enemy's ranks. When the Romans adopted the stirrup, first used by the Persians, they became, like their enemies, able to fight on horseback, instead of taking part in what was simply a mounted charge. Before the end of the fifth century the Romans had again borrowed from Persia the equipment of the Cataphractarii, in which horse and rider were protected by garments of chain mail, a material made of iron links which remained in use till it was superseded by the complete plate armour of the fourteenth century.

The barbarian threats to the frontiers of the Empire made it increasingly difficult for the Romans to send legions back to Britain to repel the invasions of the Saxons. In 368, however, they sent from Gaul a force under an exceptionally able general, Theodosius, accompanied by his son Theodosius, and the latter's young friend, Magnus Clemens Maximus. With a force of cavalry, against high numerical odds, they repulsed the Saxons and reconstituted the demoralized local government. This expedition was a demonstration of the power of cavalry against an unmounted adversary. Cavalry, again, gained an overpowering victory, this time against the Romans, for the Goths at Adrianople. After this crushing defeat, the Romans summoned young Theodosius to Rome and appointed him First Officer commanding the cavalry of the Empire, and Emperor of the East. His friend Maximus remained in Britain, putting down the Picts and Scots. His success made his soldiers worship him, and he collected the best part of the troops who should have stayed in Britain and set out with them to gain Rome for himself as his friend had gained Constantinople. From Gaul he sent back to Britain for the last of the troops who were manning Hadrian's Wall, and after their withdrawal the Wall was never manned again. Maximus marched on Rome and gained the city, but two years later he was killed in battle against his one-time friend Theodosius.

Though he had done irreparable harm to Britain by leaving her unprotected against the savages, and had gained such a short-lived victory for himself, Maximus commanded the wholehearted enthusiasm of the Celtic storytellers because he had conquered Rome. With his name debased to Macsen, he figures in one of the collections of Welsh tales in the Mabinogion, whose writing down was of course much later than its composition. Beram Saklatvala[3] points out that the history of Maximus accounts for the extraordinarily far-flung conquests ascribed to Arthur; Malory, writing in the fifteenth century, taking his material from much earlier writers, repeats that Arthur, in preparing to invade Rome, sent summons to Alexandria, India, Africa and Araby, Egypt, Damascus, Damietta, Cappadocia, Tarsus, Turkey, Pamphilia, Syria and Galatia. 'We are seeing, with the eyes of one of Maximus' veterans, the battle line of Theodosius, Emperor of the East. This list was one of the deep memories of the soldiers and their descendants.'

Effective Roman control of Britain is said to have died with Maximus. The beautiful, stately façade remained but a series of blows would bring it down. Local kings and tribal chieftains, living as a Celtic society with the cleanness and comfort of a Roman civilization, were now coexisting with small bodies of Saxon settlers, for whom, in the blissful emptiness of a land with a very small population, there was plenty of room. The Romanized inhabitants lived in their villas on the produce of their estates, worked for by their slaves. A flourishing trade between Britain and the Continent supplied them with wine and oil, dried fruit, jewellery, pottery, glass and silverware of a rich, elegant description. In the Roman-British galleries of the British Museum are the silver dishes chased with piping fawns and dancing nymphs, the glass urns and bowls of aqueous blue and dark emerald, the silver spoons and beakers, the iron-work braziers and window grilles, which were in use in Britain in the fourth and fifth centuries. As the loosening of Roman authority allowed the villa-owning class to evade taxation, the wealth and luxury of their households increased very much. At the same time the towns, lacking administration, began to decay. The instinct of self-defence caused the Britons not to refortify them, but to repair and adapt, wherever they were available, the great circular earthworks which had been constructed hundreds of years before.

A state of uneasy calmness was shattered in 395 by another invasion of the Barbarian Alliance, the Saxons, Picts and Scots. Rome dispatched another brilliant general, Stilicho, to aid the Britons. He drove off the invaders and restored peace, but he could not be spared to maintain it, and he was obliged to withdraw the troops he had brought with him to fight the Goths.

Some remnants of an army were still left in Britain, and in 407 it was proved again how dazzling and entrancing, beyond all bounds of common sense, was the lure of conquering the Eternal City. Because his name was Constantine, the soldiers elected an undistinguished subordinate as Emperor, and he, withdrawing such trained soldiers as Stilicho had left, marched with them on Rome to repeat the triumph of his namesake. He was killed in battle against the Emperor Honorius.

The Britons under threat of imminent invasion wrote to the Emperor appealing for help, but they were told they must fight for themselves. In 410 Rome was sacked by Alaric the Goth; this cataclysmic event loosed the barbarian hordes all over Europe, and the Saxons poured into Britain again.

In spite of the official refusal of help, there is some evidence that the Romans did send one more expedition to Britain. The historian Gildas, a Celtic monk, referring to the campaigns of Theodosius and Stilicho, calls this the Third Rescue. Writing of it in the sixth century, he makes two facts clear: first, that it was sent against the Saxons – 'The Roman forces', he says, 'drove our enemies' bands beyond the sea . . . for it was beyond those same seas that they had transported, yearly, the plunder they had gained, no one daring to resist them.' His second point is that the success was that of a cavalry commander. 'The Romans sent forward, like eagles in flight, their unexpected bands of cavalry, as a mountain torrent swelled with numerous streams and bursting its banks with roaring noise, with foaming crest and yeasty wave rising to the stars, does with one of its billows overwhelm every obstacle.'

Despite this triumphant victory, defensive action against the Saxons was destined to be a losing one; however they might be repulsed, they came on again, wave after wave. Even at the height of its power, the Roman authority could not, perhaps, have kept them out for ever, but in the fifth century the nature of Roman power had changed, and it was under new auspices that Rome sent an expedition to Britain in 429. The Roman Emperor, administering the cult of Emperor-worship, had been called Pontifex Maximus, and within a decade of the sack of Rome, the Bishop of Rome had adopted this title, claiming a supreme authority over all branches of the Christian Church. To establish the supremacy of the Christian religion, it was felt necessary to insist on an absolute uniformity of belief, and therefore heresies, or, in modern language, deviations, were to be crushed remorselessly. Britain had a heresy of its own, initiated by the Welsh monk Pelagius, who denied the doctrine of original sin. This idea had taken some hold among the Christians in Britain and a mission to combat it was dispatched under Germanus, Bishop of Auxerre. The mission was a pastoral one, but its arrival coincided with an invasion in Flintshire of a combined force of Picts and Scots. Germanus, though now a bishop, was an old soldier, and when he offered to conduct their defensive operations, the Britons thankfully put themselves under his orders. He posted his troops in a valley which was crossed by a river. When the enemy were advancing up an apparently deserted ravine, Germanus emerged holding his cross aloft and shouted 'Alleluia!' The ambushed Britons repeated the cry in a series of ringing shouts which terrified the invaders and caused them to fall back. The river they had forded easily at their own pace proved a deathtrap to panic-stricken fugitives, and of those who escaped slaughter, many died by drowning. This spectacular and extraordinary victory was not only important from a military standpoint: its role in history was pivotal. It firmly associated the defeat of barbarians with the ability and heroism of a Christian leader. This conception was a basic one in the image of Arthur.

In 425, the most powerful of the local British kings was Vortigern, who ruled from Wales to the south-east of Britain. He had four actual or potential adversaries: the Picts, against whom the unmanned walls of Hadrian and Antoninus were now no defence; the Scots, who invaded from bases in Wales; the Saxons, who were a perpetual menace on the south-east coasts; and, finally, a party of the Romano-British, whose object was to restore the practical, intelligent, beneficent rule of a Roman-inspired authority, and to crush, not the barbarians only, but those native rulers who appeased them. Faced with a threat from all four parties, Vortigern decided to fight off three of them by making an alliance with the fourth, giving the Saxons lands and maintenance in return for their military services. As

Vortigern ordering the execution of his
enemies, from a fourteenth-century
Italian MS.

22

the Celtic forces in the west demanded the expulsion of the Saxons, Vortigern
was obliged to commit himself to the latter more and more completely. When
another contingent, three shiploads, arrived led by two tall Saxon chiefs, Hengist
and Horsa, who offered to send back across the North Sea for still more of their
countrymen who would defend the King from all his enemies, Vortigern closed
with their offer. Among the Germanic tribes whom Hengist and Horsa at once
imported, some were Jutes, whose name has become lost in the course of time;
others were Angles, who by inexplicable chance gave theirs to this country.

During the next eight years, the Saxons fulfilled their treaty obligations with a
brutality that made them utterly abhorred. Vortigern married Hengist's daughter
Rowena; as this woman had a reputation for great beauty, the match came to be
regarded as one of those – admittedly few – cases where a king has made an
unsuitable marriage purely on grounds of sexual infatuation, of which Edward IV's
to Elizabeth Woodville, Henry VIII's to Anne Boleyn and Edward VIII's to Mrs
Simpson were later examples.

The Saxons had done their work so vigorously that their services were no longer
required; when they were told that their pay would now cease and they must live
on the lands already granted to them, which included the whole county of Kent,
their resentment knew no bounds. Like other immigrants, they had come to the
country in great numbers, bred with extraordinary rapidity and sent home for the
families of their relatives; they then announced themselves discontented with the
conditions that had been granted to them. In 442, they broke out of their territory
and fought Vortigern's army at the indecisive but terrible battle of Aylesbury.
From that engagement they went on to unchecked pillage and slaughter. They
were now abroad in the land as conquerors; some of the Britons fled as refugees
to Armorica, others died at the Saxon's murderous hands or lived like starving
animals in the wrecks of their sacked houses.

The massacre and destruction took place in the era called the Dark Ages, a
period pointed only by scraps of information written down long after the events,
with, however, one astonishing exception: Gildas, writing before the middle of the
sixth century his *Liber querulus* or 'Book of Complaints on the Destruction and
Conquest of Britain', gives an account not only inspired by bitter personal feeling,
but full of copious information. He was in a frame of mind we can easily recognize.
As we look back to the Victorian era when, whatever its drawbacks, industry, thrift
and self-respect were national virtues, and deplore our mounting crime rate and
the lewdness, ignorance and bloody-mindedness of a considerable part of the
population, so Gildas looked back to the Romans, and to the collapse of their
authority as the cause of the nightmarish conditions which followed it. As he says,
'The subject of my complaint is the general destruction of everything good and the
general growth of everything evil throughout the land.' With all the vividness and
vindictiveness of his race, he makes one see and feel, as well as merely know, what
it was like when the remains of Romano-British civilization, the towns and villas
and farms, were cut off and destroyed by the Saxon hordes in their savagery.

non gur pietr. Si pe
as contes quen ner
fer quen fer auidugs

quan il lesfut fitte l
nelef euft onqs uer

He begins with a description of Britain, which seems always to have aroused a passionate love in its writers: 'this land of such dear souls, this dear, dear land'. With the limits imposed by lack of geographical knowledge, he calls it 'the island of Britain, situated on almost the utmost border of the earth'. It is famous, he says, for twenty-eight cities, 'embellished by castles, with walls, towers, well-barred gates and houses with threatening battlements built on high'. So much for a contemporary picture of London, Lincoln, York. More lovingly still he describes the landscape: 'decked, as a man's chosen bride with jewels, with lucid fountains, abundant brooks wandering over white sands, transparent rivers, lakes which pour forth cool torrents of refreshing water'.

He says in his preface: 'It is my present purpose to relate the deeds of an indolent and slothful race, rather than those who have been valiant in the field.' He does in fact mention a few names, but his striking omission of any reference to the one name we would expect to find, is accounted for by this statement, the very reverse of our own method of printing every name of news-value. It is clear that Gildas found his chief stimulus in lamenting the calamitous withdrawal of the Romans and execrating Vortigern for his opening the door to the Saxons which Gildas regarded as the conduct of a vicious lunatic. He says of the Roman retreat: 'No sooner were they gone than the Picts and Scots . . . hastily land again in their canoes, differing from one another in manner but inspired by the same avidity for blood.' We can sympathize with him when he says that these savages were 'more eager to shroud their villainous faces in bushy hair than to cover with decent clothing those parts of their body that required it'. 'Now', he says, 'came the casting away of our nation.' Vortigern and his crew sealed its doom by inviting 'like wolves into the sheepfold, the fierce and impious Saxons . . . oh! darkness desperate and cruel!' 'In the midst of the streets lay the tops of tall towers, tumbled to the ground . . . fragments of human bodies covered with livid clots of coagulated blood, looking as if they had been mangled in a press, with no chance of being buried save in the ruins of the houses or in the ravenous bellies of wild beasts and birds.'

But, within this horror and destruction, a centre of resistance was forming. One of the few characters Gildas names is Ambrosius Aurelianus, who, he says, was 'the sole survivor of his Roman family'. Gildas describes him as 'modest, strong and faithful', a description of the typical Roman soldier. He was a cavalry man, for Gildas says that, 'though brave afoot, he was braver still on horseback'. 'The Britons', he says, 'fled to him like swarms of bees who fear a coming storm. They fought the war', he adds, 'with Ambrosius as their leader.' Ambrosius's first attack was not upon the Saxons but on Vortigern, who had betrayed the country to them. The latter took refuge in a castle in Flintshire. Ambrosius burned it down and Vortigern died in the conflagration. That Ambrosius was now the authority in the west is shown by the fact that it was by his permission that Vortigern's son was allowed to rule some of his father's kingdom while Ambrosius turned his forces to the south-east. The passionate determination to preserve a civilization to

A castle, and its occupant the defeated
Vortigern, burnt by Ambrosius, from a
fourteenth-century copy of an older chronicle

BRITAIN BEFORE ARTHUR

25

which its remains – the buildings, the aqueducts, the roads – bore such a splendid testimony, was strengthened by contempt for an enemy who could not value these things. They destroyed the towns because they wanted only to live in village communities, they made fires on the mosaic pavements, they allowed the heating and water systems to fall to ruins since they did not care about washing themselves. Frightful as they were, they had no military discipline. As Tacitus said, they fought for pleasure and for loot. They recognized loyalty only to the chief of a small community based on family ties.

The struggle between two civilizations, two eras, was something of a deadlock. It was impossible to get the Saxons out, but at least their advance was checked. In 488, Ambrosius pursued Hengist into the north-east and the Saxon chief was killed in battle, but the Saxons themselves were, in the last resort, undefeatable. Notorious for the rate at which they bred – a fertility which had driven them to seek other lands – they were now so firmly settled in the south-east of Britain that to eradicate them was impossible; but could they be contained in the districts they already occupied? Could the north-west and the south-west be held against them? Ambrosius had inspired a resistance in his despairing countrymen, and had proved that, in a pitched battle, mounted soldiers had the advantage of those who fought on foot. He continued a strong defensive action, and now he had a second-in-command whose fame was to prove world-wide and immortal.

ti sunt. usq; ad decu̅ & ualenanu̅. anni
sunt sexaginta noue. · an̅

an̅	an̅ xxx.	an̅
an̅	an̅	an̅
an̅	an̅	an̅
an̅	an̅	an̅
an̅	an̅	an̅
an̅	an̅	an̅ lxx.
an̅	an̅	an̅
an̅	an̅	an̅ Bellu̅ badonis in q̅
an̅ Pasca co̅	an̅	arthur portauit crucē
mutatur. sup di	an̅	d̅m n̅ri ihu xp̅i. trib;
en dnica cum	an̅ xl.	dieb; & trib; noctib;
papa leone·ep̅r	an̅	in humeros suos &
rome.	an̅	brittones uictores fuer.
an̅ ·& Brigida	an̅	an̅
sca nascitur.	an̅	an̅
an̅	an̅	an̅
an̅ Sc̅s patrici⁹	an̅	an̅ Sc̅s colu̅cille nasc̅.
ad d̅n̅m migra	an̅	Quies sc̅e brigide.
tur.	an̅ ·l·	an̅
an̅	an̅	an̅
an̅	an̅	an̅ lxxx.
an̅	an̅	an̅
an̅	an̅	an̅
an̅	an̅	an̅
an̅ xx.	an̅ Ep̅r ebur pau	an̅
an̅	lat in xp̅o an̅	an̅
an̅	no· ccl· etatis	an̅
an̅	sue	an̅
an̅ quies benigni	an̅	an̅
ep̅i.	an̅	an̅ xc.
an̅	an̅ ·lx·	an̅
an̅	an̅	an̅
an̅	an̅	an̅ Guerth ca̅ lan̅ in q̅
an̅	an̅	arthur & medraut
an̅	an̅	corruer. & mortalitas

(left margin, partially visible)
...merdote
...ruchi be
...uocat.
...cesrad
...a̅m
...ep̅r obe
...ecit be
...bi;
...it decc
...egnu̅
...onnan
...osuual
...e dolu̅
...cecidit
...ercioru̅
...se uictor
...nerat bap
...dicit.
...ad constan
...lia sexcen
...nu repriu̅t
...o & rubelio
...ccc· septu
...e stilhcone
...nu̅ placide
...ginta octo
...no̅ um· usq;
...mbrosii.
...loppdo̅m
...ru̅ auc
...nta the
...nsulib;·
...n saxones
...cc & cauro
...cesimo anno
...n̅ri ihu· xp̅i·
...u uener moz

The Easter Annals, dating from the early
eleventh century, that give the only factual
evidence for the existence of Arthur

2 Fact and Legend

In 1220, an abbot was addressing the monks in his chapter house: 'Seeing that many, especially of the lay brethren, were asleep, and that some were even snoring, he cried out: Hark, brethren, hark! I will tell you of something new and great. There was once a mighty king, whose name was Arthur!' The effect was electric. The abbot then said: 'Had they not come to a sad pass, when they would not stay awake to hear of holy things, but were agog at the mention of Arthur?'

For over a hundred years Arthur's fame had been blazed over Christendom. The Prior of Tewkesbury had written in 1170: 'What place is there . . . to which the winged praise of Arthur has not extended? Who is there, I ask, who does not speak of Arthur the Briton, since he is but little less known to the people of Asia than to the Bretons, as we are informed by pilgrims who return from the Eastern lands? The peoples of the East speak of him, as do those of the West, though separated by the breadth of the whole earth. Egypt speaks of him, nor is the Bosporus silent. Rome, queen of cities, sings his deeds, and his war, and known to their former rival Carthage, Antioch, Armenia and Palestine celebrate his feats.'

This far-flung fame would scarcely have been achieved in a later world, where there were more stories to compete, but even so it was extraordinary: the story was not only spellbinding: it aroused deep, passionate conviction. In 1146, Hermann de Tournai related that some canons of Laon Cathedral were in Cornwall on a fund-raising mission. They arrived at Bodmin carrying an image of Our Lady which they declared had power to heal. A man with a withered arm presented himself, but before the healing influence could be invoked, an unseemly fracas had broken out. 'Just as the Bretons are wont to wrangle with the French on behalf of King Arthur, the man began to dispute with one of our company, saying Arthur was still living.' So great was the feeling aroused, 'it came to bloodshed', and the cure could not be performed.

The power of arousing total commitment in the hearer is the essential quality of a tale that is to be world famous. Arthur's story has it to an exceptional degree. The extent to which its hearers identified themselves with it is shown by the broken heads in Bodmin market-place.

But who was he?

His fame has lasted for fourteen centuries and brought him, a magnificent figure, into our own childhood. It is natural for an adult to assume that he was never anything but a character of romance. To find who he was one must go back

Interpreted by Merlin to Vortigern, a Saxon
victory over the Britons symbolized as the
Red Dragon vanquished by the White

28

through centuries until figures can be descried only looming through a mist, among stretches of blank darkness. The supremely exciting moment is that of realizing that he did exist.

Because Easter is a movable feast, it was necessary to draw up calculations as to when it would fall for the next given number of years. These calculating tables, kept in various abbeys, were called the Easter Tables. They were arranged in columns and the right-hand column was left blank. In this were noted down events of outstanding importance. The entries in these columns are called the Easter Annals.

It is accepted that the date of a manuscript containing the Annals is considerably later than that of the events noted in the Annals; but the experts are agreed that, when new tables of calculation were drawn up, the chief events from previous tables were carried over to the current ones.

In the British Museum is a bundle of documents known as the *Historical Miscellany* which contains a set of Easter Tables, and in its column of annals occur two entries: of the first, the interpretation of the date is disputed, as the scribe dated the entry from the year the Annals were begun; it is put at A.D. either 499 or 518. It reads: 'Battle of Badon, in which Arthur carried the cross of our Lord Jesus Christ on his shoulders for three days and three nights and the Britons were victors.' The second entry, for 539, reads: 'The Battle of Camlann, in which Arthur and Modred perished. And there was plague in Britain and Ireland.'

The validity of these two fragments is demonstrated by Leslie Alcock.[4] The gist of their claim to be historical evidence is that the Battle of Mount Badon is mentioned also by Gildas, who gives its date as that of his own birth; that he describes it as 'almost the last slaughter of the enemy', after which, during his lifetime, the Saxon advance from the south-east to the south-west was checked; and that, in a history notorious for its avoidance of proper names, Gildas, though he does not give Arthur's, gives that of the battle, thus implying its singular importance.

The Annals say Arthur fought for three days and three nights, and this is made credible by Gildas's calling the battle a siege: *obsessio Badonici montis*. Arthur's carrying the cross on his shoulders is explained by reading 'shield' for 'shoulder'.

The site of the hill called Badon is much disputed, but it is assumed that it must lie across the route of the Saxon advance from Kent and Essex. It has been suggested by K. H. Jackson (citing Gildas)[5] that a decisive battle of the time around 500 'suits remarkably the known history of southern England, from which it appears that the Anglo-Saxon penetration of the south-east during the first half-century of the invasion was stopped about 500, when it had reached the borders of Salisbury Plain in Berkshire and Hampshire, and was not resumed until another half-century later.' Badbury near Swindon in Wiltshire, Badbury Hill in Berkshire, Badbury Ring in Dorset and a hill outside Bath in Somerset have all had their claims seriously considered. It is not known whether Arthur and his warriors held

the summit, or were the besiegers who scaled it; at all events the result was a massacre of the Saxons. Badon is entitled to rank as one of the great battles in the history of this country. This reference, and the one to Arthur and Modred both dying in the battle of Camlann, are the irreducible base on which the towering superstructure of Arthur's fame has been erected.

In the *Historical Miscellany*, these two entries in the Easter Annals are the most exciting, because they have a validity not equalled by anything else; but next in importance is a collection made by the Welsh monk Nennius in the mid-eighth century. He says: 'I have heaped together all that I found from the annals of the Romans, the writings of the holy fathers; and the traditions of our own old men.'

Nennius's collection in the *Historical Miscellany* is known as the *Historia Brittonum*; it begins with a recapitulation of other works, including a calculation of the six ages of the world, beginning with the Flood; then comes what is called the Independent Section, information for which Nennius is the only authority. This relates the career of Vortigern and his encouragement of the Saxons; Nennius gives the story of Vortigern's discovering a clairvoyant boy with prophetic powers called Ambrosius, whose mother confesses that he was begotten on her by an incubus. The castle Vortigern is attempting to build will not stand up and the boy tells him to drain the pool he will find under its foundations. When this is emptied, a red and white dragon are discovered in it; they fight each other, the white vanquishing the red. The boy explains that the fight foretells the Saxon victory over the British.

After this fable comes a passage which, but that it is written so much later, would be as precious as the entries in the Easter Annals. It begins with the indication of a date: 'After the death of Hengist, his son Octha came from northern Britain and settled in Kent, whence come the kings of Kent.' The accession of Octha, under the name Aesc, is dated in the Anglo-Saxon Chronicle as 488. Nennius continues: 'Then Arthur fought against them in those days, with the Kings of the Britons, but he himself was the leader of the battles.' This shows that several kings, rulers of small British kingdoms, had formed themselves together after the retreat of the Romans, that they united against the Saxons and that Arthur was the general commanding their combined forces. Not only does Nennius imply in this statement that Arthur was not a king himself; in another section, *The Marvels of Britain*, he calls him a soldier merely; he speaks of Cabal, the dog of Arthur the Soldier, and of the grave of Anwr, son of Arthur the Soldier.

The next passage is momentous and mysterious; it is a list of twelve battles fought by Arthur, of which only two have sites that can be identified. The first, Nennius says, was fought on the River Glen. This may have been the Glen in Northumberland or the Glen in Lincolnshire. The second, third, fourth and fifth were fought on the River Dubglas, '*in regio Linnius*', which may mean Lindsey in Lincolnshire. The sixth was at Bassas, a name which has not been translated. The seventh was the Battle of the Caledonian Wood, which is believed to mean a forest in Strathclyde. The eighth was at Tor Guinnion, and this, though not geographically found, is distinguished by the anecdote that here Arthur carried the image of Mary, Ever-virgin, on his shoulders, through whose virtue and that of Jesus Christ, the pagans were routed. The ninth was fought at the City of the Legion, the Roman name for Chester. The tenth was on the shore of Tribruit; this sounds like another, unknown, river, but it is suggested that it may mean 'the many-coloured shore'. The eleventh was on the mountain called Agned; the twelfth was on Mount Badon, and here, Nennius says, nine hundred and sixty fell in one onslaught made by Arthur. 'No one overthrew them except himself alone.' This would be perfectly credible if Arthur were in sole command of a force of cavalry. The final sentence, 'In all battles he stood forth as victor', sounds a natural way of speaking of the commanding officer in a victorious campaign. Though the terrain cannot be plotted precisely, the battles would seem to have been fought over an area stretching from Strathclyde in the north-west eastwards, either to Northumberland, or to a region considerably south of it, in Lincolnshire; from Chester in the west, to some point south-west, where the engagement of Badon Hill culminated in a victory so overpowering that it brought the campaign to a close and established peace for fifty years.

Whatever the details, the outline is unmistakable: of a terrific action, offensive and defensive, fought with a high degree of mobility over a very wide area, with brilliant, amazing success. It could not eradicate the Saxons, but it saved the south

The section of Nennius's *Historia Britonum* describing Arthur's twelve great battles, and RIGHT Christian symbolism on a banner such as Arthur carried at the Battle of Badon

uit de siniltrali parte brittannie ad reg
nu cantorū · & de ipso oras reges cantor.
unc arthur pugnabat contra illos.
millis dieb; cū regib; brittonū · s. ipse dux erat
bellorū · Primū bellū fuit mostiū flumin
nis quod dicit glein · sedm & tciū & qr
tū & quintū · sup aliud flumen quod
dicit dubglas · q̄ inregione linnuis ·
Sextū bellum sup flumen quod uocā
ē bassas · Septimū   fuit bellū
in silua celidonis · id: cac coit celidon ·
Octauum fuit bellū incastello gunin
on · Inquo arthur portauit imagine
sc̄e marie ppetue uirginis sup hume
ros suos · & pagani uersi s in fugā in
illo die · & cedes magna fuit sup illos
p uirtutem dn̄i nr̄i ihu xp̄i & p uirtutē
sc̄e marie uirginis genitricis ei · Nonū
bellū gestū in urbe legionis · Decimū
gessit bellū in litore · Fluminis quod
uocat tribruit · Undecimū factū:
bellū in monte qui dicit agned · Duo
decimū fuit bellū in monte badonis ·
in quo corruer in uno die n̄ genti sexa
ginta uiri de uno impetū arthur.

of Britain, west of Kent, from destruction by them. The description of their horrible brutality, their slaughtering and burning, their overpowering senseless vandalism, makes us see why the commander who routed them in a series of pitched battles, of which the climax was the one fought on a boundary of Salisbury Plain, became the image of the hero and saviour, whose death his people refused to believe in, whose return was yearned for and expected throughout centuries.

These are the only unassailable facts so far known about Arthur, but there are certain reasonable assumptions. The chief is that he was a cavalry commander. The widespread nature of the terrain implies that his force was highly mobile. The Black Book of Carmarthen, a manuscript collection of the twelfth century,

Camlann, the last battle of Arthur, who lies
mortally wounded while his sword projects
from Modred's corpse

32

whose contents are infinitely older than this compilation, contains a poem on the
Battle of Llongborth, now Southampton, fought by Arthur with cavalry:

> Before Geraint, the enemy's scourge,
> I saw white horses, tensed, red. . . .
> In Llongborth I saw spurs
> And men who did not flinch from spears . . .
> In Llongborth I saw Arthur's
> Heroes who cut with steel.
> The Emperor, ruler of our labour. . . .
> Under the thigh of Geraint swift chargers,
> Long their legs, wheat their fodder,
> Red, swooping like milk-white eagles. . . .
>
> (from John Morris, *The Age of Arthur*)

The apposition of white and red may mean that the horses were piebald, or that,
being white, the stains of blood showed on them vividly.

The absence of horse-furniture in their graves suggests that the Saxons were not
horsemen, but the British fighters were celebrated in British and early Welsh
poetry as mounted warriors. The Gododin, another poem in the Black Book of
Carmarthen, but attributed to the end of the sixth century, says of a hero: 'He
showered spears in fight from his bounding, wide-coursing horse.' This poem
also contains something that would be ranked with the entries in the Easter
Annals as evidence of Arthur's existence, if only it were certain that it was not a
later interpolation. It says that a warrior in his heroic feats of arms 'glutted black
ravens on the city ramparts, though he was not Arthur'. His feats were second only
to those of the hero.

The Battle of Llongborth speaks of Arthur as Emperor but the ascription of
Emperor or King is later than the historical evidence. The earliest mentions of
Arthur speak of him simply as Arthur. Nennius calls him *miles*, a soldier and leader
of battles, among kings. The vision of him as a military commander merely, is so
ancient that an indescribable magic invests a poem found in a Scots work of 1549.
This, *The Complaint of Scotland*, is a manifesto against the havoc wrought by the
English at the battles of Flodden and Pinkie Clough, but in part of it a shepherd
and his wife sit down to entertain a guest by telling tales. The author does not give
the substance of these, he only names their titles. Some of these have a haunting
quality, such as 'How the King of Eastmorland Married the Princess of Westmorland'. One is referred to only by its first two lines:

> Arthur knycht he rode on nyght
> With gilten spur and candle-light.

Dr Furnivall believed that this was the opening of a ballad he had never been able
to trace. The glamour of the lines is enhanced by the sense of their incalculable
age, before Arthur has been metamorphosed into a king. An attractive theory,
again in support of the idea of Arthur as a mounted warrior, is developed in *The*

la place. En li q̃ .j. gñr moꝛtalite del
ꝟ artu et de moꝛdꝛes son fil la vil
urent tout destruir.

vant li rois artus voit
celui cop si dist trop do
lant qha a ciel pꝛ sum

Black Horsemen: English Inns and King Arthur. By tracing all the English inns which bear the sign of the Black Horse, S. G. Wildman[6] deduces that lines connecting the places where they stand, mark the frontiers and hinterlands of the regions Arthur held against the Saxons. Quoting from D. M. Goodall,[7] he says that, at Housesteads on the Roman Wall, a group of Frisian cavalry was posted, the Cuneus Frisiorum. D. M. Goodall suggests that the departing Romans sold off their horses to the British, and that the Frisian horses, which were large and black, crossed with the native black Fell pony, produced the mounts used by Arthur's army, which combined the staying-power needed for transport and the mettle of a battle charger. The idea of black horses contradicts the picture of white ones in the Battle of Llongborth, but it is possible that both black and white were used, or that the hero and his companions had been imagined on white horses, the rarity of a white animal investing it with a romantic quality, a convention often seen in fairy tales; for example, the milk-white steed of the Queen of Elfland in the ballad of *Thomas the Rhymer.*

A speculation very well grounded is the outcome of the immense feat of excavation and research on the hill in Somerset known as Cadbury Castle. This enormous hill fort, overlooking the little village of Cadbury near Glastonbury, has a long tradition of association with Arthur. It is a mound 250 feet high whose summit extends over 18 acres. The mound is girdled with four ridges, one above the other, the remains of defence works. The research of the 1960s proved that it had already been inhabited between 500 and 400 B.C.; that the Romans found it occupied and massacred some of the inhabitants, removing the rest to live on ground level, and that afterwards the fort was dismantled and the hill-top ploughed over.

The most exciting stage of the excavations revealed that the hill had been re-fortified about A.D. 470; this was proved by the presence, tamped into wall trenches and post holes, of pottery shards, their edges still sharp, which belong to the 'Tintagel Pottery' group, dated in the fifth century. The buildings of the period contemporary with Arthur have been identified by their remains as a defence work on the summit, consisting of a timber frame, banked inside with earth and rubble and faced with dry stonework, a gate in the south-west curve of this, with a timber threshold, two 5-foot doors' leaves and a watch tower over it, and, in the centre of the plateau, occupying a dominant position, a great hall, 60 by 30 feet, gabled at each end with a lofty thatched roof but low walls, probably of wattle and daub.

The image of a feasting-hall, of the kind evoked by the Cadbury research, is one that rises in the mind when reading the tenth-century Arthurian story *Culwych and Olwen.* Culwych claims admittance to Arthur's hall, and is told he cannot enter as the feast is already begun. He sends an imperious message, and the porter, bearing it, describes his noble presence. Arthur says: 'A shameful thing it is to leave in wind and rain such a man as thou tellest of.' At the words, the wind sweeps across the summit of Cadbury Hill, and the rain teems against the thatch.

The association with Arthur is a local one of very long standing. There was a belief that Arthur slept inside a hill, 'near Glastonbury'. There is no legend of his sleeping inside Glastonbury Tor, and the only other great hill in the neighbourhood is Cadbury, where hollow underground spaces give colour to some such legend. At the end of the sixteenth century, the historian William Camden found the local inhabitants calling the hill Arthur's Palace; he himself knew only that it had once been a Roman fort.

The name Camelot was first given to Arthur's supposed capital by the twelfth-century French romancer Chrétien de Troyes. There is no historical warrant for it and indeed the idea of the capital only comes into the story after the general Arthur has been mythologized into a king. 'Camelot' is thought to be a Frenchman's corruption of Camalodunum, the Roman name for Colchester. By the sixteenth century it had become accepted as that of Arthur's capital city: when John Leland the antiquarian visited Cadbury in 1542, and saw the great hill with the four ridges encircling it and heard the villagers speak of it as Arthur's Palace, he was convinced that it must be so; his conviction drove him to call it Camelot and to misinterpret the name of the neighbouring village, Queen's Camel; he said the latter must originally have been Queen's Camellat.

The ascription of the name Camelot, unfounded in history and supported by a false etymology, has been most unfortunate, for it has tended to obscure the genuine claims of Cadbury to be Arthur's fortress. These have, however, been demonstrated by the excavations. As Leslie Alcock[8] says, 'The immensity of the hill-top fortress and the strength of its defences show that it was the station of some commander of great importance; it was rebuilt in an era consistent with its having been occupied by Arthur and its site would make it suitable for the headquarters of a leader who was fighting a campaign in the south-west of England, concluded by a battle waged on the perimeter of Salisbury Plain.'

Leland's insisting on calling the hill fort Camelot creates an ambience of unreality; but his comment contains a valuable piece of visual reporting, of a date four hundred years nearer to Arthur than our own: 'Good Lord, what and how many deep ditches are there here? . . . What dangerous steepness?' It is clear that he saw the four ridges much more sharply cut, their sides presenting a much steeper appearance than they do to us, worn down and overgrown with grass, their outlines altogether softened. Leland also picked up the local tradition of association with Arthur, whose value his talk about Camelot has obscured. The people said that, on nights of full moon, Arthur and his warriors rode about the hill and that there was once picked up a silver shoe, cast by one of their horses.

The two notes in the Easter Annals on which the historicity of Arthur is founded both speak of his presence at battles. Mount Badon can be only vaguely located; the site of Camlann is obscurer still. One theory places it at Birdoswald, on the River Irthing, the Roman Camboglanna at the west of Hadrian's Wall; another, on the River Camel in Cornwall. If, as the later development of the story says, Modred was Arthur's son begotten on his sister, and that Modred betrayed him,

then the entry 'Arthur and Modred perished' must mean that they fought each
other, though it does not say so. That the battle was fought in the course of a
civil war rather than against the Saxons is, it has been suggested, borne out by the
situation of the small, independent kingdoms, firmly cemented by the Saxon
menace and falling apart when that menace was removed during the long period
of peace that Arthur's victories had secured.

The idea that Arthur took up arms against a member of his family is suggested
by another entry among those Nennius had 'heaped together' under *Marvels of
Britain*. He says that at the source of the River Gamba in Herefordshire is the
grave of Arthur's son, Anwr, whom his father slew. The measurements of this
grave, Nennius says, are never found to be the same when taken twice running; he
himself had proved this. This may suggest a psychic disturbance connected with
some painful event.

36

The statement in the Annals is merely that Arthur and Modred perished, but references to Arthur's death after this entry very soon begin to say that it is not known where he was buried. A poem inscribed in the Black Book of Carmarthen, called *Verses on the Graves*, says: 'A grave for March, a grave for Gwythur, a grave for Gugann of the Red Sword; concealed till Doomsday the grave of Arthur.' Writing in 1125, the great historian William of Malmesbury said, in his *Gesta Regum*, that though the tomb of Arthur's nephew Gawain had been discovered 'on the sea shore', during the reign of William the Conqueror, 'the tomb of Arthur is nowhere seen, whence ancient rhymes fable that he is yet to come'. The great image of Arthur the saviour was touched with supernatural light because the site of his earthly remains had never been found, so that men could say he had not died.

The earlier of the two Easter Annals' entries says that Arthur bore the cross on his shoulder, or shield, and gained his victory through the might of Jesus Christ. The Christian faith, ascribed to him in the very first mention of him in history, became one of the leading characteristics of his *persona* in the great medieval version

of it; he fought the paynims, and his most distinguished knights devoted themselves to the quest of a visionary experience, the sight of the Holy Grail. But, between the earliest record of him as the defender of Roman-Christian Britain and the splendid medieval figure of the greatest Emperor in Christendom, is a sphere of Welsh poetry and prose, cloudy but lit with a fitful brilliance, where Arthur moves among companions whose names were once those of Roman and Celtic deities. In the Black Book of Carmarthen there is a dialogue between Arthur and his gate-keeper. The latter, before he opens the gate, demands to be assured of Arthur's identity and of those of the companions he brings with him. Arthur numbers among his troop men whose names Loomis identifies with those of gods of a previous era: Mabon, son of Modron, was once Apollo Maponus, a god of Roman Britain; Manawidan, son of Llyr, was the Irish sea-god, Manannan; and Lluch Lamhfadyan, Lluch Llaunnyauc, the Irish god of sun and storm. Such a stature had Arthur achieved, dim and mighty, walking under forest boughs with ancient gods as his companions.

Two of the earliest known architectural
decorations recording the Arthurian legend,
at Modena and BOTTOM Otranto

3 Early Arthurian Tales

Arthur was a commander who fought a campaign to restrain a Saxon advance across a part of the small country of Britain. The spreading of his story into Europe, so unexpected and improbable, is generally accepted as the work of Breton *conteurs*. Armorica was now called Brittany or Little Britain, from the numbers of Britons who in successive immigrations had taken refuge there. They had kept in touch with their cousins in Britain, and without a word of writing, the transmission of British history and legend had been effected, as flowers and fruit trees were brought here from foreign lands through their seeds being carried in the crops of birds.

The agency of the Breton *conteurs* is acknowledged over and over again. William of Malmesbury speaks of 'this Arthur, about whom the Bretons rave even today'. Breton lays were cited by French romancers of the twelfth century as the origins of their stories. The Welsh profession of bards, or chanters and reciters of heroic tales to entertain a chief and his household, depended for its theatrical success, first on there being a good story to tell, then on the memory and dramatic powers of the reciter, and on the emotional receptivity of the hearers. All these qualities were in high perfection among the Celts, and anyone who can remember listening, as a child, to a good storyteller, has an insight into the extraordinary power of this oral diffusion which spread the Matter of Arthur into France, Italy and Germany. An astonishing evidence of this diffusion is found on the arch over the north door of Modena Cathedral: a semicircular frieze depicting a woman in a moated tower on which six knights are advancing, three from each side. The woman's figure is inscribed *Winlogee*, and three figures defending the tower are given as *Burmaltus*, *Mardoc* and *Carrado*. One of the advancing knights has the inscription *Artus de Bretani*. Loomis says the name Winlogee is 'a transitional form between the Breton Winlowen and the French Guinloic'. This then is one of the very early mentions of Guinevere in Arthur's story. The carving presumably illustrates the expedition made by Arthur to rescue Guinevere when she had been abducted by Modred, Arthur's son, and been held captive by him in a tower while Arthur was away fighting Lancelot. The story is given in what is supposed to be a life of Gildas by Caradoc of Lancafarn, written down at some time in the first half of the twelfth century. The date of the carving over the cathedral porch is judged to be between 1099 and 1120.

The transformation in people's imaginations of Arthur from a military commander to a king had begun by the tenth century. The Welsh poem on the battle of Llongborth calls him Emperor. John Morris[9] says that, though the verbal form of the poem is considerably later than the event, 'any elegy composed in or near the time of Arthur would have been in British, not Welsh', but he considers it to be a Welsh rewording of a British poem composed not long after the fifth-century battle.

The most famous Welsh story, *Culwych and Olwen*, of the late tenth century, shows the status of Arthur in transition; he is not called King, but he is shown, a powerful and supernaturally gifted chieftain, presiding over his court. In another famous Welsh tale, *The Dream of Rhonabwy*, of the twelfth century, he is addressed as Emperor.

These two tales are part of the Mabinogion, of which there are two manuscripts, one known as the White Book of Rhydderch, written down between 1300 and 1325, and the other as the Red Book of Hergest, written down between 1315 and 1425, some four hundred years later than the origin of *Culwych and Olwen* and two hundred years later, perhaps, than *The Dream of Rhonabwy*.

The young hero Culwych wants to wed Olwen, the daughter of Giant Ysbadadden, and when he wonders where to seek help, his father merely says: 'Go to Arthur.' No explanation of the great warrior is needed. The description of Culwych riding to Arthur's court is one of the world's most beautiful evocations of a young man riding out on his adventures. He rides a four-year-old horse, 'shell-hooved'; he has a battle-axe that would draw blood from the wind, a gold sword and a gold shield, 'the hue of heaven's lightning therein'. 'Never a hair-tip stirred on him, so exceeding light his steed's canter under him on his way to Arthur's court.'

When he arrives, the porter will not admit him to the hall as the feast has already begun, but at last, overborne by the young man's imperious commands, he goes to Arthur, whom his words show to be, already, a conqueror of widest renown: 'I was with thee of old in India the Great and India the Lesser. . . . I was in Egrop, and in Africa was I, and in the islands of Corsica. . . . I was there of old when thou didst conquer Greece with the east . . . but never saw I a man so comely as this, who is even now at the entrance gate.' Arthur with great graciousness sends for the young man to come in, and at sight of him promises him all the help in his power, 'as far as wind dries, as far as rain wets, as far as sun runs, as far as sea stretches, as far as earth extends'. Arthur promises that the hero shall have any of his own possessions, except his personal properties; the list of these shows that since the early, the very early mention of him, he had become the theme of a body of storytelling: he now has a sword, Caledfwlch; a spear, Rhongomyniad; a shield, Wynebgwrthucher; a dagger, Carnwennan; a ship, Prydwen; a dog, Caball; a mare, Llamrei; and the name of his feasting-hall is Eliangwen.

Of his followers, some two hundred in all, who promise their help in the suit of Olwen, many are mere outlandish names; others are dowered with magical attributes: Sgilti Lightfoot never used a road – 'so long as there were trees, along the tops of the trees he would go.' There was Clust, who could hear an ant getting up in the morning fifty miles away, and Medyr, who could aim at a wren in Ireland and shoot between its legs; in the catalogue of mingled brilliance and nonsense, there is one thrilling item: the mention of three men who are said to have fought at Camlann: Morgan, son of Tegid, who was so ugly that no one attempted to wound him because they thought he was a devil; Sandde, 'Angel Face', whom no one tried to wound because they thought he was an angel; and Cynwyl the Saint, who was 'the last to part from Arthur'. Are these vestigial traces of three warriors who were in that mysterious battle? The fact that the action of Culwych and Olwen must be taking place after Arthur got his mortal wound, is nothing. The teeming procession of figures is brought to an end by a bevy of ladies, 'the gentle, gold-necklaced maidens of this island'; the foremost of them being 'Gwenhwyfar, the first lady of this island, and Gwenhwyach, her sister'. This mention of Guinevere as Arthur's wife, earlier even than the carving of her over the cathedral porch at Modena, has also an echo of the strange, persistent theme of 'the double Guinevere'; Gwenhwyfar has a sister whose name is almost identical with her own.

Arthur and his warriors discover the whereabouts of Olwen, and when her father, Giant Ysbadadden, demands the performance of a series of preposterous tasks as the price of her hand, Arthur undertakes to lead an expeditionary force to execute them. The most spectacular of these is the hunting of the boar Twrch Trwyth, for the sake of the comb, razor and scissors between his ears, which the giant requires for his barbering on his daughter's wedding day. This exploit takes Arthur to Ireland. 'Arthur gathered together what warriors there were in the Island of Britain . . . and what there were in France and Brittany and Normandy and in the Summer Country and what there were of picked dogs and horses of renown.' He explains to his men that the boar had once been a king whom God for his wickedness had changed into a swine. The quarry was located in his forest lair and Arthur sent an interpreter to him. It is startling to hear of this great commander, one of the military geniuses of history, that the interpreter he sent 'went in the form of a bird' and alighted as such above the lair of the boar and his seven piglets. The one who spoke for his father was Grugyn Silver-Bristle: 'Like silver wings were all his bristles; so what way he went through woodland and meadow one could discern from how his bristles glittered.'

Grugyn Silver-Bristle refused Arthur's overtures and declined to give up the comb, razor and scissors, adding: 'Tomorrow in the morning we will set out hence and go into Arthur's country and there will we do all the mischief we can.'

The boar and his family set out by sea towards Wales. Arthur, his host, horses and dogs go on board 'and in the twinkling of an eye they saw them in the sea'. The hunt begins, through the Irish Sea and over the land of Wales: the enormous prospect before the mind's eye is enhanced by the words 'Arthur and all the hosts of the world came thither.' Twrch Trwyth is at last overtaken and driven into the Severn, but though he is in the water, two warriors seize from between his ears the razor and the scissors. He escapes with the comb and Arthur chases him into

42 Cornwall. 'Whatever mischief was come by before that, was play to what was come by seeking the comb. But from mischief to mischief, the comb was won from him.' Twrch Trwyth was then driven into the sea once more 'and from that time forth never a one hath known where he went'; and Arthur 'went thence to Celliwig in Cornwall to bathe himself and rid him of his weariness'.

The tale proliferates with tasks and adventures, ultimately crowned with success, and culminating in the wedding of Culwych and Olwen, 'and she was his only wife so long as he lived'; but, unlike later groups of stories in which Arthur and his court serve merely as a framework for adventures of individual knights, here Arthur's part is energetic and leading. This picture of his prestige, his prowess, his kindness, is fully developed by the middle of the tenth century, probably in its oral version some hundreds of years earlier. There is an episode at the end which already shows the respect and protectiveness his followers feel for him, encountered again and again through the next five centuries. The final demand of Ysbadadden is for the blood of the Black Witch, who is found at the

Britain from the Roman to the Anglo-Saxon period, showing Roman sites, the British kingdoms of Scotland, Wales and Cornwall, the Anglo-Saxon incursions, and the places traditionally associated with Arthur

1	DUBRIS Dover	21	Southampton, battle of Llongborth
2	RUTUPIAE Richborough	22	Salisbury
3	DUROVERNUM Canterbury	23	Stonehenge
4	LONDINIUM London	24	South Cadbury
5	CAMULODUNUM Colchester	25	Glastonbury
6	VENTA ICENORUM Caistor	26	Tintagel
7	VERULAMIUM St Albans	27	St Michael's Mount
8	NOVIOMAGUS REGNENSIUM Chichester	28	Malmesbury
9	VENTA BELGARUM Winchester	29	Caerleon
10	ISCA DUMNONIORUM Exeter	30	Tewkesbury
11	AQUAE SULIS Bath	31	Badbury Hill
12	CORINIUM DOBUNNORUM Cirencester	32	Uffington (Badon?)
13	GLEUM Gloucester	33	Badbury Rings
14	Worcester	34	Badbury
15	RATAE CORITANORUM Leicester	35	Aylesbury, site of battle A.D. 442
16	LINDUM Lincoln	36	Lindsay
17	DEVA Chester	37	Camboglanna, Birdoswald (Camlann?)
18	MAMUCIUM Manchester	38	Caledonian Forest, Strathclyde
19	EBURACUM York	39	River Tribruit
20	LUGUVALLIUM Carlisle	40	River Glen, Northumberland

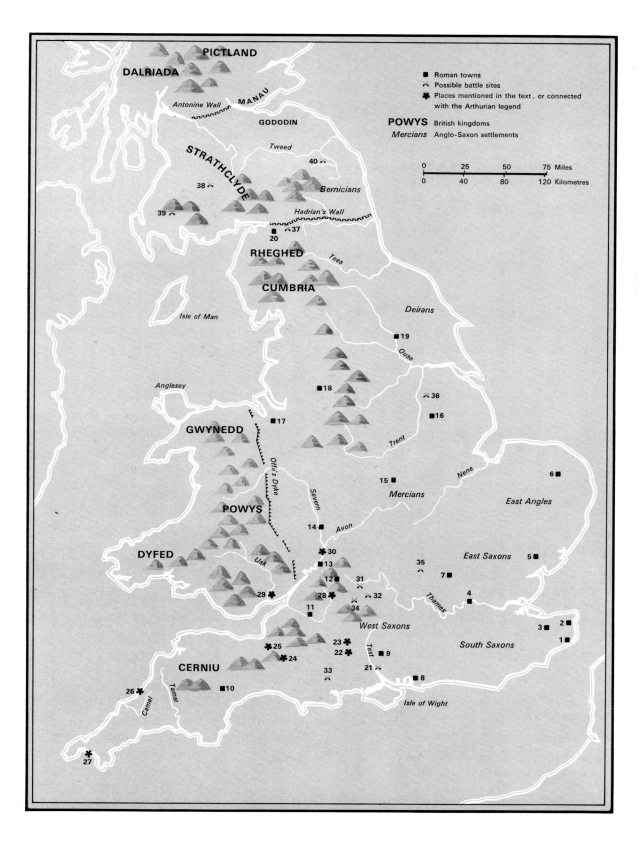

PICTLAND

DALRIADA

Antonine Wall

MANAU

GODODIN

■ Roman towns
✕ Possible battle sites
✴ Places mentioned in the text, or connected with the Arthurian legend

POWYS British kingdoms
Mercians Anglo-Saxon settlements

0   25   50   75 Miles
0   40   80   120 Kilometres

Tweed

STRATHCLYDE

40 ✕

38 ✕

Bernicians

39 ✕

Hadrian's Wall

✕ 37

20 ■

RHEGHED

Tees

CUMBRIA

Deirans

Isle of Man

19 ■

Ouse

Anglesey

18 ■

36 ✕

16 ■

GWYNEDD

17 ■

Trent

Offa's Dyke

15 ■

Nene

6 ■

POWYS

Severn

Mercians

East Angles

14 ■

Avon

DYFED

✴ 30

East Saxons

5 ■

Usk

13 ■

35 ✕

12 ■

31

7 ■

29 ✴

28 ✴

✕ 32

Thames

4 ■

11 ■

34

3 ■   2 ■

West Saxons

1 ■

✴ 25

23 ✴

South Saxons

✴ 24

22 ✴

9 ■

CERNIU

Test

26 ✴

33

21 ✕

Tamar

10 ■

8 ■

Camel

Isle of Wight

27 ✴

44

head of the Valley of Grief in the uplands of Hell. Two of Arthur's men enter her cave but she sends them out screaming. Arthur then prepares to go himself, but his companions Gwyn and Gwyther say: 'It is not seemly or pleasant for us to see thee scuffling with a hag. Send Long Amren and Long Eiddil into the cave.' These two were sent in, 'but if ill was the plight of the first two, the plight of those two was worse, so that God knows not one of the four could have stirred from the place but for the way they were all loaded on Amrei, Arthur's mare'. Then Arthur 'took aim with Carwennan his knife and struck her across the middle until she was as two tubs'. He not only inspired and encouraged the feats of others, he stepped in and took on himself those for which his followers had not the spirit or the physical power.

Another Welsh version of Arthur, belonging to the eleventh century, is found in the Mabinogion. In *The Dream of Rhonabwy*, Arthur is spoken of as an Emperor; the tale is one of the strangest productions. The dreamer comes along a road from which he can see a ford of the Severn, where the river passes from England into Wales. He has the power, experienced in dreams, of being able to see figures a long way off as clearly as if he were close to them. He and his friends are overtaken by a youth who tells them he is called Iddawg the Embroiler of Britain. When Arthur sent him to Modred to remind the latter that Arthur was his uncle and foster-father and to ask for peace, Iddawg suppressed the message and spoke words of scorn and hate which brought on the battle.

Meanwhile 'a mile from the ford on either side, they could see the tents and the pavilions and the mustering of a great host. And they came to the back of the ford.' The time scheme as well as the range of visibility is dreamlike, for when the dreamer sees Arthur seated on a flat island in the river, though he has just been told of the Battle of Camlann, it appears that Arthur is waiting for the Battle of Badon to begin. Arthur, who is now called Emperor, is engaged in *gwydbyll*, a game played with gold pieces on a silver board. His opponent is Owein, who is attended by a flock of ravens: Loomis explains that the ravens were the bird-forms of Owein's mother, the goddess Modron, and her companions. At the approach of Iddawg, accompanied by the dreamer and his friends, Arthur says: 'Where, Iddawg, didst thou find those little fellows?' 'I found them, Lord King, away up on the road.' The Emperor smiled wryly. 'Lord,' said Iddawg, 'why art thou laughing?' 'Iddawg,' said Arthur, 'I am not laughing; rather, how sad I feel that men as mean as these keep this island, after men as fine as those that left it of yore.' *The Dream of Rhonabwy*, with its eerie effects of space and brightness, its symbolic pictures, gives the impression of an actual dream. In history and tradition, in the conscious workings of imagination, in the subconscious imagery of dreams, Arthur's idea was present in the mind.

It is on the face of it strange that Arthur was adopted as a hero, not only by the British whom he had defended but by the Saxons whom he had utterly defeated; but, in the fifty years during which peace was enforced on them after the Battle of Badon, the Saxons lost much of their ferocity and turned their capacity and

industry to the arts of peace, at which the Germans excel when they give their
minds to them. Their chief contribution was agricultural; they drained the marshy
valleys of the south of England and cultivated them with their heavier ploughs.
Man is a worshipping animal and this is particularly true of the Germanic peoples;
the grief of the vassal whose lord is dead is poignantly shown in the Saxon poem
The Wanderer, written down in the Exeter Book of 975:

> Long ago I wrapped my lord's remains
> In darkness of the earth and sadly thence
> Journeyed by winter over icy waves.
> . . . He understands
> Who long must do without the kind advice
> Of his beloved lord.

A feeling of desolation and of suffering from the cold were emotions the Saxons
turned very readily into their poetry. Cadmon's line chills the blood:

> The wolves sing their dread evensong.

The body of their verse speaks a longing for protection.

Their greatest poetic achievement, *Beowulf*, is not a story of Arthur, but it
reveals an emotional climate in which men's thoughts turned with longing to the
idea of a saviour. The Danish king Hrothgar had built a magnificent feasting-hall,
but at night, when the feasters were asleep, Grendel, a monster who lived at the
bottom of a neighbouring mere, came in at the door of the hall, seized and mangled
the sleepers and carried them off to devour. Beowulf, the hero, comes with his
men to Hrothgar's aid and, after a frightful struggle with Grendel and his mother,
pursues them to their lair in the bottom of the lake. He kills them in their subaqueous cave, and rises to the surface of the mere again, where his men have been
waiting for him in agonized anxiety as the turbid waters bubble with blood. The
poem reads as if it came directly from the subconscious without the usual trans-
formations of the conscious mind. There is the gilded hall, the lights, the
enthusiasm of a great feast, the lapse into helpless sleep, and then:

> out in the darkness
> The monster began to walk . . .
> He moved quickly through the cloudy night
> Up from his swampland sliding silently
> Toward that gold-shining hall.

The terror is so near to us, yet we can hardly put a name to it. It was called up with
fearful vividness in 1973 when a woman came by night, broke into the ground
floor of a house where a baby was sleeping in its cot, took it out through the window
and drowned it in a pond half a mile away.

The darkness, the agony of fear, the longing to hear in a story about a champion,
a hero, a protector, no matter of what race or for whose benefit, are a part of the
mental landscape in which the idea of Arthur grew to such strength.

Arthur, sword in hand, faced with a giant
roasting a pig on Mount St Michael

4 Growth of the Legend

After Arthur's death it appeared that the Britons could make no sustained resistance to the Saxons. Wales remained unconquered but the rest of Britain was divided into the Saxon kingdoms of Kent, Sussex, Essex and Wessex, and the Anglian kingdoms of East Anglia, Bernicia and Mercia.

The Saxons developed a civilization which could not have been foreseen by those who had suffered from their savagery. Their religious foundations, their scholarship, their art, their agriculture, their social structure in which the family was the most important unit, gave them a way of life that had become valuable and beautiful when it, in turn, was hideously attacked by the Danes who murdered and looted, and burned down cities, abbeys and farms. Alfred the Great mounted against them one of the great resistance movements of history, and it is strange that with all we know of his courage, his ability and intellect, he has never been touched by the glamour that attaches to the almost unknown Arthur. The Danes were a seafaring race and no doubt contributed something to our ideas of ship-building, but the event that had most influence on our national consciousness was not their invasion, but that of the Normans. This had a very great effect on the development of Arthurian legend; it set a scene against which a hero, a saviour, fought against an ogre or devilish tyrant in a neighbouring stronghold, and it provided an audience of Norman gentry who, since they were obliged formally to acknowledge the King of France as the overlord of their Norman estates, were glad to hear that Arthur, the British king to whose power their duke had succeeded, had conquered France, so that, in fact, they themselves, *vis-à-vis* the French king, were in the superior position.

Boullainvilliers, in his *Essai sur la noblesse de France* of 1732, put forward the theory that the origin of giants in folk tales was that they were oppressing feudal lords. This carries with it a dreadful conviction. William the Conqueror laid the foundations of this country's greatness by enforcing the king's rights as feudal overlord of the whole realm, crushing the minor kingdoms which had divided it. This he did by inhuman severity: he could have done it in no other way. He maintained his supremacy by the building of castles. These were first put up as wooden erections: William brought over one in sections in his invasion fleet. They were then rebuilt in massive stonework, with a rapidity that shows not only the skill of the master masons brought from Normandy, but the pressure exerted on the local forces of slave labour.

Combat in chain mail between Arthur and
the Emperor Lucius

48

The barons who had come over with the Conqueror were licensed by him to build castles on the fiefs he granted them. Here, unassailable in their solid stone keeps, they could tyrannize as they pleased over their humble neighbours living beneath a thatch of straw. Robert de Bellême had been licensed to build castles at Shrewsbury, Bridgnorth and Ticknall, and he made these holds the scenes of cruelties so ghastly that they appalled the people even of that savage time. After a career of bargaining for his allegiance with the Conqueror's three sons, Robert of Normandy, William Rufus and Henry I, he was at last arrested by the latter and put into prison, from which he never came out.

William Rufus, on his father's death, immediately secured the English crown. While his brother Robert was thinking of taking it, William bolted to Winchester and secured the treasure kept in the castle. This fabulous heap of gold and silver was known as the King's Hoard, and represented the financial assets of the monarch, which then meant actual handfuls of gold and silver coin.

William's rapacity was devouring. The Conqueror, though rigid in his exactions, had been a defender of the Church. William Rufus said that God had never done anything for him, therefore he could not be expected to do anything for God. When the Norman abbot of Glastonbury had tried without success to get the monks to leave off their Gregorian chanting and adopt a style of singing which he preferred, he brought the archers of his escort into church and had the monks shot down at the altar steps. The Conqueror had deposed him for this; William Rufus allowed him to return to his office on payment of five hundred pounds of silver.

But though he tyrannized over Church and people, William Rufus had a veneration for knighthood. Towards knights, whether followers or adversaries, he behaved with a high courtesy and generosity, and an exact obedience to the laws of chivalry. His court attracted hardy and skilful warriors from all over Christendom and the King maintained them as privileged companions. In the late eleventh century the armour worn by knights was a hauberk, or short-sleeved shirt of chain mail worn over a leather undercoat. The helmet was a steel cap with a steel nose-guard worn over a coif of chain mail. The term 'mail' came from the Latin *macula*, meaning 'spot', a picture-word for the effect of mesh. The mail was made of interlocking links of metal, each link connected with four surrounding links. The best kinds were manufactured abroad. William of Malmesbury says that, in the reign of Henry I, the quays of London were piled high with costly imports, including coats of mail from Mainz and Regensburg.

Over the hauberk, a belt supported the scabbard of the sword. The latter had been used as a slashing implement by the Saxons and the Danes; the Normans developed the use of the sword's point. The blade, about 3 feet long, was made of steel and had its weight reduced by a groove down the centre of both surfaces. The grooves acted also as blood-gutters. The steel-clad, mounted swordsmen were vulnerable to opponents similarly armed, or to the deadly force of an arrow in flight; otherwise they were invincible. William Rufus allowed his household knights to live off the land. They not only commandeered food and women; they

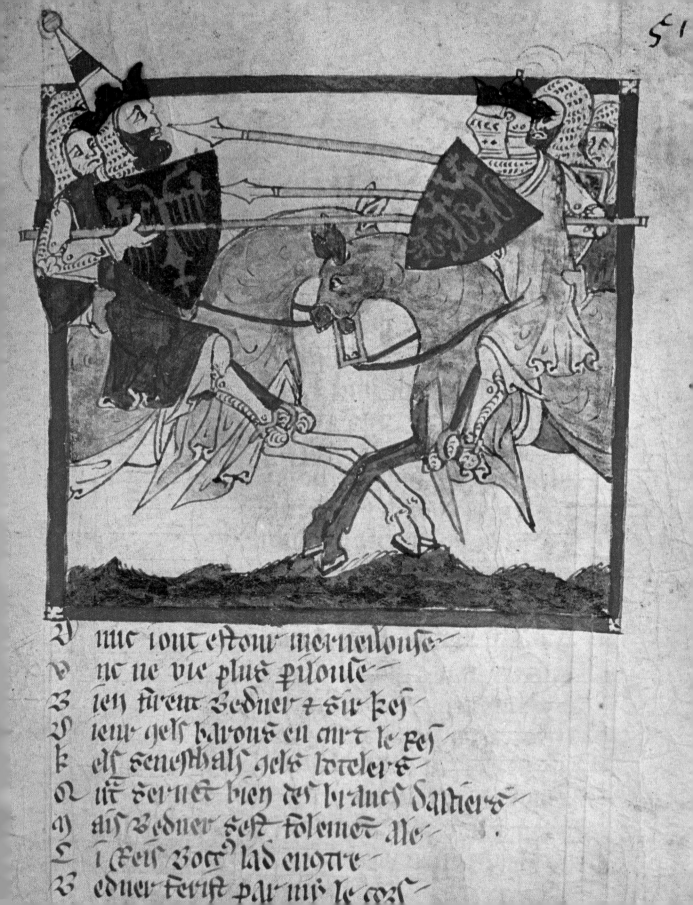

V nuc iout eſtour merueillouſe
V ne ne vie plus priſouſe
B ien furent Bedner ⁊ ſir kes
V ieur gels barous eu cuit le kes
k els ſeneſthals gels lotelers
O nt ſernet bien des braues halriers
J dis Bedner ſeſt folemet ale
L i Beiſ Boct⁹ lad enotre
B edner feriſt par mi le cops

showed their senseless arrogance by staving in the barrels of mead they had not been able to drink, and selling or burning the provisions they had not been able to eat. When country folk heard that the King and his retinue were approaching, they took to the woods.

In spite of his barbarity, William Rufus had a certain grandeur of mind. Westminster Hall as we see it now was rebuilt by Richard II, but in its original form as built by William Rufus it was said to be the most magnificent building erected in England or France since the Romans. Here the King held his great Whitsun feasts. As instituted by the Conqueror, the King's seasonal feasts were the great social occasions of the Middle Ages. The Easter Feast was held at Winchester, the Whitsun in London, the Christmas at Gloucester. Many of the adventures of the knights of Arthur's court take their rise because of the King's refusing to sit down to the feast until some adventure shall have declared itself.

William Rufus's successor, his brother Henry I, was said to have had twenty illegitimate children; of his two legitimate ones, his daughter Matilda was married to the Holy Roman Emperor Henry VI, his son William was drowned in the shocking wreck of the *White Ship*, when a drunken crew ran her on to the rocks outside Barfleur. When the news was brought to the King, he fell down in a dead faint, but the consequences of the tragedy went far beyond the father's grief; they brought on the darkest period in English history. It was also an era in which the leading figures were strangely connected with the development of Arthurian romance.

Matilda was widowed in 1125, and the following year the King forced his barons to recognize her as the heiress of the English crown. In 1128 she was married to Geoffrey, Count of Anjou, surnamed Plantagenet from the sprig of broom he had adopted as a badge. Matilda despised her husband, who was eleven years younger than she, and the marriage, to her, was one of gnawing discontents, but it produced one of the greatest of monarchs, Henry II, and the Plantagenet dynasty which divided with the Tudors the claim to be the greatest of the English royal lines.

Another heir, however, put himself forward in the old King's lifetime, his nephew Stephen of Blois, son of the Conqueror's daughter Adela. Except that he had their physical courage, he was the very opposite of his three predecessors: tall, fair, handsome, charming and weak. It was clear that he would not be a tyrannical ruler, and as the holders of the Norman fiefs detested the Angevins, they supported Stephen's claim against Matilda.

The latter's great ally in England was her half-brother Robert, Henry I's favourite bastard whom he had created Earl of Gloucester. He was a man of chivalrous nature, great cultivation and remarkably loyal to his sister's cause. But for the unfortunate bar sinister he would have made an excellent king.

The difficulties of the situation were soon beyond Stephen's control. Besides his brother Henry, Bishop of Winchester, who had deserted him from rage at not being made Archbishop of Canterbury, Stephen was faced with three dissident and immensely wealthy clerics: Roger, Bishop of Salisbury, who had been Henry I's chancellor, and his nephews Nigel, Bishop of Ely, and Alexander, Bishop of Lincoln. Afraid that they would betray him as Henry of Winchester had done, Stephen seized on the excuse of a street brawl begun by the Bishop of Salisbury's men, to arrest all three of them. The clergy were now violently hostile to the King, and in 1139 full-scale warfare began. Matilda, supported by Robert of Gloucester, landed in England, but while Gloucester made his way to his headquarters in Bristol, Matilda fell into Stephen's hands; Stephen, like the good-natured fool he was, let her go and she joined Gloucester at Bristol. The invasion was now extremely serious. Hostilities culminated in a battle outside Lincoln, where Stephen opened the engagement according to the rules of chivalry, with his knights drawn up in ceremonial formation, waiting for the signal to attack. Matilda's motley forces fell upon them with disorderly energy and broke their stand. Stephen fought with magnificent courage, wielding an old Danish battle-axe that, when his sword was lost, someone put into his hand; but he was captured and taken off to Bristol Castle, where his cousin Matilda ordered that he should be kept in chains. She then proceeded to London, where she announced herself Queen and demanded a huge subsidy. Her haughty bearing so much infuriated the citizens that they rang the tocsin, which brought all their fellows pouring into the streets, and Matilda fled ignominiously to Oxford.

While he was covering his sister's retreat, Gloucester fell into the hands of Stephen's queen, the gentle and charming but high-spirited Matilda of Boulogne. Months of negotiations had failed to gain her husband's release from his vindictive cousin and Queen Matilda now went over her rival's head. Stephen was still imprisoned in Bristol Castle, and now that Gloucester himself was captured, the castle was in the charge of his wife. Queen Matilda threatened the Countess of Gloucester that, if the King were not immediately released, the Earl should be sent to one of the Queen's own castles in Boulogne. After nine months of his chains, the King was thus able to rejoin his wife. He now besieged Matilda in Oxford, in the four-storeyed tower of Oxford castle. He began the siege in September; three months later, when the Cherwell was frozen and the landscape white with snow, Matilda and some of her ladies, all dressed in white clothes, escaped out of the tower by night and stole away unperceived down the river to Wallingford, where helpers were waiting with horses. From there she made her dangerous way to Bristol. It was said that, while the pursuit was on, her men got her out of a town by shrouding her as a corpse and carrying her away in a coffin.

The death of Robert of Gloucester in 1147 left her without effective support and she withdrew from England for good the following year. In that year, Stephen and his Queen kept Christmas at Lincoln, where the King attended mass on Christmas Day wearing his crown and afterwards held a great Christmas feast.

The terrible stain on Stephen's disastrous reign was that, though he had gained the titular supremacy, the Norman barons, without a strong king to control them, reverted to the cruelties of an earlier epoch. Three hundred and seventy-five castles had been built without royal licence, and by bargaining alternately with Stephen and Matilda, the barons secured to themselves larger and larger gains. The worst of them all, recalling the hideous Robert de Bellême, was Geoffrey de Mandeville, who seemed as though he would establish a separate principality. Stephen at last arrested him and, with his usual hopeless folly, offered de Mandeville the choice between hanging and giving up his place as the governor of the Tower of London and all his castles in Essex. De Mandeville, once let go, marched north-east with his private army and seized a large fief in Cambridge-shire, where he fortified the Isle of Ely. From this stronghold he conducted a reign of terror which, though it lasted only a year, is said to have destroyed more victims than the war of Stephen and Matilda. His career, even, of plunder, burning and massacring, was not so horrifying as his method of sending spies to detect anyone who had concealed property, and abducting them for vile torture to make them reveal it. The Anglo-Saxon Chronicle, instituted by Alfred, was kept in several abbeys on the basis of a common plan to which the abbey scribes added local details. It is sinister indeed that the famous passage on the barons' cruelty in Stephen's reign, which ends with the words 'Men said openly that Christ and His saints were asleep', was added in the chronicle kept at Peterborough, the abbey within twenty miles of Ely.

The stronghold was almost unapproachable through reeds and fen, but Stephen laid siege to the borders of the fief and de Mandeville met his death at Burwell in 1144. He had taken off his helm for the heat; an arrow struck him in the head and he died of the festering wound.

Meanwhile Matilda's son Henry Plantagenet, who on the death of Stephen's son was destined to be the heir to the crown, was building up a position of strength. His father had given up to him the Duchy of Normandy, and at his death left him Anjou, Touraine and Maine. He gained the great Duchy of Aquitaine with the hand of Eleanor, from whom her husband the King of France allowed himself to be separated, that her son by Henry Plantagenet might be born in wedlock. On Stephen's death in 1154, Henry II began his splendid career of putting down the Norman barons and laying the foundations of our rule of law.

5 The First Recorders

The tale that the Breton *conteurs* had carried to France, and to the Norman castles
of England, was based on historical truth, but much of it had developed into fairy
lore, an aspect accentuated by the hero's mysterious death and unknown grave;
but in 1135, with the suddenness of a revelation, a new presentation of Arthur was
before the world: that of a professional soldier, a crowned king, famous for his
generosity and his knightly example, established in a court, not in a nameless fairy
realm, but in the actual Welsh town of Caerleon-on-Usk, one who presided over
tournaments at home, and who, abroad, instead of taking part in the ridiculous
adventures of a folk-tale, achieved a formidable series of conquests, annexing
Scotland, Ireland, Norway, Denmark and Gaul, and who was only recalled from
an assault on Rome itself by the outbreak of treachery at home.

The popularity of a best-seller is often a more interesting study than the work
itself, and the amazing success of Geoffrey of Monmouth's *Historia Regum
Britanniae*, which survives in two hundred manuscripts and was known before the
end of the twelfth century in France, Spain, Italy, Poland and Byzantium, is at
least as interesting as the stories it narrates.

Geoffrey of Monmouth was a Welsh or Breton monk born in Monmouth, and
he chose to site Arthur's court in the city of Caerleon, built out of Roman remains,
within twenty miles of his birthplace. The final ingredient in the magic brew of
his success eludes us, but we can recognize certain of its elements. He had a
technical gift for writing which enabled him to gather up legends already known
and loved and present them in a compact and gleaming whole; although he said
he was writing a history, he put down what he knew to be lies, for interest's sake
and with an immense appearance of conviction; above all he pitched on the one
British king, or king so-called, in the *Historia*, who was going to interest the
readers and hearers most. The procession begins with the mythological Brutus who
came from Troy to colonize Britain, and ends with the mythological Cadwallo.
It covers ninety-nine kings in all, and of the entire work one-fifth is devoted to the
imaginary history of Arthur.

Geoffrey himself did not perhaps invent so very much; he took existing legends
and, adding some few unassailable facts, put them forward as history. His contribution to the story of Arthur is the assertion that he was the son of Uther
Pendragon, that he ruled from Caerleon-on-Usk, that his prime minister was the
magician Merlin, and that when mortally wounded he was borne away to the
Island of Avalon.

The rocky promontory at Tintagel, which
Uther Pendragon took with the help of
Merlin's magical powers

54

Loomis shows that Geoffrey found a Welsh legend of a seer called Myrddin. He found in Nennius the story of a marvellous boy called Ambrosius, of clairvoyant powers, who prophesied to Vortigern the latter's destruction and the final victory of the Saxons over the Britons. By a masterstroke, he identified this boy with Merlin ('Ambrosius, who was also called Merlin'). This brought Merlin into the orbit of Ambrosius Aurelianus, and therefore established the connection between Merlin and Arthur, for Ambrosius Aurelianus was said by Geoffrey to be the brother of Arthur's father, Uther Pendragon. The two basic elements of the Arthurian legend were now combined.

Loomis further says that Geoffrey found a Cornish legend of Arthur's begetting at Tintagel by Uther Pendragon, on Igerna, the beautiful, chaste wife of Gorlois, Duke of Cornwall; this was brought about through Merlin's powers, which gave Uther the likeness of Gorlois, deceiving the faithful wife, whom Uther afterwards married when his men had slain Gorlois in battle. Arthur was therefore conceived in the glamour of overwhelming passion, and had the legal advantage of being born in wedlock.

The Easter Annals had said that, in the battle of Camlann, Arthur and Modred perished. The assumption (borne out by *The Dream of Rhonabwy*) is that they fought each other. Geoffrey states that they did, and that Modred had forcibly married Guinevere in Arthur's absence. Using a tradition of the greatest interest, since it refers to Camlann (which, however, he does not name), Geoffrey says that Arthur pursued Modred 'into Cornwall as far as the river Camel'. In this encounter Arthur receives his death-wound, and though one of the most interesting features of the historical story was that Arthur's grave was unknown ('whence', as William of Malmesbury said, 'ancient ditties fable that he is yet to come'), Geoffrey names the retreat to which Arthur was borne; he himself does not identify it with a place on the map, but he says it was Avalon. The name is sometimes derived from 'Glass Island', sometimes from 'Isle of Apples'. Geoffrey gives it the latter derivation. He was the earliest of widely read writers to name it at all.

Geoffrey's decision to say that Arthur was conceived at Tintagel (his birthplace is not stated, but it may be assumed that this was Tintagel also) is one of the instances of his genius for effect. Tintagel is one of the places it is not necessary to see to understand its impressiveness. The enormous, lofty folds of cliff that look as if they were pouring from the summit to the shore far down below, and the sea, sometimes peacock-blue, lying passively against the little stony beaches, sometimes lead-coloured, racing landward and exploding into towering foam, work so powerfully on the imagination that to say Arthur was conceived above that sea, within sound of those breakers, is to impregnate the story and the place with a mutual magic. The site now consists of a headland whose connection with the mainland has been partly eroded. In Geoffrey's time they were joined by what must have been a formidable ridge of rock.

When Uther Pendragon seeks counsel as to how he may come at Igerna, his friend Ulfin says: 'And how shall we give thee any counsel that may avail, seeing

that there is no force which may prevail whereby to come unto her in the Castle of Tintagel? For it is situate on the sea and is on every side encompassed thereby, nor none other entrance is there, save such as a narrow rock doth furnish, the which three knights could hold against thee, though thou wert standing there with the whole realm of Britain beside thee.'

When Geoffrey was working on the *Historia*, the isthmus and the island were the scene of ruins of a series of Celtic monastery buildings, dating from about A.D. 350 to 850. The first Norman castle to be built on the island was that of Reginald, Earl of Cornwall, another of the illegitimate sons of Henry I, who completed it about 1145. Geoffrey, if he were in the neighbourhood, would have seen or heard of the building; the ruins of the monastic buildings he may well have supposed to be those of a previous castle, such as Gorlois might have held.

Geoffrey says that Arthur, when he succeeded Uther Pendragon, was a boy of fifteen. He determined to free the land from Saxons, and 'assembled all the youths that were of his allegiance'. This youthful army fought great engagements at York and Lincoln. The Battle of Badon Geoffrey sites at Bath. In preparation for it, 'Arthur, donning upon himself a coat of mail worthy of a king so noble, did set

56

upon his head a helm of gold graven with the semblance of a dragon.' In this he did as any twelfth-century knight might do; but Geoffrey harks back to Welsh legends when he names the pieces of armour: the shield Pridwen (a confusion with the ship Prydwen in which Arthur voyaged to Annwyn), his lance Ron and his sword Caliburn, though the naming of swords was an ancient practice lasting into the Middle Ages. Charlemagne's was called Joyeuse, and Geoffrey says, on whatever authority, that Julius Caesar's sword was called Saffron Death. This might perhaps refer to the colour of a steel blade stained with dried blood. (A similar idiom is found in the 'bright brown blade' spoken of in the ballad *Glasgerion*.)

Arthur's victory at Badon is followed by a campaign vanquishing the Irish and the Scots, whom he determines to do away utterly. When they were at his mercy, 'he yielded him to treating them with a cruelty beyond compare'. Only the intercession of the Scottish bishops prevailed on him to spare the miserable remainder of the population. Geoffrey approves of this savagery; he also applauds the similar behaviour of Arthur's army against the inhabitants of Norway: 'When they had won the victory, they over-ran and set fire to the cities, scattering the country folk, nor did they cease to give full loose to their cruelty until they had submitted the whole of Norway as well as Denmark to Arthur.'

After the Scottish campaign, Arthur 'took unto himself a wife, born of a noble Roman family, Guinevere, who did surpass in beauty all the other dames of the island'. So early is the acceptance of Guinevere's astonishing beauty.

Arthur's next martial expedition is the one which may have done most towards making his story so successful in the castles of Anglo-Norman nobility. He is described as invading France, where the issue is to be decided by a single combat between him and the Roman tribune Flollo. The account of the contest is a professional one:

'Taking their stand opposite each other and couching lance in rest, they forthwith set spurs to their steeds and smote together with a right mighty shock. But Arthur who bore his spear the more heedfully, thrust the same into the top of Flollo's breast, and shielding off the other's blow with all the force he might, bore him to the ground. Then, unsheathing his sword, he was hastening to smite him, when Flollo, on his legs again in an instant, ran upon him with his spear levelled, and with deadly thrust into his destrier's chest, brought both horse and rider to the ground.'

The fight is continued on foot until Arthur, excited by the sight of his own outpouring blood, gives his opponent the final stroke. 'Flollo fell, and beating the ground with his heels, gave up his ghost to the winds.'

For the next nine years Arthur devotes himself to the conquest of France. When he had achieved it, he did as William the Conqueror had done in England: 'Many provinces did he grant to the noblemen who served him in his household. . . . At last, when all states and peoples were established in his peace, he returned to Britain at the beginning of the spring.'

ntost quilz furent entrez ou
np fans plente dattente ilz
allerent les lances lun cotre
ultre z ferirent cheuaulx des
perons qui les emporterent de
le roideur quil sambloit que
fust fourdre tellement frai
ent ilz la terre resonnee. si fe
ent en ce venir lun sault ens
nis si durement qil comunt

qui prestement retourna z auoit
la sacquiet son espee pour ferir
le dit flolon le quel flolon es
toit ia releuez come tous cofus
z honteux. et en tresriant deste
de venuier sa honte auoit ahers
sa lance qui lj estoit volee par
et sen vint de grant ire embrase
deuers le roy et assist sa lance
ens es ars du cheual artus tel

Geoffrey now describes the great Whitsun feast which Arthur held at Caerleon to celebrate his victorious return, and to hold his coronation.

Richard Barber[10] points out that though, in Geoffrey's description, Caerleon is correctly sited, near to a river bringing in ships from the sea, surrounded by meadows and woods, the city itself and some of the ceremonial of the feast are drawn from Byzantium, the only eastern city of Christian customs. In the First Crusade, undertaken in 1096, which succeeded in capturing Jerusalem from the Turks, the Greek Emperor allowed the Crusaders to pass through Byzantium; this opened a way to increased traffic with the East in silk, spices, swords and glassware; it also sent travellers' tales to the Crusaders' homes when they went back. The Second Crusade, to capture Edessa, was not undertaken till 1147; Geoffrey therefore was working on the results of the first. He says of Caerleon: 'Passing fair was the magnificence of the kingly palaces thereof with gilded verges of the roofs that imitated Rome.' He says Rome, but the separation of the men and women for the feast, Barber points out, was a Byzantine custom. The appearance of Guinevere at the coronation is purely classical. 'The Archbishops and pontiffs led the Queen, crowned with laurel', while four visiting queens 'did bear before her, according to wont and custom, four white doves'.

Much of Geoffrey's descriptive detail is totally unrelated to historical fact, as his saying that there were three archbishops, but the description of the feast, based, it is suggested, on the great Christmas feast held by Stephen at Lincoln when the King wore his crown to go to Mass, contains the first written description of a tournament in England: 'Presently the knights engage in a game on horseback, making a show of fighting a battle, whilst the dames and damsels looking on from the top of the walls, for whose sake the courtly knights make believe to be fighting, do cheer them on for the sake of seeing the better sport.'

The next great event in this passage of the *Historia* is Arthur's reception of the demand of the Roman Emperor, Lucius Hiberius, for Britain's tribute. The origin of this is explained[11] as Geoffrey's alteration of an episode of Welsh tradition, that of Arthur's war with an Irish chieftain, Llwch the Irishman; 'Llwch' being latinized as Lucius, and 'the Irishman' being changed, by accident or design, from 'Hibernus' to 'Hiberus'. The method is characteristic of Geoffrey, aggrandizing the circumstances out of all knowledge by making an obscure Irish chieftain the Emperor of Rome.

The demand for tribute, fiercely and haughtily resented by Arthur, causes the latter to embark with a vast army recruited from his dependencies, to conquer Rome itself by way of teaching the Emperor a lesson. 'Sixty thousand were reckoned from the Island of Britain alone, of armed men with all equipment. But the kings of the other islands, inasmuch as they had not yet taken up with the custom of knights, promised footsoldiers, as many as were due from them, so that out of the six islands, to wit Ireland, Iceland, Gothland, the Orkneys, Norway and Denmark, were numbered six score thousand.' Then there were the contingents summoned from the Duchies of Gaul. 'Altogether these made one hundred and

eighty-three thousand, beside those on foot who were not so easy to reckon.' In this way Geoffrey combined the vividness of an immense exaggeration with a show of conscientious accuracy.

As Arthur is crossing with his troops to Barfleur he dreams that a flaming-eyed dragon and a bear meet in the sky; the dragon kills the bear and casts it down to earth. This dream struck the imagination of the hearers very much; it is repeated by all the followers, translators and adapters of Geoffrey of Monmouth, including Malory. It is interpreted for Arthur as meaning the prophecy of his victory over some giant; the King himself thinks it more likely to foretell his conflict with the Emperor.

Either interpretation is borne out by events. In a passage of horrible crudeness, recalling the dark ages of folklore rather than the court life of the twelfth century, Arthur finds, on St Michael's Mount, an old woman wailing over her nurseling Helena, whom a hideous giant has tried to ravish. Before the rape could be effected, the child died of fright, whereupon the giant raped the old woman. Arthur seeks out this giant, whose chops are smeared with the blood of half-eaten swine, and after a fearful struggle, kills him. This is another of the adventures in which Arthur takes not only the leading part but one in which no one else could have succeeded.

The fight with the Emperor is joined at Autun and after a long, resounding description of the campaign, occupying eight chapters, the Emperor falls by a spear-thrust 'from a hand unknown'. Arthur orders that the body should be borne to the Roman Senate 'with a message to say that no other tribute was due from Britain'.

Arthur remains in Gaul, 'bringing the cities of the Burgundians into his allegiance'; the following summer he is preparing to advance on Rome when he receives news that his nephew Modred, whom he has left as Regent of Britain, has 'set the crown of the kingdom upon his own head and linked him in unhallowed union with Guinevere the Queen'. Arthur's return to Britain begins the civil war, ending in the fatal battle of Camlann, where he and Modred are slain, and after which, Guinevere, 'smitten with despair, fled from York into Caerleon, where she proposed henceforth to lead a chaste life among the nuns and did take the veil of their order'.

Geoffrey gathered up a skein of traditions as to Arthur's survival and place of retreat: British, Breton, Welsh, the place is always a paradise, surrounded by water. He chose the strand that called it Avalon. He said: 'The renowned King Arthur himself was wounded deadly, and was borne thence into the Isle of Avalon, for the healing of his wounds, where he gave up the crown of Britain unto his kinsman Constantine, son of Cador, Duke of Cornwall, in the year of our Lord 542.'

The Easter Annals give the entry 'The battle of Camlann in which Arthur and Modred perished, and there was plague in Britain' opposite the year 537. It is interesting that when he was totally fictitious in most of his material, Geoffrey was so nearly accurate in this important date.

The *Historia Regum Britanniae* might be called the first of the international best-sellers. Its popularity spread to a degree that is amazing, seeing that the part responsible for the success, the story of Arthur, contained none of the features that came afterwards to be regarded as the most important parts of it; Geoffrey says nothing of the Round Table, or of the quest for the Holy Grail, nor does he use the two great stories which in later centuries overshadowed Arthur's own; Lancelot and Tristan were figures added by later hands. Of Merlin he says very little in connection with Arthur, but the magician nevertheless plays a leading role in the *Historia*. When Geoffrey has established his identity with that of the clairvoyant boy Ambrosius, and made the link with Arthur, he devotes the next book, Book VII, to the Prophecies of Merlin. These are wild and whirling words of which only a few passages can be picked out as conveying anything which, albeit with the advantage of hindsight, might be reckoned of prophetic value. Geoffrey seems to have used his usual method of throwing in a small quantity of fact and stirring it up with a great brew of imagination; in this case the result is so tempestuous and unintelligible as to be quite confounding. The facts where discoverable are those which Geoffrey, writing in 1130 or 1135, could put into the mouth of someone supposed to be living in the sixth century, with the effect of genuine prophecy.

'The lion's whelp shall be transformed into the fishes of the sea' sounds impressive as a prophecy of the disaster of the *White Ship*. 'The shape of commerce shall be cloven in twain, the half shall be round' is supposed to be based on an ordinance of Geoffrey's own time, that instead of obtaining halfpennies by breaking the silver penny in half, round halfpennies should be coined. His cleverest passage is where he says of Arthur: 'The islands of the ocean shall be subdued into his power and the forests of Gaul shall he possess. The house of Romulus shall dread the fierceness of his prowess, and doubtful shall be his end. Renowned shall he be in the mouth of the peoples and his deeds shall be as meat to them that tell thereof.'

The reference to Arthur's conquest of Gaul and his advance on Rome, in a work which was to recount them a little later on, was of course highly effective with people who believed that the whole body of prophecy would be found true if only they could understand it. Even more impressive, in the perspective of centuries, is the prophecy that people shall make money by writing about Arthur and his deeds.

The terse, allegorical method Geoffrey uses is copied from the usual language of prophecy; it can be compared with that used by Nostradamus four hundred years later; but Nostradamus, in the sixteenth century, prophesied explicitly, *inter alia*, the English Civil War, the French Revolution, and the rise of Hitler. To compare his utterances with Geoffrey's apocalyptic and vague pronouncements – 'The helmet of Mars shall cast a shadow and the rage of Mercury shall pass all bounds . . . the Scales of the Balance shall hang awry until the Ram shall set his crooked horns beneath them. The tail of the Scorpion shall breed lightning and the Crab shall fall at strife with the Sun. The Virgin shall forget her maiden shame and climb up on the back of the Sagittary' – makes Geoffrey's sound empty and absurd, and almost like a take-off of the prophetic style.

The extraordinary thing is that, like the rest of his work, they had a *succès fou*. They were transcribed, independently of the *Historia*, and issued with commentaries. The great prestige accorded to Merlin as a seer naturally enhanced the ascendancy of Arthur and appeared to confirm the historical truth of the fictitious image. Some years after finishing the *Historia*, Geoffrey produced a final work, a verse narration of the *Life of Merlin*. This contains one very important passage; in it, the Welsh bard Taliesin is supposed to give an account, fuller than the one in the *Historia*, of Arthur's being carried to Avalon, now described as a fairy island, inhabited by the mystic number of nine ladies, one of whom is Arthur's sister, Morgan le Fay. The latter plays inconsistent parts in Arthur's story, sometimes showing hostility towards him, sometimes affection. She is said in some versions to live beneath a lake. In Breton villages, water fairies were called morgans. 'In her own chamber she placed the King on a golden bed, with her own noble hand she uncovered the wound and gazed at it long. At last she said, health would return to him if he were to stay with her for a long time. . . . Rejoicing, therefore, we committed the King to her.'

The personality combined with the success of Geoffrey are such, it is not surprising that he was connected with many influential people in Stephen's sensational and calamitous reign. He was a canon of the Chapel of St George, a learned society which, before the foundation of the university, occupied premises in Oxford Castle. Since he held this appointment between 1129 and 1151, he was domiciled either in the castle or near it when Matilda made her escape from it, dressed in white, across the wintry landscape.

Walter, Archdeacon of Oxford, was Geoffrey's patron. Geoffrey says in the *Historia*, giving confirmation to the importance of oral transmission, that he could never find in writing any account of the kings before Arthur or of those who succeeded him, 'although', he says, 'their deeds be as pleasantly rehearsed from memory by word of mouth in the traditions of many people, as though they had been written down'. While he was thinking about this, the Archdeacon, he says, 'offered me a certain most ancient book in the British language that did set forth the doings of them all . . . told in stories of exceeding beauty'. He has, he says, 'been at pains to translate this volume into the Latin tongue'.

This device of the pretended source, so often used by fiction-writers since – a diary discovered in a trunk, a packet of letters in a cupboard – was then so fresh that the mere assertion of it carried conviction and invested Geoffrey's statements with authority. The existence of the British book is now generally disbelieved; the strange thing is, unless it is naïve to think it strange, that though the *Historia* was finished before 1140, the Archdeacon did not die till 1151. He must therefore have been a party to the deceit himself.

Geoffrey dedicated the work to the great Robert of Gloucester. 'Let it be held to be thine offspring, as thou thyself art offspring of the illustrious Henry, King of the English.' In another copy, this dedication is followed by one to Galeran, Count de Meulun, 'our other pillar of the state'. This baron was the brother of Henry I's faithful adviser, Robert de Meulun, but Galeran himself became a supporter of Stephen, and in another copy yet, the dedication reads: 'To Stephen, King of England, nephew of the illustrious Henry, King of the English.'

William of Malmesbury – of whom Stubbs said: 'He was the first writer, after Bede, who attempted to give to his details of dates and events such a systematic connection as entitles them to the name of history' – was also a protégé of Robert of Gloucester. He said that the Earl combined nobility, military science, personal elegance, surpassing magnificence, learning and justice.

Geoffrey had another patron of great distinction. When Stephen arrested the Bishop of Salisbury he had also imprisoned the latter's nephew Alexander, Bishop of Lincoln, depriving him of the castles he had built at Sleaford, Newark and Banbury. Alexander justified the King's mistrust by giving his allegiance to Matilda, but after this virago's retirement he was received into Stephen's favour once more and at the great ceremony held at Lincoln, in 1146, when the King went to Mass on Christmas Day wearing his crown, the Bishop of Lincoln naturally occupied a position of dignity and splendour. It is said in some accounts that Stephen underwent a second coronation at Alexander's hands.

The Bishop had, at all events, regained and improved upon his original footing. Geoffrey says: 'There was none other, whether he were cleric or layman, that did retain so many knights and nobles in his household, whom his gentle holiness of life,' as Geoffrey put it, 'and his bountiful kindness, did allure to his service.'

It was Alexander, Geoffrey said, who, having heard many tales about Merlin and his prophecies, encouraged Geoffrey to collect these and write them down; this Geoffrey had done, putting aside his work on the *Historia* for the purpose. When the latter was produced, the Prophecies were interpolated as Book VII, with a dedication to the Bishop.

Alexander's work on Lincoln Cathedral caused him to be known as Alexander the Magnificent. He beautified the West Front, and the sight of that towering achievement, of inspiration and of technical skill, makes it hard to understand how a man whose mind could superintend the creation of this dazzling richness and grace, could take so seriously the prophecies of Merlin. It is, however, possible that having at first only heard of them, the Bishop had been disillusioned by them when he saw them written down at length, for Geoffrey in the last resort was disappointed; his final work, the rhymed *Life of Merlin*, is dedicated to Alexander's successor in the see, Robert Chesney, in the hope, the dedication says, that this bishop will do more for the writer than his predecessor did.

William of Malmesbury's *Deeds of the Kings of England* was finished ten years before Geoffrey's *Historia*. In it he had already dealt, as an able historian, with the historical existence of Arthur and the accretion of legend around it. Speaking of the holding-back of the Saxon advance by Ambrosius Aurelianus, he says it was achieved through the military genius of Arthur, adding: 'This is that Arthur of whom the trifling of the Bretons talks such nonsense today; a man clearly worthy not to be dreamed of in false fables, but to be proclaimed in veracious histories, as one who long sustained his tottering country and gave the shattered minds of his fellow citizens an edge for war.' When Geoffrey finished the *Historia*, he wrote in a concluding paragraph that he made over the recording of Welsh kings to Caradoc of Lancafarn, 'as I do those of the Saxons to William of Malmesbury, and Henry of Huntingdon, whom I bid be silent as to the kings of the Britons, seeing that they have not that book in the British speech which Walter, Archdeacon of Oxford, did convey hither out of Brittany'.

They had not; it was a question whether Geoffrey of Monmouth had ever had it either – one readily solved by William of Malmesbury, who wrote in *Novella Historia*, 1142, 'Everything this man wrote about Arthur and his successors, or indeed about his predecessors, from Vortigern onwards, was made up, partly by himself, partly by others, either from an inordinate love of lying, or for the sake of pleasing the Britons.'

The annoyance of the conscientious historian was exacerbated by the fiction-writer's success; but this success was not owing only to the skill of Geoffrey; it was created also by the eagerness of a large audience to hear the story told.

6 English Interpretations

Geoffrey of Monmouth had begun his *Historia* with the adventures of Brute, the descendant of Aeneas who had fled to Italy after the Sack of Troy. The influence of the *Historia* was so compelling, that as Brute was said by it to have colonized England, this country was called by writers, for the next four hundred years, Troynovaunte or 'Second Troy'. Another result of Geoffrey's influence was that Brut became a term meaning, simply, 'Chronicle'. Two poems based on the *Historia*, one French, one Anglo-Saxon, were written under this title, though neither of them mentions Brute, since they open at the reign of Constantine, the father of the immediate predecessor of Vortigern.

Wace the Frenchman was born about 1100 in Jersey, then a part of the fief of Normandy. His childish impressions of life on a small island made him a graphic writer on shipping and seafaring. He was taken to Caen to be educated and spent his life between Normandy and France, with, however, at least one visit to England.

Eleanor of Aquitaine, whom Henry II had married in 1152, was the first of that series of damnable French queens which continued with Eleanor of Provence, Isabella of France, Margaret of Anjou and Henrietta Maria. Though Eleanor was thirty years old to Henry's nineteen, she had considerable attractions of a savage kind; but as Henry, at the time he seduced her as Queen of France, or allowed her to seduce him, was on the verge of establishing his claim to the English throne, her possessions – the great Duchy of Aquitaine and a fleet of thirty ships – perhaps worked as powerfully for her as any personal qualifications. Egotistical, passionate, vindictive and treacherous, she made Henry pay dearly for the advantages she brought. She alienated her sons, Geoffrey, Richard and John, from their father, and she was said to have murdered Rosamond Clifford, the lovely, gentle creature with whom the tormented King found comfort in the forest retreat of Woodstock. She was, at the same time, intellectual and cultivated; the troubadours of her native Aquitaine boasted of her in their verses that she could read and write. She was a desirable patron, and within five years of her becoming Queen of England, Wace dedicated his *Brut* to her.

Wace says, in another of his chronicles, that he addresses himself, 'to rich folk who possess revenues and silver', for, after all, 'it is for them that books are made'. His cast of mind is typically French, sceptical and lucid. He says that he went to the forest of Broceliande, the wooded district in Brittany where marvels were said to have occurred, hoping that he might see something of the kind himself, but: 'A fool I went and a fool I returned.' When he comes to Book VII of the *Historia* he says he will not translate the *Prophecies of Merlin*, as they are unintelligible.

This evidence of his way of thinking seems to give a trustworthy air to his opinions on the balance of legend and historical fact in the story of Arthur and to the extent to which oral transmission had preserved it. 'Such rhymes', he says, 'are neither mere base lies nor gospel truths . . . the minstrel has sung his ballad, the story-teller told over his story so frequently, little by little he has decked and painted till . . . truth stands hid in the trappings of a tale.'

While some of his passages are direct translations from Geoffrey of Monmouth, Wace appears to keep his rich, sophisticated audience all the time in mind. He streamlines the narrative, leaving out unnecessary detail and declamatory speeches and he reduces the description of Arthur's barbarities towards the Picts and Scots. Where he expands he does it to great effect, particularly in his description of Arthur's setting sail for France; here he shows a first-hand knowledge of seamanship: 'When the last man had entered the last ship, the sailors raised the anchor and worked the galleys from the haven . . . they pulled stoutly upon the hoists and ropes so that the ships ran out to sea. . . . At the captain's bidding they put the helm to port, to lee, as they might better fill their sails with the wind. As need arose, the shipmen drew upon the cords and bowlines or let the canvas fall upon the deck . . . thus loosing and making fast, letting go and bringing quickly to the deck, hauling and tugging at the ropes, they made on their way.'

Wace gives, although without detail, a strong impression of Guinevere's beauty, and though other storytellers imply that she was childless since there is no mention of children by her, Wace states that she was: 'Arthur cherished her dearly for his love was wonderfully set on her, yet never had they a child together, nor betwixt them might get an heir.'

His unique contribution to the written legend is the Round Table. This was not his invention; he says it was already famous. 'Arthur', he says, 'made the Round Table, so reputed of the Britons. This Round Table was ordained of Arthur, that when his fair fellowship sat to meat, their chairs should be high alike, their service equal and none before or after his comrade.'

Interesting as Wace's version of the story is, even more so is the evidence it gives of a great body of word-of-mouth storytelling about Arthur. The parts of this to which writers gave a form has remained; the rest has disappeared like morning dew. From what he says, Wace must have heard much that, having weighed, he did not put down. His final paragraph is most remarkable; it is impartial and sober and yet it has a haunting sadness like that of the Jacobite lament 'And will ye no come back again? Better lo'ed ye canna be': 'He is yet in Avalon, awaited of the Britons, for they say and deem he will return from whence he went and live again. . . . Men have ever doubted, and as I am persuaded, will ever doubt, whether he liveth or is dead. . . . To Constantine, Cador's son, Earl of Cornwall and his near kin, Arthur committed his realm, commanding him to hold it as King, until he

Miniatures from the thirteenth-century
chronicles of Wace: Arthur and his soldiers
setting out by sea, and RIGHT Arthur crowned

ENGLISH INTERPRETATIONS

returned to his own. The earl took the land to his keeping. He held it as bidden, but nevertheless Arthur came never again.'

The story of Arthur had been already told in Latin, Welsh and French. Between 1189 and 1199, in the reign of Richard Cœur de Lion, Layamon, a priest of Arley Regis in Worcestershire, made a version based on Wace's *Brut* in Anglo-Saxon verse, the first presentation of Arthur in the English language. Layamon was deeply impressed by the story: he says of himself: 'It came into his mind, a happy thought, that he would tell the noble deeds of the English, what they were named and whence they came who first possessed the English land.' He is perfectly clear in his distinction between the Britons and 'the Saxish men', and the work closely follows Wace and through him Geoffrey of Monmouth, in presenting Arthur as a mighty hero who defeated the Saxons. Geoffrey was Welsh or Breton, Wace was French, and their eager, imaginative participation in Arthur's victories was natural enough; but Layamon was Anglo-Saxon, writing in the language of the Anglo-Saxons, and his enthusiasm for Arthur's destruction of the Saxon hosts is surprising. One is led to suppose that, after six hundred years and more, he looked back to Britons and Saxons as all 'English', as people today look back on the Cavaliers and Roundheads of the Civil War, and that he took his side, as we do ours.

The difference between the French and Anglo-Saxon temperaments is implicit in a comparison of the two works. Layamon says Arthur 'was winsome where he had his will but exceeding stern with his enemies'. Wace says: 'He was one of love's lovers, a lover also of glory.' Layamon has none of Wace's scepticism; he wholeheartedly accepts the supernatural and adds to Geoffrey's marvels some of his own, culled from who shall say what vanished regions. He says that at Arthur's birth, fairies attended. 'So soon as he came on earth, elves took him; they enchanted the child with magic most strong; they gave him might to be the best of all knights; they gave him another thing, that he should be a rich king; they gave him the third, that he should live long; they gave him the prince-virtues, so that he was most generous of all men alive.' Arthur's resplendent reputation in the racial memory needed the explanation of magic.

Layamon's poetic passages are something quite out of the range of the elegant and sensible Wace. The famous one, of Arthur's exulting over the bodies of the drowned Saxons lying in the Avon, is one of the strangest in English poetry: 'How the steel fishes lie in the stream . . . their scales float like gold-dyed shields, there float their fins as if they were spears.' Unlike Wace, who toned down such passages, Layamon took a keen delight in imagining violence and cruelty wreaked on people who were on the wrong side: 'The Britons laid on them, as men should do on the wicked; they gave bitter strokes with axes and with swords.'

Similarly, he gives Wace's account of the Round Table a more savage cast. He confirms the idea that the story of the table was Celtic (he says it was of Cornish origin), and he depicts Arthur in vivid colours as authoritative and ferocious. A shocking brawl arises as to the seating order in the hall. 'Then approached the King out of his chamber, with him an hundred nobles, in helms and hauberks, each bore in his hand a white steel brand. Then called Arthur, noblest of Kings, "Sit ye, sit ye quickly, each man on his life! And whoso will not that do, he shall be put to death."' When order is restored, Arthur commands that the man who began the riot shall be dragged away in a halter and left submerged in a fen; his male relatives are to be beheaded and the female ones to have their noses cut off. When this was done, 'Men took all the dead and carried them to burial places. Afterwards men blew the trumpet with noise full merry . . . gleemen there sang, harps gan resound, the people were in joy.' When Arthur goes to Cornwall, he encounters a carpenter, who says: 'I will work thee a board exceeding fair, that thereat may sit sixteen hundred or more, all turn about so that none be outside. And when thou wilt ride, with thee thou mayst carry it and set it where thou wilt, after thy will; and then thou needst never fear, to the world's end, that ever any moody knight at thy board may make fight, for there shall the high be even with the low.' When the table is made trial of, all the knights seated there, 'each spoke with other as if it were his brother'.

Layamon had expanded Wace's story of the Round Table, but he puts in a striking incident which does not occur either in Wace or Geoffrey of Monmouth. He says that when Arthur, having defeated the Roman army in Gaul, is about to set out for Rome, he has a dream foretelling the news that Modred and Guinevere have betrayed him. Loomis believes that the dream should be accepted as traditional: its dreamlike symbolism and its prophetic quality make the suggestion a highly interesting one. Arthur dreams that he is sitting astride the roof of his hall, from where 'all the lands I possessed I there overlooked'. Modred with an axe begins to hew down the supporting posts; Guinevere appears and begins to pull down the roof. Arthur, dislodged, falls to earth breaking his right arm, but with his sword in his left hand he cuts off Modred's head, which rolls along the ground. 'And the Queen I cut in pieces with my dear sword and afterwards set her down in a black pit.' When the truth, so foreshadowed, is known, Arthur's nephew Gawain declares that he will hang Modred with his own hands and that Guinevere shall be torn to pieces by wild horses.

Layamon admits that the Britons have told many falsehoods of Arthur, but people, he says, will always do this when speaking of those they love. He himself claims to give the true account. The battle of Camlann, he says, was fought in Cornwall on the River Tamar. 'There fought together innumerable folk . . . there might no man in the fight know any warriors, so was the conflict mingled.' In the matter of Arthur's death he follows Wace and Geoffrey, saying the King was borne away to Avalon to be healed and that afterwards he should return; but he was the first to say, or rather the first to write, that a boat came to shore from the sea, 'floating with the waves' (the Tamar is a tidal river), and in it two beautiful women, who 'took Arthur anon and bore him quickly and laid him softly down, and forth they gan depart'. No one, he says, knight or lady, can tell more of the King than that.

It is strange to be reminded that Layamon's version is forty years later than that of Wace; passionate, gloomy, brutal, illumined with passages of an intensely poetic cast, the Anglo-Saxon seems archaic compared with the earlier, light and accomplished French; but it is Layamon who is inspired by the real Matter of Arthur. To him it was not only a story, it was a faith. Wace had said: 'Arthur came never again.' Layamon's last words were: 'But whilom was a sage hight Merlin; he said – his sayings were sooth – that an Arthur should yet come to help the English.'

Tristan playing the harp to King Mark,
from a tile made by the monks of Chertsey
in the fourteenth century

7 Lancelot and Guinevere

The suddenness in the change of atmosphere from the Celtic treatment of Arthur's story, to that of two famous twelfth-century French writers, is like that of the first warm day of spring; but in the work of both of them, Arthur himself is a figure of minor importance; their stories concern knights who were members of his court. For the next two hundred years Arthur's function is to provide a framework.

One of the writers was a charming woman of whom very little is known. Marie de France is said to have been a half-sister of Henry II, to have spent some time in the circle of his English and Norman courts and to have been made by him abbess of a nunnery at Shaftesbury. This suggests that she combined her distinguished literary talent with a disinclination to be married. Her writings were *lais*, verse renderings of knightly stories already known, and she says frequently that these stories were current among the Breton *conteurs* from whom she heard them.

Her most famous *lai* is her rendering of the story of Tristan and Iseult, which she calls *Chèvre Feuille*, 'The Honeysuckle'. This tale, known as early as A.D. 1000, is of purely Celtic origin, but it has no essential connection with Arthur. The king in the story is Mark, King of Cornwall. The magnetic pull of Arthur's name caused the story to be attached to the body of legend surrounding him, but though Tristan is said to be one of Arthur's knights, his character is quite at variance with the accepted picture of chivalry. He is not famous for his skill as a jouster, but he has great physical agility; one of the stories about him was that when Mark's suspicions were aroused, the King had flour sprinkled on the floor around Iseult's bed, and Tristan defeated the stratagem by leaping to her bed from the chamber door. In another version of the story, when he had been captured by Mark and sentenced to be burned alive, he asked permission to say his prayers in the chapel at Tintagel and escaped by leaping from a window on to the rocks below. He distinguished himself in fighting when a fight was on, but unlike other knights, he was said to be a hunter. He was also a harper, and when wounded in the service of King Mark, asked to be put alone in a boat with his harp, at the mercy of the waves. Chrétien de Troyes said of him, in *Érec*, that he never laughed. These traits suggest a Celtic character rather than a figure of sophisticated romance. Marie de France adds an indescribable charm of simplicity and total *engouement* to the mutal passion. Once the honeysuckle has twined about the hazel tree, they die if they are separated. Tristan carves on a hazel-stem:

> *Belle ami, si est de nous,*
> *Ne vous sans moi, ni moi sans vous.*

72

The story, with the addition of the love philtre, was retold in numerous versions in the twelfth century, the most famous being those of Thomas of Britain and Gothfried of Strasbourg. The details varied but the essential facts remained unaltered: that Tristan went to Ireland to seek the Princess Iseult as a bride for his uncle, Mark; that on their voyage back to Cornwall they drank by mistake a love philtre which Iseult's maid Brangwen had prepared for the Princess's bridal night with Mark: that a complete mutal infatuation engulfed them and that when they arrived in Cornwall they were already lovers. Then begins the morbid but riveting tale of her marriage to the half-suspecting Mark and the continuation of her amour

with Tristan; the discovery and his flight to Brittany, where he marries a Princess because her name is Iseult, but cannot bring himself to consummate the marriage. When he is dying from the wound of a poisoned arrow he sends a message imploring Iseult of Ireland to come to him, and commanding that his returning barque is to spread white sails if it is bringing her, and black if it does not. When the white sails are seen coming in, his wife Iseult tells the dying man that they are black. His anguish brings on death and Iseult arrives, to die beside him.

The power this story exerts over the minds of the hearers is undying; poetry and music have added to it, but without the force of the story itself they could have done nothing. The hush in which the audience waits for the opening notes of

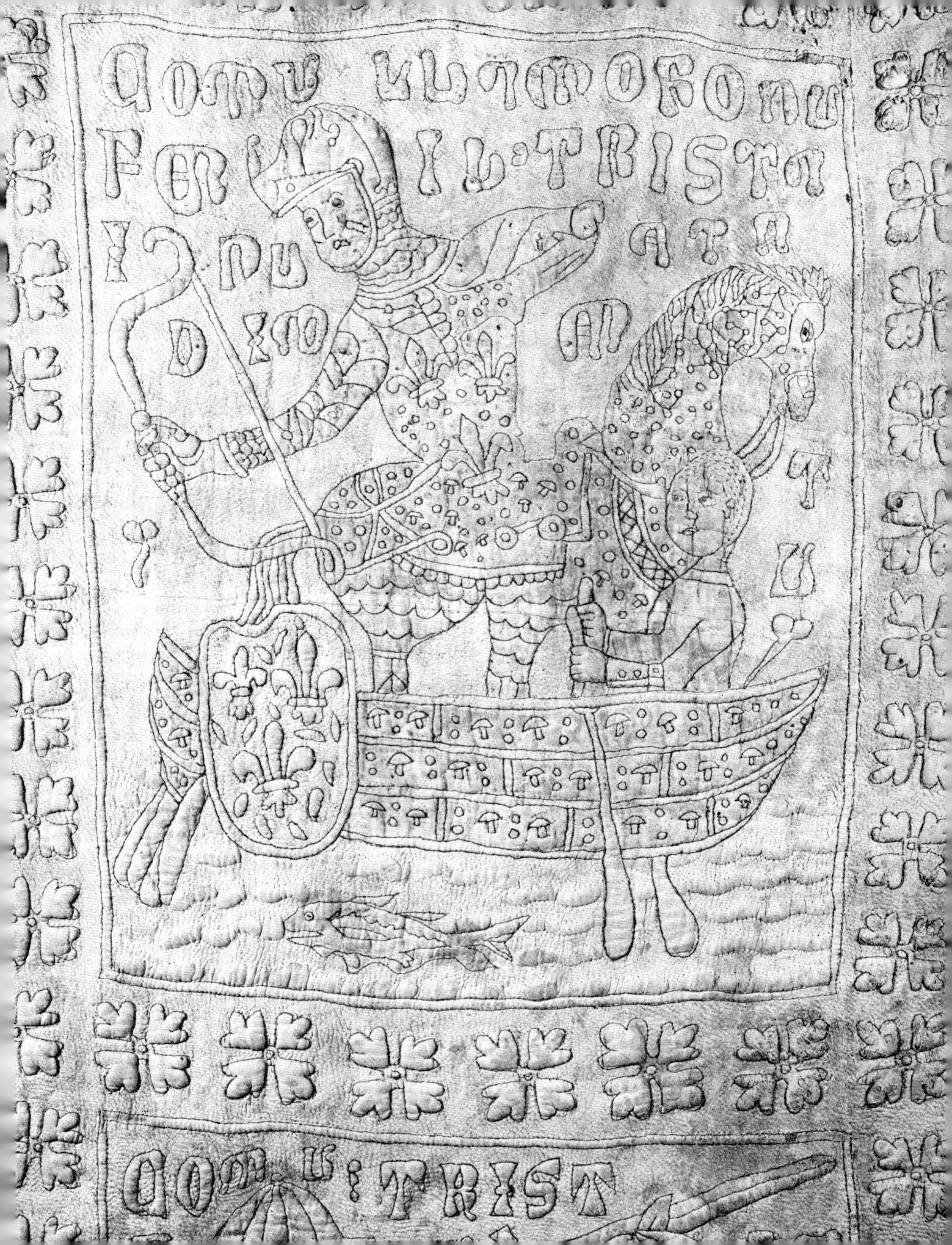

'O sink hernieder, Nacht der Liebe!' is not a tribute to Wagner's music only, but to the story that has travelled eleven hundred years to reach that moment in the opera houses of Dresden, Munich, Milan, Rome, Paris, London.

The story of Tristan and Iseult is *sui generis*; but other stories of Celtic Britain were given an enormous accession of fame by the most successful romance-writer of the twelfth century. Chrétien de Troyes wrote at the court and under the patronage of Marie de Champagne, the daughter of Eleanor of Aquitaine by her hapless first husband, Louis VII of France. This Princess, married to the Count of Champagne, had inherited from her mother an interest in romantic literature and the *amour courtois*, that strange system of carrying on a love affair by a set of complicated rules, so that it resembled the movements of an elaborate and stately dance. The rigid bargaining by which medieval marriages were arranged, in which family interest was everything and the feelings of the boy and girl were nothing, led naturally to the convention that romantic love was a state that could exist only outside of marriage. This idea was held merely within the small range of fashionable society; to many ordinary people, marriage seemed, as it still does, a very satisfactory way of life. As Chaucer said, at the end of *The Franklin's Tale*:

> Who could tell, but that he wedded be,
> The joy, the ease and the prosperity
> That is betwixt a husband and his wife?

But the *amour courtois* had the glamour of sophistication and permissiveness; as an added attraction it was frowned on by the Church, since it both condoned adultery and encouraged the worship of women.

Of Chrétien's five surviving tales, *Érec et Énide* is the story of a knight of Arthur's court falling in love at first sight with a very beautiful, gentle girl, marrying her, and then, led by a misunderstanding, putting her through a series of severe trials to prove her devotion to him, with the result of a gloriously happy reconciliation. There is no *amour courtois* in this tale, it is a straightforward one of passion, marriage, misunderstanding and the triumph of love. Érec sets out on his adventures from Arthur's court, he brings his bride back to it, and receives cordial and generous treatment from Arthur and Guinevere, but the story could take place in an altogether different milieu. The second story, *Cligés*, is even more loosely attached; the hero's father, Alexander, Emperor of Constantinople, visits Arthur and recovers Windsor Castle for him from the hands of a treacherous regent. He falls in love with Soredamours, one of Guinevere's ladies, woos her and takes her back to Constantinople. The adventures of their son Cligés are quite independent of Arthur's court. *Yvain*, a French version of the Welsh tale, *The Lady of the Fountain*, is more closely connected with its background of Arthur's court. Yvain sets out from it for an adventure in the forest of Broceliande, where, whoever entered a certain glade and struck a block of emerald suspended there, would create a mighty storm, after which a knight would appear and challenge him. Yvain slays the knight and makes a conquest of his widow. They are about to be married when Arthur arrives to see how the adventure has turned out, and though the French romancers have shorn him of his active part, the welcome bestowed on him by the lady's people is a reflection of the feeling he had once inspired: 'At the King's arrival, the town resounds with the joyous welcome which they give. Silken stuffs are taken out and hung aloft as decorations, and they spread tapestries to walk upon and drape the streets with them while they wait for the King's approach. . . . Bells, horns and trumpets cause the town to ring so that God's thunder could not have been heard. The maidens dance before him, flutes and pipes are played, kettle drums, drums and cymbals are beaten . . . the crowd pressed close as they cried with one accord: Welcome to the King of Kings and Lord of Lords!'

The unfinished *Perceval*, or *Le Conte del Graal*, is a story which crystallizes the legends current about the Graal, though in such perplexing form that volumes of exposition have been written on it. The first verses contain a passage very interesting from the aspect of Arthur. Perceval's mother, who had lost her brothers and her husband by their deaths in tournaments, had determined to bring up her infant son in a forest retreat in the foothills of Snowdon, where he would never hear the name of knight. One morning in May the boy is in the depths of the woods, and though he can see nothing for the leaves, he hears the noise made by five approaching knights. 'Every moment their arms banged against the branches of oaks and hornbeams, lances knocked against shields, mail grated.' From this noise he supposes they must be the demons who live unseen in the heart of the forest. Then he sees them, coming out of the trees: 'When he saw their glittering hauberks, their bright helmets, lances and shields – things he had never seen before – when he saw green and vermilion shining in the sun, and gold and sky blue and silver, he cried out in amazement: These are angels!'

His mother's precautions are overthrown in one moment. When he hears that they are knights and are attached to the court of Arthur, he declares he will go with them, 'to the King who makes knights'.

The attraction of the sight of knights on horseback, and their armour, is reflected by Chrétien over and over again. Érec puts on a hauberk, 'all made of worked silver in tiny meshes triple-wove, and it was made with such skill that I can assure you, no one who had put it on would have been more uncomfortable or sore because of it than if he had put on a silk jacket over his undershirt'. In the course of his adventures, Érec is riding along the hillside, 'when, behold! the knight comes tearing down over the top of the hill, mounted upon a powerful steed which tore along at such a pace, that he crushed the stones beneath his hooves and bright gleaming sparks flew off in all directions as if his four feet were all ablaze with fire!'

He does not evade the grim side of combat, either. 'Drawing the swords from their scabbards, they each wound and injure the other and there is no mercy on either side. They deal such blows on the helmets that gleaming sparks fly out, and the swords recoil, they split and splinter the shields, they batter and crush the

hauberks, in four places the swords are brought down on the bare flesh! If their swords had lasted longer, they would never have retreated, nor would the battle have come to end till one of them, perhaps, had died.' When the knights had gained each other's thorough respect by this contest, 'Each one cut off long wide strips from the bottom of his shirt and bound up the other's wounds.'

Chrétien records an ominous sight, such as must often have been encountered. Arthur and some knights go to look for Sir Kay, who has undertaken an adventure. 'As they approached the forest they saw Kay's horse running out . . . the horse was running wild, the stirrup straps all stained with blood, and the saddle bow was broken.' The warmth and sensitiveness of Chrétien's response to sensuous impressions is enchanting. When Arthur is ceremonially greeted by the Lady Laudine whom Yvain has married, she says: 'Welcome a hundred thousand times to the King my Lord!' The King replies: 'I wish all good luck to your fair body and your face, you lovely creature!' Then, clasping her round the waist, the King embraced her gaily and heartily, as she did him, throwing her arms about him.' His world was

Arthur finding Sir Keu, wounded by
Lancelot in a fight to decide which of them
should take a prisoner to the King

LANCELOT AND GUINEVERE

77

one of charming freedoms, as it would seem the English one never was. He was
surrounded by luxury and brightness, which he took the trouble to describe: clean
tablecloths, polished silver, snow-white sheets, a bed, 'covered with a yellow cloth
of silk and a coverlid of gilded stars'. The felicity of some of his phrases is astonishing. Yvain awoke in a garden and found himself 'naked as ivory'.

The tale in which Arthur is a main character, even with an inferior role, instead
of merely a figure in the background, is *Lancelot*. The amateur student of the
Matter of Arthur is continually reminded that the earliest written form of a story
is probably several hundred years later than its actual origin; and it would seem
that the body of a legend did not advance by the creation of individual storytellers, but by a gradual accretion of detail and moulding of action, produced by
generations of repetition. Was there a great and striking exception to this process
in the creation by one writer of the story of Lancelot and Guinevere?

The character of Lancelot as a distinguished member of Arthur's fraternity was
well known by the twelfth century and Loomis[12] has established that there are

Lest le liure de messire lancelot du lac ou
quel liure sont contenus tous les fais et les ch...

et ramenees a la ioie pardurable. Ou saint ...
par qui toutes choses sont mises hors des m...

LEFT Lancelot's birth, life and quest for the Holy Grail depicted in four miniatures at the opening of a fifteenth-century French MS., and BELOW a lady in bed greeted by Lancelot, according to the custom, often illustrated in medieval MSS., by which men and women saw each other naked without shame

traces in his origin of the Welsh warrior Lluch Llauynnauc and the Irish deity Lugh Lamhfada. The origin of his name, Lancelot of the Lake, in the last decade of the twelfth century, is given by the Swiss writer Ulrich von Zatzikhoven in a translation of a lost Anglo-Norman romance. This says Lancelot was the son of King Ban of Benoic, a district of Brittany. At his father's death he was seized away by the Lady of the Lake, a water fairy, who brought him up in her subaqueous palace. In another version of Lancelot's story (the *Lancelot* of the Vulgate Cycle) it is said that the water which covered her palace was an illusion merely. This sounds like some psychological image; it also recalls the practice of *tregetours* or conjurors, who practised mass-hypnotism. Chaucer in *The Franklin's Tale* says:

> For oft at feastes, I have heard well say
> That tregetours within an halle large
> Have made come in a water and a barge
> And in the halle rowen up and down.

That as late as the 1380s an audience was so susceptible of hypnotic illusion shows how easily the legends could be believed.

Von Zatzikhoven's story says that at fifteen years old Lancelot is armed by his foster mother and sent to Arthur's court. He fights a combat on behalf of Guinevere but there is no word of any adultery between them. Lancelot himself has casual amours with two women, then he marries a faithful and lovely wife. His story

80

includes many well-known elements: he releases with a kiss, *Le Fier Baiser*, a girl who had been changed into a dragon. The story is very interesting because some of its details are of very great antiquity. The description of one of the castles Lancelot attacked, sounds like the drawing of an archetypal dream: 'The mountain was a crystal, round as ball, on which stood a strong castle. The gateway was as hard as a diamond. Outside and in, it was of gold, like a star-cluster.'

It shows that, in the second half of the twelfth century, the story of Lancelot, his upbringing by a water fairy, his reception at Arthur's court, his championship on one occasion of Guinevere, was well known, and that the story did not give him as Guinevere's lover.

Who first said that he was? Chrétien de Troyes at the beginning of *Lancelot* says that he is writing this tale at the behest of Marie de Champagne, that she dictated to him the *matière*, the material, and the *sen*, the style in which it should be written. As this is, apparently, the first written account of the love affair, it might be argued that the Comtesse de Champagne and Chrétien had evolved it between them. What seems to suggest that the story was well known already, is that it is told in an allusive fashion, which would scarcely be understandable by someone who was hearing it for the first time. When Chrétien begins his story, Lancelot is already the lover of the Queen and his passion leads him into such trances of self-forgetfulness and such slavish absurdities, it has been suggested that when the Countess of Champagne dictated the *sen*, she asked for the story to be treated in a manner bordering on caricature.

At the outset of the story, a recreant knight, Meleagant, has driven off many of Arthur's subjects and holds them captive in the water-surrounded land of Goirre. He at last captures Guinevere herself. Lancelot overcomes him in single combat and so procures all the captives their release. Loomis finds in this the story introduced by Caradoc of Lancafarn into his *Life of St Gildas*, a personage into whom the passionately vindictive author of the *Liber querulus* appears to have been translated. This work, written before 1130, relates how Arthur's queen was captured by Melvas (transmuted by Chrétien into Meleagant), the King of the Summer Country, who bears her off to the Isle of Glass – the French scribe misread *Voirre* as *Goirre*. Arthur, with a large army recruited from Devon and Cornwall, besieges Melvas and rescues Guinevere. This is one of several accounts representing Guinevere as a captive.

Chrétien's version makes the lamentable alteration that Guinevere is not rescued by her husband but by her lover. Arthur is presented as a good-natured, gracious but ineffective man, hopelessly reduced in stature. The court of Champagne, after all, were not Bretons; they were not interested in the idea of the heroism of a military commander who had rescued a part of England from the savages; they were listening to a tale of fashionable life, in which King Arthur was necessarily cast for the part of cuckold. He was not a *mari-complaisant*, he did not know he was being injured, but graciousness and good humour were his leading characteristics. When the ladies arranged an unofficial tournament so that among

pour aler a ceanote Et quant il veint sloilli
one fenestre quieltoit endroit le lit sa fille et
quant illot ouuerte si mist sa teste dedans.

t il regarda si bit sa fille qui teno
le chk entre ses bras/ et illui et
quant il oit ce fioit. Alas quar
ie tousiours tarde. et ses cha
bellant qui auetse li siuent
seuez li demandent Sire quaues
ous. ne bous chaut fait il. alez bous courchie

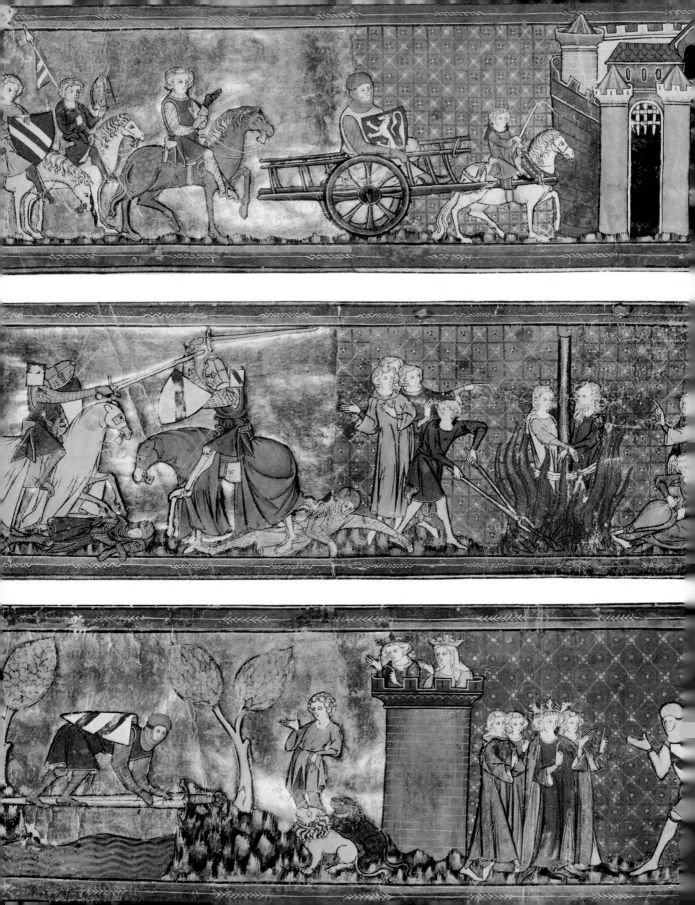

the collection of knights they might find themselves husbands, they asked the King a favour. 'He promised it, whatever their desire might be.' They said they wanted the Queen to grace this rather unusual occasion. 'And he, who was not accustomed to forbid, said he was willing, if she wished it.'

Lancelot's entry on the scene seems to make it clear that Chrétien's audience knew the story before he retold it. Lancelot is not named at first. He is coming to the Queen's rescue, and his horse founders. At that moment, an executioner's cart in which criminals are taken to the gallows comes by, driven by a dwarf. The surly driver offers him a seat in the cart, and so great is the degradation of being carried in this vehicle, he hesitates while he takes two steps only. He then throws false shame aside and mounts the cart. It is never explained how the Queen knew of his hesitation, but she regards the second's faltering as a heinous offence against herself and afterwards behaves towards Lancelot with the degree of exaggerated hostility and resentment which, with his servile acceptance of it, has given rise to the idea that the story was intended as a skit on the *amour courtois*. 'Reason', Chrétien says, 'is inconsistent with love's dictates.'

When Lancelot is fighting Meleagant before the walls of the latter's castle, the Queen is looking down and one of her damsels says: 'Lady, for God's sake and your own as well as ours, tell me, if you know, the name of yonder knight?' The Queen replies: 'The name of the knight, I know' – and it is spoken in the story for the first time – 'is Lancelot of the Lake.' The girl leans out and cries loudly: 'Lancelot, turn about and see who is taking note of thee!' When Lancelot turns round and sees the Queen, he is so besotted he cannot take his eyes off her and Meleagant harries him at will. The girl calls to him again, to exert himself, and thereupon he begins to drive Meleagant about so that he himself is always facing the Queen. The rescue of the captives is celebrated with a great tournament, and here Guinevere gives rein to her caprice and vanity, by ordering Lancelot first to do his worst, so that his failure is mocked and despised, then sending a message telling him to use his powers to the full, so that he achieves a spectacular victory.

This leads to a reconciliation with the Queen, and the episode of their first meeting at night. Lancelot comes to the wall of Meleagant's castle, in which is the window of the Queen's bedroom, and sees her 'in a very white chemise' looking out through the iron bars. They hold hands and he says he would for anything be inside, with her. When he hears her say that she wishes it too, he declares that nothing shall keep him out and begins to tear the bars out of their sockets. His hands are lacerated but he is barely conscious of them. 'He comes to the bed of the Queen whom he adores and before whom he kneels, holding her more dear than the relic of any saint. And the Queen extends her arms to him, embracing him, presses him tightly against her bosom, drawing him into the bed beside her . . . her love and her heart go out to him. . . . Now Lancelot possesses all he wants, when he holds her in his arms, and she holds him in hers. Their sport is so agreeable and so sweet, as they kiss and fondle each other, that such a marvellous joy comes over them as was never heard or known. But their joy will not be revealed

82

by me, for in a story it has no place. The most delightful satisfaction was that of which our story must not speak.'

Chrétien expresses as much delight in Lancelot's achieving the Queen as he does in his hero's triumph in the tournament. There is great caution, great apprehension, but the bliss is unalloyed by any pangs of remorse.

It is in the *Lancelot* of the Vulgate Cycle that Guinevere exclaims: 'It would be better for me that I had never been born.'

li rois eſter. uos en uoiera deus auicune
part auſi com il aſet eſpee. Lors regardet
uers lanue ſtreual et uoit uenu auſi
come abeſoing une damoiſelle monte
ſeur un paleſtroi blac et uenoit uers
aus gin aleure.

8 'Glastonbury Is Avalon'

Out of a reign of thirty-five years, Henry II spent only twelve in England; though he did so much for this small realm in the time he had to spare for it, most of his maniacal energy was devoted to maintaining the enormous realms he held in France. In 1166, he secured the overlordship of the dukedom of Brittany and the hand of its heiress Constance for his son Geoffrey of Anjou. A party of the Bretons, led by Roland of Dinan, were loyal to their dispossessed ruler, Conan, and in 1168, a curious work in verse was produced by Étienne de Rouen, a monk of the Abbey of Bec. He called it *Draco Normannicus*, 'The Norman Standard'. The poem opens with what appears to be a letter written by Roland of Dinan, to Arthur. Calling himself Arthur's standard-bearer, he implores Arthur for help against Henry II. Arthur, it seems, is now abiding at the ends of the earth, but he answers this appeal by writing a letter to the King of England. He recalls his own victory over the Saxons, his contest with Modred, and his retreat to Avalon; now, he says, he rules in the antipodes. If Henry wants to know any more about him, let the English king consult Geoffrey of Monmouth. Arthur is now collecting his forces in the woods of Cornwall and he warns Henry to leave the Bretons alone. The author then says, in his own person, that Henry was not alarmed by this letter; he read it aloud to his smiling counsellors, but he undertook that, when he had completed the conquest of Brittany, he would hold it as Arthur's vassal. This is a very interesting instance of a famous person, while actually living, being used as a character in fiction: a practice which, in films and plays, is only just finding acceptance now. E. K. Chambers[13] says that the writer is 'not quite serious'; but, serious or not, it was a dangerous game to play with Henry II; there have always been people who will believe anything, and who was to say how this might be taken? Geoffrey, like all Henry's sons, instigated by their odious mother, rebelled against his father; he died in 1186, and in 1187 his posthumous son was born, 'much desired of the people', and christened Arthur.

The great abbey of Glastonbury had been founded in the fifth century. On its site was the small wattle-and-daub church of very great antiquity, which, it was claimed, was the first Christian shrine to be erected in Britain. The disastrous fire in 1184 which destroyed it, destroyed as well nearly all the abbey buildings. With these went also the community's rich stores of gold and silver vessels, brocaded vestments and illuminated manuscripts; losses which made priests abroad, who had never seen Glastonbury, weep to hear about. A massive programme of re-

Glastonbury Abbey, where according to
legend Arthur and his Queen are buried

Glastonbury Abbey, where according to
legend Arthur and his Queen are buried

building was set on foot, to which Henry II gave generously, but the undertaking called for immense sums, and something to attract crowds of pilgrims would be very useful.

Giraldus Cambrensis, the vivid, agile, intellectual Welshman of partly Norman descent who accompanied Henry II to Wales was brilliant both in absorbing impressions and in writing them down in a racy and topical manner. ('It is better to be dumb', he said, 'than not to be understood. New times require new fashions.') He produced between 1193 and 1199 a work, *De Principis Instructione*, in which he recorded that Arthur had been a patron of Glastonbury Abbey, and though fables had spread abroad fantastic stories of his end, his body had in fact been found buried in the precincts of the Abbey in 1190. It was lying between two stone pyramids, which marked the sites of other graves, 16 feet in earth and enclosed in a hollow tree-trunk. On the underside of the makeshift coffin was a stone, and under this stone, a leaden cross on which Latin words were incised, affirming: 'Here lies entombed the renowned King Arthur with Guinevere his second wife in the Isle of Avalon.' Giraldus says two-thirds of the coffin was filled with a man's bones of unusual size, the remainder with the bones of a woman, among which was a tress of yellow hair, fresh and beautiful. A monk seized hold of this, and it crumbled to dust in his grasp. The man's bones, shown to Giraldus by the Abbot, Henry of Sully, included an enormous thigh-bone and a skull of giant capacity, with ten wounds, nine of them scars but the tenth of great depth, unhealed, assumed to have been the cause of death.

According to Giraldus, the monks had been led to find these remains, partly by inscriptions, almost obliterated, on the stone pyramids, partly through visions received by members of the community, but chiefly by the advice of Henry II himself, who had been told by an old British singer that Arthur's body would be found 16 feet in earth in the bole of a hollowed oak.

The discovery was extremely apropos for all concerned. As a tourist attraction the Abbey soon proved its worth, and it provided a retort to the Bretons, and also to the intransigent Welsh, who had resisted Henry II with all but decisive success, if either of these peoples were founding their hopes on the return of Arthur.

Étienne de Rouen had told the English King, if he wanted to know more, to consult Geoffrey of Monmouth. If Henry II took this advice, he did it to some purpose. His 'old British singer' was fit to stand beside Archdeacon Walter's 'ancient book in the British tongue'. Henry II died in 1189, but the following year the 'discovery' at Glastonbury was carried out with a vigour and an attention to detail that the King himself could hardly have bettered. It is, Chambers points out, significant that Adam of Domerham, writing his chronicle in 1291, and therefore speaking from hearsay, says nevertheless that, on the day of the exhumation, the Abbot gave orders that the area to be dug should be surrounded by curtains.

The question as to whether the inscription on the leaden cross – *Rex Inclitus* – referred to a genuine burial of Arthur, is not difficult to decide; one of the very few facts we may claim to know about Arthur is that he was not a king. The puzzle is that Giraldus Cambrensis, the first person to record seeing the inscription, is the only one whose record contains the words *cum Wennevaria uxore secunda*. Two antiquaries of the sixteenth century, John Leland and William Camden, saw the cross or a facsimile of it. Leland quoted the inscription without the reference to Guinevere. Camden made a drawing of the cross with its incised letters, which were, he said, 'made after a barbarous manner and resembling Gothic characters', and they, again, merely read: *Hic jacet sepultus inclitus Rex Arturus, in insula Avalonia*. Camden calls this cross 'the first copy in the Abbey of Glascon'. Did he use 'copy' in the sense in which we speak of a copy of a first edition, or did he use it in the sense of imitation? If it means a copy of the original cross, then, as Richard Barber[10] says, the cross Giraldus saw might have been recognized as of later date than the sixth century, and been replaced by a more convincing forgery. This does not explain why the words 'with Guinevere his second wife' should have been added or left out. They are a disturbing echo of the theme of 'the double Guinevere'.

The bones were reinterred in two marble coffers with arms and images on the lids, in a chapel then standing near the south doorway of the great church.

Geoffrey of Monmouth had said that Arthur was borne away, mortally wounded, to Avalon. When Arthur's bones were supposedly found at Glastonbury, with the funerary cross saying that he was buried in the Isle of Avalon, Glastonbury became Avalon, once and forever. William of Malmesbury, in his *Gesta Regum Anglorum*, of 1125, had said merely that the British called Glastonbury Inis Witrin, the Glass Island. Caradoc of Lancafarn in his *Life of Gildas*, of 1136, says that the British called it Ynis Gutrin, the Glass Island again. Giraldus Cambrensis and Ralph, Abbot of Coggeshall, in his *Chronicon Anglicanum*, were the first two writers to say that Glastonbury was Avalon.

William of Malmesbury spent some years between 1129 and 1139 as a guest in Glastonbury Abbey, minutely studying the archives of which there was so splendid a collection before the fire, and writing a comment on them: *De Antiquitate Glastoniensis Ecclesiae*. This work is considered to be of very great value, dealing as it does with the time before the Abbey's foundation by Ina, the Saxon King of Wessex, in the eighth century. That it should be credible that a small Christian church stood there at such an early date, is in itself a tribute to Arthur's work in holding up the Saxon advance to the west. If the Saxons had overrun Somerset in the fifth or early sixth century, such a sacred building would have been destroyed ruthlessly. By the time the Saxons were able to advance again, it has been said, they would not have razed a Christian shrine. The *De Antiquitate* was incorporated by William into his *Gesta Regum Anglorum*, which he dedicated to the Abbot of Glastonbury, Henry of Blois, the brother of Stephen, whose record of rapacious treachery between Stephen and Matilda was combined with that of a highly cultivated churchman. This document of course remained in the Abbey, and it escaped destruction in the fire, for several statements connecting Arthur with Glastonbury were inserted into it by forgers during the next two hundred years.

In the Castle of the Holy Grail: Perceval
presented with the Sword by the Fisher King
while the Grail is borne to the table

88   E. K. Chambers says that anything in the *De Antiquitate* which does not occur in
the parallel passages of *De Gesta Regum*, is an interpolation. In three places the
forgers call Glastonbury the Isle of Avalon, whereas William of Malmesbury
himself never gives it another name than Inis Witrin; and Arthur, whom he
never mentions in connection with Glastonbury, is described in another of the
forged interpolations as buried with his wife 'in the grave-yard of the monks
between two pyramids'. The forger adds that he was mortally wounded by
Modred near the River Camber in Cornwall, and being taken to Avalon, for the
healing of his wounds, died then, 'in the summer about Pentecost, being nearly
one hundred years old or thereabouts'.

It was a cruel stroke of fate that the great historian who had spoken so severely
and so justly of Geoffrey of Monmouth's impudent farragos about Arthur, should
have his own painstaking, deeply considered work manhandled like this, marred
with the sort of irresponsible fiction against which he had protested so vigorously.
This baseless identification of Avalon with Glastonbury and the reputed discovery
of the bones of Arthur and Guinevere brought streams of pilgrims with their
coins to the new abbey buildings; it had also another consequence.

The legends connected with the Holy Graal which came in the thirteenth
century to form a very important part of the story of Arthur's court, are of con-
fused and obscure though fascinating origin. The etymology of the word 'Graal'
is doubtful; it is sometimes traced to the medieval Latin word *gradalis*, a cup or
dish. The early forms of this legend, although ostensibly Christian, contained
elements of folklore so irrelevant to any Christian interpretation that they were
dropped by later writers. By the fifteenth century the image had been drastically
simplified; it had become the apparition of the Chalice out of which Jesus Christ
had given the Apostles wine to drink at the Last Supper. Radiant with the light of
supernatural gems, it appeared sometimes between the hands of an angel, sometimes moving of itself; the experience of seeing it was to be gained only by knights
who had kept themselves chaste.

In the early versions, however, as told by Chrétien de Troyes and other twelfth-
and thirteenth-century romancers, the apparition of the Graal was the climax of a
complicated story. A young knight, sometimes Gawain, sometimes Perceval, is
guided to a river where he sees a man fishing. This is the Fisher King. The knight
is invited by the latter to his castle above the riverside. When he arrives his host is
there before him, lying on a couch from which he cannot move without help. He
has been wounded through the thighs and while the wounds are unhealed his
land remains arid and sterile. The Fisher King is a courteous and generous host.
While he and the guest are at dinner a ritual procession makes its way through the
hall; it consists of a damsel bearing a dish, followed by another with a carving-
platter, accompanied by a squire carrying a bleeding lance and servitors with
candelabra. They are going to feed the Fisher King's father, unseen in his chamber,
who is kept alive by one consecrated wafer borne in the damsel's dish.

This inexplicable scene is conveyed with such magic by Chrétien de Troyes in

Perceval, or *Le Conte del Graal*, the reader believes it contains a meaning which he cannot see: 'Two flambeaux lit up the hall, nowhere in the world could you find a place lit up more brilliantly. A great fire of dry logs cast up a clear flame. . . . The tall and strong columns of the fireplace were of massive brass. Two servants carried each a candlestick of enamelled gold; in each candlestick ten wax lights were burning.' The damsel was carrying the Graal 'between her hands', and 'so great a lightness spread about the hall, the wax lights paled like the stars or the moon when the sun rises'. Of purest gold, the Graal was inlaid with precious stones, 'richer and more varied than might be found in earth or sea; no gem could compare with those found in the Graal'.

A constant feature in the Celtic legends is the quest for a magic vessel; Arthur himself had sought one in *The Spoils of Annwyn*. The vessel produces food and drink of a delicious, life-enhancing kind. Another frequently occurring element is that a region called the Waste Land is lying infertile and desolate because its ruler has been wounded in the genitals and until he is cured his land cannot revive; this stricken ruler is called the Fisher King and inhabits the Castle of the Graal, standing above a river shore. Here the hero of the quest is lavishly entertained and at dinner sees the ritual procession pass through the hall. The hero beholds it with mute amazement and therefore the Fisher King is not released from the evil spell. Had the hero demanded an explanation of what he saw, the spell would have been dissolved.

The Fisher King has been identified as a derivative of the Irish god Bran; on the banks of the Dee, a salmon river, are the ruins of a castle, Dinas Bran. The origins of the connection of the Fisher King with a Christian legend are suggested by Jessie Weston.[14] She points out, on the one hand, the prevalence of the fish symbol in the early Christian faith: the Icthys anagram applied to the word 'Christ', Christ's calling the Apostles 'fishers of men', the Pope's 'ring of the

fisherman'. On the other hand, Miss Weston maintains that the origins of the Fisher King are much earlier than Christian. She says: 'The Fish is a Life Symbol of immeasurable antiquity and the title of Fisher has, from earliest ages, been associated with deities who were held to be connected with the origins and preservation of life. The first Avatar of Vishnu the Creator is a fish, and the fish was sacred to those deities who were supposed to lead men back from the shadows of death to life.'

The Fisher King, the Waste Land and the Sacred Vessel were images well known in Celtic stories spread abroad in France by the Breton *conteurs*. The identification of the sacred vessel with the Last Supper, either as the Chalice from which the wine was drunk or as the Dish from which the Passover meal was eaten, can perhaps be explained by the immense impact of the Christian faith in the early centuries A.D., which imagination wanted to set out in a story, and used, to clothe it, one of the oldest myths created by man.

The earliest known source of this legend's being connected with the French romancers, is the Welshman Bleheris, who lived from 1100 to 1150. The son of a Welsh nobleman, he was friendly with the Normans and helped them to defend Caernarvon Castle against the Welsh. Though Welsh himself, he must have spoken fluent French, and he had a most remarkable gift for storytelling. He was spoken

The Last Supper of Jesus and his disciples,
taken at a Round Table, and BELOW Galahad
introduced at the Round Table of King Arthur

re fanut or woru for ter chunles amor   et mon lr fauel le rour fouco er li pure

of later by Giraldus Cambrensis as *fabulator famosus*, and the English poet Thomas, the author of the version of *Tristan*, said of him that he was 'one who knew the history of all the counts and all the kings of Britain'. One of the additions made by another hand to Chrétien's *Perceval*, or *Le Conte del Graal*, a prologue called the Elucidation, speaks of 'Blihis' as one 'who knew all the stories of the Graal'. This suggests a direct Welsh source for the French romancers writing of the Graal.

The earliest known work to connect the Graal with Glastonbury is Robert de Boron's *Joseph of Arimathea*, written about 1200. Stories about Joseph of Arimathea were current by the sixth century. He was best known, naturally, for the reference to him in all four Gospels, as the man who gained permission from Pilate to take the body of Jesus from the cross and bury it in his own tomb. Legend said of him that he had taken a cup and caught in it the drops of blood from Jesus's feet.

Boron's *Joseph of Arimathea* is the first known work to connect the Graal with the Chalice used at the Last Supper. After adventures gathered from early Christian works, *The Gospel of Nicodemus* and *The Avenging of the Saviour*, Joseph of Arimathea, with his brother-in-law Bron and the latter's twelve sons, sets sail for the west. On the way the party are preserved from starvation by Bron (whose name is an obvious derivation from Bran, but rationalized by the statement that he was first called Hebron). Bron catches a large fish which, placed on a table opposite the Graal, provides food for everyone. He becomes identified therefore with the Rich Fisher, or the Fisher King. In Boron's story, Joseph of Arimathea does not come to England; the evangelizing mission is carried out by his companions, of whom it is prophesied that one will seek 'the Vale of Avaron'. Boron's contribution to the Graal legend was the statement, evolved or repeated from some other source, that the Graal was the Chalice of the Last Supper. His story contains so many elements of Celtic mythology, that Loomis asks: why has the story been shifted from the sixth century, the time of Arthur, where it belongs, to the first century A.D.? His explanation of the connection between the Biblical story of Joseph of Arimathea and the body of Celtic legend is that the Welsh word *cors*, meaning horn, the horn of plenty, was mistranslated as the French *cors*, meaning body. 'The two Welsh vessels of plenty, the horn and the platter, have been converted as a result of the ambiguity of *cors* into the Graal and the body of Christ.' The Castle of the Graal was named Corbenic, which Loomis sees as a corruption of Corbenoit, the Castle of the Blessed Horn.

The History of the Holy Graal in the Vulgate Cycle is the source of the statement that Joseph of Arimathea came to Glastonbury and there founded the first Christian church in Britain, but even this story does not actually mention Glastonbury; it is typical of the growth of Arthurian legend that one statement leads to an assumption, which is then made the ground of another statement. Since the Abbey of Glastonbury claimed to have within its precincts the earliest-founded of Christian shrines in Britain, therefore this shrine must have been the one raised by Joseph of Arimathea. The conviction attaching to this legend had become so powerful by the fifteenth century that English delegates to the Church

Councils of Pisa, Constance, Siena and Basle claimed, on the strength of it, to take precedence over the delegates from France and Spain.

Notwithstanding the importance the Church attached to the story of Joseph's mission, it seems never to have given its sanction to the story of the Graal. Perhaps the pagan origins of the cup and platter were understood and gave displeasure. In the world of romance, the story increased in vividness and emotional significance, but the Church, in spite of the encouragement it gave to other stories of the miraculous, gave none to this, the most pictorially striking of any. In the representation of Joseph of Arimathea in church windows, he is holding, not a cup, but two flasks or cruets, in which it was said he had collected the blood and sweat of the Saviour.

That his coming to Glastonbury was so profoundly believed at the time and is believed so still, shows that something very deep-seated in the human mind is responsible for the belief and for the tenacity with which it is held. It must be admitted there is some inexplicable influence connected with the Abbey ruins. After the superb rebuilding in the late twelfth, the thirteenth and fourteenth centuries, the Abbey was pillaged at the Reformation, the lead stripped from its roofs, its walls used as stone quarries, its remains left to decay, while the hanging of Abbot Whitehead on Glastonbury Tor is one of the most shocking stories of the Dissolution. The ruins stand now, the great fragments rising from the rich, daisy-powdered grass in their loftiness, their speaking grace, as if they had a function still to comfort and inspire.

9 Medieval Influences

The French Vulgate Cycle is a monumental gathering of almost everything known in Arthurian legend after the point at which Arthur was envisioned as a king. It does not treat him as a sixth-century British general but it is a compendious collection of everything else written or told about him, from the bringing of the Graal to Britain, to his death at Camlann. It was put together by anonymous writers between 1215 and 1230, and consists of five prose stories: *The History of the Holy Graal, Lancelot, Merlin, The Quest of the Holy Graal* and the *Morte Artu*. The diminishing of Arthur as a leader of heroic stature, begun by Chrétien de Troyes, has continued; he is no longer recognizable as the towering figure of Nennius, Geoffrey of Monmouth, Wace and Layamon; we are in a modern world; Arthur is the civilized, generous, beloved king of a court in which the most arresting feats are performed by his knights, one of whom has achieved world fame by making his king and friend a cuckold.

His most interesting role is in the *Morte Artu*, where he is naturally restored to a leading part. This tale is very interesting altogether; it contains for one thing the first known appearance in writing of the affair of Lancelot and the Maid of Astolat, with Guinevere's groundless jealousy of her, the girl's willing herself to die after her repudiation by Lancelot and of her corpse being borne down the river in her richest clothes, on a black-draped barge, a letter to Lancelot fastened in her hand.

Guinevere's jealousy is allayed, but Arthur's suspicions of her and Lancelot are kindled to a certainty by the paintings illustrating his amour which Lancelot had made on the walls of the chamber he slept in while he was a guest of Arthur's sister, Morgan le Fay. This episode is given force by a sight of the wall-paintings of the twelfth, thirteenth and fourteenth centuries. As the product of an age when very few people could read, the art had an importance we can hardly calculate. The descriptions and drawings of the remains of wall-paintings in St Stephen's Chapel, Westminster, made by antiquaries who looked on in despair as James Wyatt, in 1795, was allowed to destroy the painted surface of the walls to enlarge the chamber, that Parliament might have more space, before the whole building was destroyed by fire in 1834, give an idea of how graphic the murals had been. The Chapel had been largely built by Edward III; its decoration was carried out in gilt gesso-work, with transparent colour laid over gold and silver leaf, with marble and coloured glass. The saints and angels have a strange, startling, inhuman brightness; the figures of Edward III, in armour and crowned, followed by his five sons, of Queen Philippa and her four daughters, are so life-like that, though Lancelot was scarcely imagined as using the resources of a master painter, the idea that scenes from secret life could be conveyed on a wall with utter revelation would have a meaning for the thirteenth century it would not immediately convey to us, accustomed as we are only to graffiti of mindless obscenity.

As a result of the revelations, Guinevere is condemned to be burned alive and Lancelot rescues her from the stake itself, carrying her away to his castle of Joyous Garde. Arthur is besieging him here when the King receives a message from the Pope, enjoining him to take back his wife. Arthur obeys, but when Lancelot goes over to his estates in France, Arthur pursues him, and the war is continued until Arthur is drawn off to conquer the Romans. He has vanquished them and killed the Emperor, when news reaches him from Guinevere in England that Modred – in this story, Arthur's son, begotten unknowingly upon his sister – has usurped the kingdom. Arthur returns post-haste, and he and Modred engage their forces on Salisbury Plain, where Arthur kills him in the field but receives a fatal head wound. His knight, Giflet, conveys him to the water-side and Arthur exhorts him twice in vain to throw the sword Excalibur into the lake. The third time Giflet obeys, and a hand rises from the water, brandishes the blade and sinks with it below the mere. This, the most thrilling and impressive of all the scenes in Arthurian story, is developed, Frappier[15] suggests, from the vision in *The Quest of the Holy Graal*, where the cup and the lance are removed by a supernatural hand. In a storm of rain, a barge containing Morgan le Fay and other ladies comes to land and bears Arthur away, as in Geoffrey's *Historia*, but not to Avalon. The king's tomb is discovered a few days later in La Noire Chapelle. Lancelot and his friends return to England, exterminate the brood of Modred and become hermits at the Chapelle. Lancelot's soul at last is taken up to heaven by angels. Guinevere dies repentant as a nun.

Though most of the story is taken from already existing works, this writer has made a contribution of great effectiveness by combining the hitherto separate stories of the passion of Lancelot and Guinevere and the treachery of Modred. Another addition is made in deference to the exhumation at Glastonbury; Arthur is wounded in the head, to comply with the exhibition of the skull with its nine healed wounds and one that was assumed to have been fatal; and the King's body, instead of being borne out of sight across the water, is placed by the ladies in the Noire Chapelle, where everyone may view the tomb.

These five tales had an influence beyond that of any other versions of the thirteenth century. The Plantagenet kings, up to and including Edward III, spoke French as their ordinary language; the wealthy and educated ranks of English society read French as easily as, or perhaps more easily than, English. The enormous popularity of the cycle shows that the language was understood, and it shows also that the medium of the stories was one closely assimilated with daily life.

forslungnaist il direment Et lore respondit une
dame ala royne et dist dame vous dien dit il
estre si bon chlr come vous dites, ouil fet le royne
Car il est detoutes pars extraitz du plus bon
chlr du monde et du plus hault lignage queon
sache Atant descendirent les dames et alerent
oir vespres pour lahaultesse du ionr Et
quant le roy fut issu du mouster et il vint
au palais en hault si comanda q les nappes
fussent mises Et lore sallerent seoir les com
paignions chm en son lieu ainsi come ilz auo
rent fait aumatin Et quat ilz se furent tost
assis lors oyrent vng estoy de tonnaire si
grant et si merueilleux quil leur fu aduis q

lepalaix deust fondre Et maintes entre leau
ung ray desoleil plus cler arent doubles quil
nyauoit denant Si furent tantost par leaus
aussi come sils fussent enlumines par lagre
du saint esperit Et comencerent a regarder
lun lautre Car ilz ne sauoient dont telle clarte
leur estoit venue Et ny ot celluy qui peust par
ler ne dire mot tant furent mariz grans et
petiz Et quat demoures furent grant piece en
telle maniere que nul deulx nauoit pouoir de
parler ains regardoient tout roe bestes mues

Comet le saint graal saparut aux chlrs dela
table ronde couuert duy blac samyt z ny
ore entra leans lesang graal
couuert dun blanc samyt Mais
il ny eust onques celluy qui
leust veoir qui laportoit Si y
entra parmy leynt huye dupalais

eust cellui que peut apperceuoir q le portoit z les
palais de toutes viandes q5 feoret demander
Et maintenant quil yssit entre
fut lepalaix rempli desi bonnes
odeurs que se toutes les espices
du monde y feussent entrees et
espandues Et il ala tout entour

The society of the Middle Ages was essentially a military society. The Church-men and the merchants formed powerful castes but not so powerful as that of the knights; war was, it has been said, 'the central unifying fact of political life'. Arthur himself, in the distant century of his existence, had been a military com-mander of genius, and for succeeding centuries, one campaign after another occupied the energies of the ruling class. The Saxons fought to expel the Danes, the Anglo-Normans fought for their estates in France and to establish a grip on Scotland and Wales. The Crusaders who had served in the Third and Fourth Crusades had a strong influence on society; the Hundred Years War lasted till the middle of the fifteenth century; the Wars of the Roses filled the thirty years before 1487. The expanding commercial prosperity of England was directed towards state support for large-scale warfare, while ransom and plunder augmented the private fortunes of the knights. The military way of life was not adopted merely as a profession; it was enjoyed with a passion the English afterwards transferred to fox-hunting. The troubadour Bertrand de Born exclaims in one of his lyrics: 'I am never happy unless the rich are at feud!' He hails the spring not, like his contem-poraries, because it is the season of birds and flowers, warm weather and love-making, but as the one when knights go out to war, meadows are white with pavilions, shepherds and their flocks scurry away before advancing armies and the earth shudders beneath chargers' hooves. The troubadour Pons de Capdenil, inciting knights to enlist in the Third Crusade, reminds them that the Pope had promised absolution for all warriors who were slain in fighting for the Holy Sepulchre. 'Now is the time', he exclaims, 'when war and chivalry, the pursuits that are the most pleasant in this world, can make us free of the happier world to come!' This was indeed a double inducement, for the Church frowned on the worldliness, the extravagance, the useless danger to human life of tournaments. Innocent II had forbidden them in 1130, and knights who were killed in tourna-ments were not permitted church burial. The young hero of *Aucassin et Nicolete*, written in the first half of the twelfth century, says he prefers the idea of Hell to that of Heaven, because of all the agreeable and fascinating people who go there: 'the goodly knights that fell in tourneys and great wars, and the sweet, courteous ladies that have two or three lovers beside their husbands, and the harpers and poets, and the Prince of this World'.

The stories of the Vulgate Cycle, though they deal with the absorbing tale of the passion of Lancelot and Guinevere, and with the mystic, allegorical legend of the Graal, are all the time concerned with armed encounters, either between two knights at feud, or in casual violence, or tournaments or civil wars, and only a realization of the extreme popularity of jousting can explain why the subject, so constantly treated, was not reckoned monotonous. It was an expression in literary form of one of the ruling passions, and the appearance and court of several English kings gave a living reality to imaginings of Arthur.

Some of the Plantagenets were short and broad-shouldered, but there was a strain of height in the family. It had appeared in their ancestor Geoffrey of Anjou,

98 called Le Bel, and it reappeared in Richard I, the first three King Edwards, the Black Prince and Edward IV. Edward I was called Longshanks, and when his bones were disinterred in Westminster Abbey, the skeleton was found to measure 6 feet 2 inches; with a crested helmet on, he would have stood 7 feet high. Of

Edward III's sons, the Black Prince, Edmund of York, John of Gaunt, and Thomas of Gloucester, the rhyming chronicler Hardynge says:

> So high and large they were of all stature
> The least of them was of his person able
> To have foughten with any creature.

One of the Plantagenets most likely to call up the idea of Arthur in the beholders was Richard I. He succeeded his father in 1189; but two years before his accession the Third Crusade had been declared, calling upon the warriors of Christendom to rescue Jerusalem from Saladin, the Sultan of Turkey. Richard was a superb soldier, of enormous physical strength and the courage which earned him his famous nickname of Cœur de Lion. War was his passion, and the Crusade offered an opportunity not of fighting only, but of the exercise of chivalry; the expedition was satisfying from a military standpoint; it was also emotionally splendid. Richard, who, out of a reign of ten years, spent only six months in England, regarded his accession as a means of coining money to equip himself and the fleet of a hundred ships which were to carry his troops and horses to the coast of Palestine. A great deal of money was amassed by selling the offices of state, but even so, Richard spent it faster than it came in. The finest quality of his knights' chain mail probably came from abroad, but some armour was available from the city guilds of armourers and blade-smiths. Some of the best shields might have been made in England. In *Lancelot*, Chrétien de Troyes gives the conversation of spectators at a tournament: 'Yonder shield is of English workmanship and was made at London; you see on it two swallows as if about to fly.' The iron works in the Forest of Dean sent the King up supplies of a more homely kind: axes, picks, shovels, horseshoes and nails. When Chrétien wants to say that a knight is particularly well horsed, he says he is mounted 'on an Irish steed that bears him along with marvellous swiftness'.

Richard and his knights still wore hauberks and stockings of chain mail, but the Normans' conical steel cap had been changed to a tubular, flat-topped helmet which came down to the base of the neck and was pierced with slits at eye level and all over the face with small holes for ventilation. As the knight's face was hidden, arms were painted on his shield. The burning heat of the desert was to be made less intolerable by a linen surcoat worn over the chain mail. This also was blazoned with the arms.

On his way to Palestine, Richard put in at Cyprus, where he presented his ally, Tancred of Sicily, with what was said to be King Arthur's sword. This was noted in the chronicle of Benedict of Peterborough. Unfortunately, the chronicler says nothing as to what the sword was like, or where it came from. Richard, as can be seen from the engraving on his second Great Seal of 1199, where he appears on horseback in mail and surcoat, with face-concealing helmet, brandishing his sword, might have sat for the image of Arthur, and his conduct as a soldier accorded with it.

The Christian armies had been besieging Acre for two years. Richard arrived and captured the city in a month. He accomplished amazing feats of arms throughout the campaign, as when he raised the siege of Jaffa. Beaching his galleys immediately under the city's fortifications, he plunged into the sea and with drawn sword made for the strand. With a small company of followers, in the face of tremendous odds, he cut his way through the besiegers and entered the citadel; at once sallying out again at the head of the garrison, he drove the besiegers off. His clerk Ambroise, who wrote *Estoire de la Guerre Sainte*, exclaimed that the feat was worthy of Charlemagne.

'Courage and faith – vain faith and courage vain.' When Richard got within sight of Jerusalem he covered his eyes with his shield. He knew that with his depleted forces he would never be able to take it. News of his brother John's treachery obliged him to turn homewards and, like Arthur, forced to relinquish his object, he took the overland route, through Austria and France. He thus fell into the hands of Leopold of Austria, who handed him over to the Emperor Henry VI, on the understanding that they should share the stupendous sum demanded as a king's ransom.

Prince John, whom Richard had left as Regent, was a psychopathic criminal. With some of the Angevin ability, he was unreasonable, vicious and self-centred to the verge of dementia. Richard, who treated him with generosity and affection, had given him the overlordship of six English counties, of which he was allowed to collect the revenues. When these counties, like the rest of England, were placed under a severe impost to provide the King's ransom, John took this money also and put it in his pocket. During Richard's imprisonment, John took possession of his brother's French dominions, doing fealty for them to Philip of France. He intrigued with Philip to persuade the Emperor not to let Richard out. The Emperor, however, in consideration of the ransom's being raised from a hundred thousand marks to a hundred and fifty thousand, allowed his prisoner to depart. When the twenty-seven-year-old John crawled to his brother's feet, Richard said: 'You are a child. I pardon you but I will punish those who misled you.'

Two months after his return to England, after imposing fresh exactions for the war he meant to fight against Philip of France, Richard left the country never to return. The last five years of his life were spent in this campaign. Despite the severe taxes levied on England and Normandy, his need for money was devouring. He heard that a peasant, while ploughing, had uncovered a set of seated figures, all of gold. Like the legends of heroes in underground caverns, like the description of the subterranean *salle aux images* in Thomas of Britain's *Tristan*, this idea found a ready acceptance with those who heard it, including Richard himself. No description of the find appears to exist, but it was believed to be a great treasure-trove. Richard claimed it as overlord, but the lord on whose estate it had been found refused to give it up, and Richard besieged him in his castle of Chaluz. Here he was wounded in the shoulder; the wound became poisoned and the King died on the evening of April 6, 1199. He had chivalrously pardoned the archer who had shot him. It was his sister Joanna, Countess of Toulouse, who had the man flayed alive and hanged.

John might have sat for Modred's picture. His son, Henry III, was aesthetic but incompetent. Having married Eleanor of Provence, a beautiful child of thirteen, he was, and remained, infatuated with her, and incurred the violent resentment of the English by the preposterous sums he spent on clothes and jewels for her and himself, and the plunder which he allowed to a pack of her voracious relatives. The likeness to Arthur reappeared in Henry III's son, Edward I, who, tall, warlike and great, was pre-eminently a warrior and a king. Three years before his father's death, when he had put down the rebellion of Simon de Montfort and could leave his father the King, of whom he was very fond, in safety and comfort, Edward had embarked for service in the Fourth Crusade. He was recalled to England by his father's death in 1272.

On his crusade he had apparently had with him a collection of Arthurian stories which he gave to an Italian in his train, Rusticiano de Pisa. Some years later Rusticiano produced the collection, with a preface saying that he had translated the stories from 'the book of Messire Edward, King of England, at the time that he passed beyond the sea in the service of our Lord God to conquer the Holy Sepulchre'. He also says that the book contains passages from *'plusiers histoires et plusiers chroniques'*, which he extracted to please the Prince. The matter showed Edward's early interest in the Arthurian theme.

Edward I was the first king since the Norman Conquest to arouse the people's wholehearted enthusiasm. They regarded him as entirely English. He was impressive from his presence, his personality, his attitude to government, and the warlike action he took against the Welsh, whom he subdued, and against the Scots, whom, though he became known as Scotorum Malleus, he was never able to subdue.

His great programme of castle-building was carried out to maintain his ascendancy in West Wales. Beaumaris, Conway, Caernarvon and Harlech were built on a plan learned from France, in which round towers replaced rectangular ones because they afforded a much wider lookout. The castle was surrounded by a curtain wall on which the 'drum towers' rose at intervals all the way round. The first three were built for him by the Master James of St Georges, whose services Edward borrowed from Philip of Savoy. Beaumaris was built in two years; the force of four hundred masons and two thousand labourers employed on it was larger than the local population. It was natural that, when the King's mind was so much on castle-building, he should order a toy castle to be made for his six-year-old son, Prince Edward. In 1290, Master John Brodeye, cook to the Lord Edward, was paid forty-four shillings for a castle made of wood, 'with divers colours and other things bought for it'.

In 1278 King Edward and his Queen, Eleanor, were keeping Easter at Glastonbury Abbey, and Edward ordered the opening of Arthur's tomb. He may have felt that he would acquire reflected glory from this celebration of the king from whom he claimed descent, and also, like Henry II before him, that it would be a good thing for the Welsh to be reminded once more that Arthur was well and truly dead. It was found that, in the reburial of 1190, the skeletons had been put each in a marble coffer, decorated with coats of arms with an image of the King above his bones and one of the Queen above hers. The Queen's crown was intact but the King's had been wrenched away. These coffers were standing in a chapel near the south door of the great church. When they were opened, the skulls were removed as relics, the rest of the bones were placed in a black marble coffer with two lions at each end of it and an image of King Arthur at its foot. Leland saw the coffer

Arthur, from whom many later kings claimed descent, shown in the fourteenth century to have been overlord of thirty kingdoms, some wholly fictitious

standing before the high altar of the great church, in 1534. It was presumably destroyed at the Dissolution.

Edward not only ordered a sumptuous reburial of Arthur's supposed remains; when he appealed to the Pope to support his claim to be King of Scotland, he quoted Geoffrey of Monmouth,[16] who had said that Arthur had established Angusel as King of Scotland; therefore, Edward said, Arthur was overlord of Angusel, and by descent the King of England was overlord of the King of Scotland.

Edward had established a form of tournament called the Mensa Rotunda, which was held in honour of the Round Table and which may have been a dramatic representation, as certain combatants took the lists in the character of some of Arthur's knights. In 1284, to proclaim his victory over the Welsh, Edward held a Mensa Rotunda at Nevin in Caernarvon. At this ceremony, the chronicler of the Waverley Annals says: 'The crown of the famous King Arthur which the Welsh had long held in the highest honour, was ceded to the Lord King with other precious objects. Thus the glory of the Welsh, against their will, was transferred to the English.' As in the case of Arthur's sword, bestowed by Richard on Tancred, there is no word about the provenance of the crown. It must have been very old, since the Welsh had cherished it as a relic for so long. It was not likely to have been a jewelled chaplet, such as Henry III spent so much for (Eleanor of Provence had nine wreaths of precious stones, all at one time), but it was probably some piece of Celtic enamelled metal-work highly interesting in itself, though its connection with Arthur was imaginary.

There must, on some level, be a close connection between the literature which people find absorbing, and the idiom of their own existence. Edward could have taken his place as a character in those romances where kings built castles and erected costly tombs. In 1290 his wife Eleanor died at Lincoln while he was in arms against the Scots. He temporarily abandoned his warfare and accompanied her bier from Grantham down to Westminster. Thirteen crosses, surmounting lofty Gothic spires of exquisite tracery, rose in his wake, to mark each place where her body had rested on the way. Emotion was translated into visual splendour. Music, too, was a delight to him and a consolation. A payment of twenty shillings was made to Meliora, the harper of Sir John Mautravers, 'for playing on the harp while the King was bled', and one of six shillings and eightpence to Walter Lovel, the harper of Chichester, 'whom the King found playing on his harp before the tomb of St Richard at Chichester Cathedral'. One is reminded that Tristan was a harper.

France · Norvef · Albanie · Orkeneie · hirland · Roynbai

Danmark · Germem · Dovingale · Rauene · Armon · Angeon

Island · Gichland · Almain · Gruffon · Galie · Gres

Aragon · Espaine · mede · libue · Arge · Caipre

Surrie · Babiloine · Sorri · Beethie · Tores · Rome

tore que bous deuses esta qui par de longue
bous nauez estache ce chlz qui agist naure qui
est aussi gentilz home come bous estes. Mar
estor ne lentedi mie. En nom dieu fait lestuiere
il dort que ia dieux ne li aist et dit que se ses suie
ne fust malade quille meist sus de son cheual.

Ors hauta le troncon de la
lance quil tenoit si seul chlz
estor enn le bis si quille fist
boler en pieces et puis le prist
par le foam si le sacha li mlt
duuement si que par vn pou
quil ne chei a terre et le fist
venir sur les deux pies derriere. Et estor laista
son pense si bit lestuier qui bien sambleit selon
si li dit que se pensoit li quil nauoit le col busse et
pourquoy beau sire fait estor pourquoy sire
fait il si comenca a iurer trop duuement le dif
feable fait il bous auoient endormi que par vn
ror que bous nauez a estache. I. chlr naure et

10 Arthur and Chivalry

The feature which most closely connected social life with life as described in the Arthurian romances, was the rise, growth and enormous popularity of tournaments. Though condemned by several popes as a mischievous indulgence, leading to 'the death of the body and corruption of the soul', this pastime was followed with insensate enthusiasm, from the early twelfth century onwards; in spite of papal prohibition, one was held during the Second Crusade itself, outside the walls of Antioch.

The fact that, in England and France, the power of the barons was being restrained and private war on an unlimited scale was no longer possible, made the barons eager for some outlet for martial energy which would also provide the chance of rewards: ransom and the horse and equipment of the defeated adversary. In its earliest form the tournament was not, as it afterwards became, a trial of skill, held in a confined space between two opponents obeying a set of complicated rules; it was a free-for-all, between armed bands who fought across whole districts, trampling cornfields and vineyards and pursuing each other through the streets of towns. Henry II forbade tournaments in England; they were altogether too reminiscent of the barons' wars which it had cost him so much time and energy to put down. His sons, therefore, who were mad for the sport, were obliged to go over to France to enjoy it. They joined a brilliant, eager, extravagant company of tourneyers in France and Flanders, who held a tournament once a fortnight. This was not only exciting but profitable; knights made up teams to share the gains of ransoms and forfeited horses and arms; the value of the rich armour and the splendid animals added a keen edge to the enthusiasm for winning. For days before the tournament, knights and their retinues descended on the scene, occupying all the available lodgings in the town and pitching their pavilions in the meadows, as Geoffrey of Monmouth and Chrétien de Troyes vividly described.

Richard I, who combined, with his love of armed combat, a rapacious instinct for getting in the money, abolished his father's edict and licensed tournaments; two knights and their clerks were to supervise each event, to prevent entrants from pursuing a private feud – a recognition of his father's purpose in banning tournaments altogether – and to collect fees from each entrant which were to be paid to the crown.

The thirteenth century changed the tournament, from war on a small scale, to a contest within a limited area, requiring a high degree of technical skill. A strict

Preparations for the Jousts of St Inghilbert
in the fifteenth century: a miniature from
Froissart's *Chronicles*

code was evolved, saying who might and who might not take part, and covering
every detail of the encounter. This could be fought either with *armes courtoises*,
blunted sword and lance, or, a very dangerous alternative, with arms *à outrance*,
naked weapons. The strong element in this brew of heady excitement was the
presence, once the lists had been defined, of an audience, including women. The
sexual significance of victory or defeat, the undertaking to defend a woman's
claims to superior beauty, or the hope of arousing admiration in one whom the
knight longed to possess, gave the proceedings a highly emotional quality, for
participants and watchers, over and above the absorbing interest of superb
masculine skill and courage. This aspect of the tournament was naturally
emphasized by romancers.

In spite of regulations, passions aroused in the lists sometimes led to murderous
attacks, and perhaps as an antidote to this danger, 'Round Table Tournaments'
were instituted in Flanders, first recorded in 1235, in which all combatants were
understood to belong to a fellowship of brothers-in-arms. The convention became
popular and was introduced into England.

Whatever efforts were made to render the passion for fighting more civilized and humane, the underlying ferocity is shown, even in so unexpected a context as *The Quest of the Holy Graal*. Galahad, riding incognito in the Waste Forest, finds Lancelot and Perceval riding together. 'They took him for a stranger, being unfamiliar with the arms he bore. So Lancelot charged him first, striking him full in the chest and snapping his lance, while Galahad met him with a blow that toppled horse and knight together but did him no other injury. Then, his lance being broken, he drew his sword and smote Perceval so hard that he cut through the helm and mail coif and had not the sword twisted in his grasp he must have killed him. As it was, Perceval lost his grip on the saddle and hurtled to the ground, so stunned and dazed from the blow that he knew not whether it were day or night.'

This unprovoked, murderous attack of two to one on a man because he was thought to be a stranger, was the sort of episode that made Roger Ascham, one of the greatest teachers of children, say that it was wrong and irresponsible to give *Morte Arthur* to boys and girls, particularly ones living in rich households where, Ascham felt, unlike his pupil the Princess Elizabeth, they had not really enough to do. The book's two leading features were manslaughter and adultery. Put it into these children's hands and they would read it, day in, day out. After that, you would have only yourself to thank.

The mania for fighting, in which, as Ascham said, 'they are accounted the noblest knights that do kill most men without quarrel', is reflected when Perceval asks his aunt where his cousin Dyabil is to be found. She says: 'More than two years have passed since I saw him, for he travels the length and breadth of Britain in the wake of tournaments.'

The wayfaring of the knights in the thirteenth-, fourteenth- and fifteenth-century romances brings a constant reminder that a great part of this land was still forest. It was calculated that, in the eleventh century, one-third of England was under forest law. While we try to preserve such trees as we have, men of the Middle Ages viewed the conquest of the woodlands as their hardest, most important task in making and keeping the land habitable. Since the time of Edward the Confessor, the great roads – Ermine Street, Watling Street, the Fosse Way, the Icknield Way – were called the royal roads or the King's Highway. They were under the King's protection, and anyone who attacked a wayfarer on one of them was liable to a fine of a hundred shillings: a penalty with which, it would seem, the knights of Arthur's court should frequently have been visited. Edward I had seen what cover encroaching woodland gave to crime, and he enacted that all brushwood was to be cleared for a space of 200 feet on each side of the public highway. It was natural that the forest depths should frighten men and give rise to the idea that they were haunted. Chrétien de Troyes's Perceval thought that the noise of the approaching knights came from the demons who lived in the heart of the woods, and in *The Quest of the Holy Graal* a hermit, anxious to learn how his friend had met his death, called up 'the Enemy' to tell him; when the Evil One had satisfied the hermit's demands, 'He departed suddenly, razing the trees in his

Eaulx fire dieux qui de reft
fant vaiffel que de toy ty
venir aues fait tant de

path and whipping up such a violent storm that it seemed as if all the fiends of hell
were tearing through the forest.' Such were the tales born of the woodland's
intense solitude and its eerie sound. But one of Lancelot's journeys in *The Quest*
has a formidableness of a practical kind: he is warned by an anchoress, 'one of the
holiest ladies in the land', who says to him: 'Lancelot, this forest is vast and
labyrinthine in its depth; a knight can ride a whole day long and never find a
house or refuge.' This would have been altogether possible in the great woods of
the south and west of England.

The French Arthurian story of the most bewitching interest is one mysteriously
connected with English ground. It is not one of the Vulgate Cycle. *Perlesvaus le
Gallois*[17] was written between 1191 and 1212, and, Nitze[18] argues, precedes the
Vulgate versions of *The History of the Holy Graal* and *The Quest of the Holy Graal*.
It is less brilliantly imagined than Chrétien's *Perceval*, and it has not the intensely
symbolical, mystical, allegorical atmosphere of the Vulgate stories. Altogether
simpler and wilder, its extraordinary fascination lies in the fact that despite its
French origin it is firmly sited in Somerset, in and about Glastonbury, and that
some of its episodes lead back to a past of far remoteness.

A colophon at the end of the book says: 'The Latin, from whence this book is
drawn, was taken in the Isle of Avalon, in a holy house of religion that standeth
at the head of the Moors Adventurous, there where King Arthur and Queen
Guinevere lie, according to the witness of the good men religious that are therein,
that have the whole history thereof from the true beginning, even to the end.'

The work which interlaces the adventures of Perceval, Lancelot, Gawain and
Arthur himself, begins with the career of Perceval. When Perceval, the guest of
the Fisher King, saw the procession pass through the hall, he ought to have asked:
'Who is served with this Graal?' His failure to put this question has resulted not
only in the Fisher King's still languishing under the evil spell, but in a general
deterioration of society. Arthur himself has become despised as a *roi fainéant* and
Guinevere begs him to exert himself. The King decides to ride out after adventures
and to make his way to the Chapel of St Austin in the woods. He tells his page to
be ready for a very early start, and the boy, all eager obedience, does not go to
bed but lies down in front of the hall fire. He now dreams that he has set out with
the King but has become parted from him in the forest and while looking for him
makes his way into a chapel where a dead knight is lying on a bier, surrounded by
tapers in gold candlesticks. Thinking the King will be pleased with one of these,
he removes the taper from a candlestick and puts the latter into the top of his
stocking. On his way out he encounters a tall, fearful-looking man in black who
charges him with the theft and stabs him in the side. The boy shrieks, and awakes
to find himself lying before the hall fire. The King, Queen and Chamberlain are
all around him, asking what is the matter. The boy relates his dream – but he is
dying; there is the knife in his ribs and the gold candlestick in the top of his
stocking.

This astonishing climax is dealt with by Jessie Weston.[14] She believes that it preserves the memory of 'an initiation carried out on the astral plane and reacting with fatal results on the physical'. The suggestion leads the mind back to the paranormal practices of the civilization that raised Stonehenge, and further still. Arthur now sets out alone and comes to the Chapel of St Austin, where he finds Mass being celebrated. The writer's use of light and jewels to express a visionary state is like that of Ezekiel: 'Thou hast been in Eden, the Garden of God, every precious stone was thy covering, the topaz and the diamond, the sapphire, the emerald, the carbuncle . . . thou hast walked up and down in the midst of the stones of fire.' The King has a mystic experience clothed in the same idiom; suddenly he sees, at the priest's right hand, 'the fairest Child he had ever seen; he was clad in an alb and had a golden crown on his head loaded of precious stones that gave out a full great brightness of light. On the left side was a Lady, so fair that all the ladies of the world might not compare them with her beauty . . . he looketh at a window behind the altar and seeth a flame come through at the very instant that Mass was begun, clearer than any ray of sun nor moon nor star, and ever more it threw forth a brightness of light. Such that an all the lights in the world had been together, it would not have been the like. . . . When Mass was sung, the voice of a holy angel said: *Ite, missa est.* The Son took the Mother by the hand and they vanished forth of the chapel, with the greatest company and the fairest that might ever be seen.'

The groundwork of the tale is the search of the three knights, sometimes accompanied by Arthur, for the mystical experience of the sight of the Graal, but the religious attitude of the writer is harsh and barbarous. The new law, Christianity, is to be enforced at the sword's point. Perceval, after a great slaughter of infidels among the inhabitants of a castle, says: 'They that are unwilling to believe in God shall die like mad folk and devils.' He 'straight way slew all the others, for that they were not minded to believe. The castle was all emptied of misbelieving folk.' The contending forces in the Crusades would have felt in the same way. Richard slaughtered hundreds of captives ruthlessly, and Saladin declared that only death should make him lay down his sword while a single unbeliever remained alive.

A more horrible reminder occurs of the practice of mutilation brought in by the Normans, when Lancelot is at dinner with a lady who entertains him on his way to the castle of the Fisher King.

'The first course was brought in by knights in chains that had their noses cut off, the second by knights in chains that had their eyes put out, wherefor they were led in by squires. The third course was brought in by knights that had but one hand and were in chains. After that came knights that had each but one foot and brought in the fourth course.' This evil fantasy calls up the hideous recollection of Robert de Bellême and Geoffrey de Mandeville. 'Lancelot beheld the martyrdom of these knights and some misliking he had of the service of such folk.' This is the Lancelot we know, but there is a terrifying vignette of him which seems to have risen from some infinitely older level of storytelling. Arthur, Lancelot and Gawain and their squire are benighted and come to an empty hall with a bright fire in it.

The squire explores the premises to see if he can find food for the horses, and comes back panic-stricken saying he has found a chamber which is in darkness, but where he can feel that some two hundred dead men are lying. 'Lancelot went into the chamber to see whether he spake true, and felt the men that lay dead and groped among them from head to head, and felt that there was a great heap of them, and came back and sat at the fire, all laughing.'

The handling of Lancelot's passion for Guinevere, however, is written with great sensibility and psychological insight. Before presenting himself at the Graal Castle Lancelot shrives himself to a hermit 'beside a spring'. The hermit exhorts him to leave this fatal passion, but Lancelot says: 'I am willing enough to do penance, as great as is enjoined of this sin . . . but so dearly do I love her, that I wish not even that any will should come to me to renounce her love. . . . The affection seemeth me so good and so high that I cannot let go thereof, for so rooted as it is in my heart that thence may it never more depart, and the best knighthood that is within me cometh to me only of her affection. . . . She hath in her such beauty and worth and wisdom and courtesy and nobleness, that never ought she to be forgotten of any man that hath loved her.' 'The more of beauty and worth she hath in her,' said the hermit, 'the more blame hath she of that she doeth and you likewise.'

In all the stories about Guinevere, she only shows unamiable traits when she is driven by the torments of her love for Lancelot. She exerted a cruel and un-reasonable caprice at the tournament in Chrétien's *Lancelot*, she gave way to causeless jealousy in the *Morte Artu*, over the Maid of Astolat, but in her relations with others she is gracious, sympathetic and generous; in *Érec et Énide*, she took pains to dress Enide for her bridal, for she was fond of them both; and until the tragic climax is reached, Arthur's love for her is undoubted. In *Perceval le Gallois*

Arthur and Gawain enter for a tournament in which Arthur is to fight incognito. A girl makes advances to him, which appears to please the King, but she does not succeed in captivating him, for 'his thought is on Queen Guinevere, in what place so ever he may be, for nought loveth he so well as her.'

In this story, the climax, the revelation of adultery is never reached. Arthur has left Guinevere behind him as Regent while he, Lancelot and Gawain made this extended expedition to fight in a large-scale tournament. Arthur distinguishes himself superbly in the lists, and the writer gives an interesting detail of his tendance after the combat. He and Gawain 'washed their hands and faces for the rust with which both of them were be-smuttered'. More than a hundred and fifty years later, Chaucer's Knight, just home from the wars, was riding to Canterbury in the woollen coat he had worn under his chain mail, 'all bismotered with his habergeon'. The rusting of mail was a perpetual nuisance. Chrétien had described the luxurious chain mail of Érec, which did not rust because it was all of silver. The usual method of cleaning mail from rust was to bury it in a barrel of sand and shake the barrel to and fro.

Jousting at Camelot: Lancelot watched from
the castle by Guinevere and her ladies.

ARTHUR AND CHIVALRY

113

When Arthur has retired from the lists, he is approached by a messenger leading a white horse and carrying a rich gold crown. He offers these to Arthur, whom he does not recognize, saying they belonged to a famous queen who has just died. Whoever accepts them must take it on himself to rescue her lands from invading enemies; from his performance in the lists, he sees that Arthur is eminently fitted for the task. 'Saith Arthur, whose was the land, and what was the name of the Queen whose crown I see? Sir, the King's name was Arthur and this crown was the crown of Queen Guinevere, who is dead and buried, whereof is sore sorrow.' Lancelot hears the words and the tears pour down his face and out through the chain-mail neckpiece at the base of the helmet. 'Had he durst make other dole, yet greater would it have been.' Arthur's own grief is indescribable. 'He holdeth the crown of gold and looketh full oft at the destrier, for love of her, for he had given it to her.' On their journey back to his kingdom, Arthur 'made the white horse to be led after him and kept the gold crown full near himself'.

The writer has already shown knowledge of a part of England: he has described Tintagel. Arthur and Lancelot and Gawain had come to 'a land . . . scarce in-

habited of any folk, and found a little castle in a combe . . . they saw that the enclosure of the castle was fallen down into a abyss so that none might approach it on that side. . . . They beheld a chapel that was right fair and rich and below was a great, ancient hall.' A monk comes to them out of the chapel. They ask him what castle it is. 'He told them it was the great Tintagel.' The writer then says that Guinevere is buried at Avalon and that Lancelot goes to visit her tomb. This passage is of the greatest interest because the scene of Lancelot's approach is unmistakably Glastonbury.

The ruins at Tintagel, which still seem to
echo the words of Perlesvaus le Gallois on
'the castle . . . fallen down into an abyss'

ARTHUR AND CHIVALRY

115

This actual landscape is dominated by the Tor, on whose summit remains only
the tower of St Michael's Church. The church replaced one destroyed by an
earthquake in 1275, but the latter, Dr Ralegh Radford[19] says, 'we may suspect was
the successor of many shrines, Christian and pre-Christian'. A church on the
summit of this commanding site may be justifiably supposed between 1190 and
1212. Below the Tor is a tree-covered hillside, now called Chalice Hill. Out of this
hillside springs the Chalice Well, enclosed in a thirteenth-century stone well-
shaft. It produces 25,000 gallons a day and in periods of acutest drought has never
run dry. The Tor with the church on its summit, the wooded hillside and the
pouring stream now enclosed in a well, are the distinguishing features of the scene.

The writer of Perlesvaus says: 'At the top of the mountain beside the valley he
seeth a chapel newly builded that was right fair . . . and a spring came down full
clear from the heights of the forest before the chapel and ran into the valley with a
great rushing.' When Lancelot ascends to the chapel, leading his horse, for the Tor
is too steep to ride, he finds two stone coffins, one prepared for Arthur and one in
which Guinevere is already lying. Before the assembled monks, 'no semblant of
grief durst he make, other than such as might not be perceived, and great comfort
was it to him that there was an image of our Lady at the head of the coffin. He
knelt down the nighest he might to the coffin, as it had been to worship the image,
and set his face and his mouth to the stone of the coffin.'

The mysterious writer has chosen to place the burials in the church at the top
of Glastonbury Tor instead of in the Abbey church at its foot, but his description
of the terrain is more interesting than whatever he says took place there. He gives
what appears to be another first-hand impression. The flat land from which the
Tor rises was once under the waters of the Bristol Channel, and though draining
had begun in the twelfth century, it still remained marsh and peat moor. Drained
by deep-cut rhines, the peat moor is there today. The land surrounding the
castle of Perceval's mother is called the Sea Moors; some of it, the Isles of the
Moors. The tyrant from whom Perceval rescues her is the Lord of the Moors.

There is yet another connection between the landscape in Perlesvaus and the
neighbourhood of Glastonbury. K. E. Maltwood[20] demonstrates, by means of
aerial photographs and ordnance maps, that in a ring about the base of the Tor,
of 10 miles in diameter, are a series of zodiacal figures whose outlines are created
by earthworks, rivers, lanes, roads, which are still more or less intact. She suggests
that they were the work of sun-worshippers about 2800 B.C. and calls the circle a
land-chart of the sky. That these shapes are recognizably those of the figures
representing the constellations is not admitted by everyone; some people feel
that the eye of faith is required; but the really remarkable feature of her research
is her work on Perlesvaus itself; the work is arranged in sections called 'branches',
divided into chapters called 'titles', and the action of the book is linked with a
journey through these zodiacal images imposed on the Glastonbury landscape.
The matter is extremely complex, requiring much learning to elucidate it, and the
outstanding aspect of it is that it is there to be explained.

116   Mrs Maltwood refers to a passage in *The Quest of the Holy Graal* which, she submits, shows the adoption by Christian legend of the zodiacal figures. Lancelot, having turned his horse loose to graze, falls asleep in a wood at the foot of a cross and dreams of a man 'all set about with stars' who ushers in a vision of two knights. The elder of them is rebuked, but 'he who came down from heaven went up to the younger knight and changed him into the likeness of a lion and gave him wings', a blending of the zodiacal Leo with the winged lion of St Mark. The writer of *The Quest* gives another pointer in this direction when he says 'The sun, by whom we mean Jesus Christ'. This is one of the statements suggesting the view that the effigies were the product of a religious belief that was practised in 2800 B.C., which Christianity had adapted to itself. Mrs Maltwood, by abstruse astrological calculations which the uninitiated cannot follow, identifies the leading characters in *Perlesvaus* with astronomical counterparts: Arthur is the Sun in the east and the last quarter of the year, Lancelot the midday sun in the south and the third quarter of the year. Whatever importance may be attached to these calculations it is clear that some, at least, of the giant effigies, in their rudely graphic outlines, may be traced, and it is also demonstrated by Mrs Maltwood that a connection is traceable between the 'branches' of the *Perlesvaus*, and the zodiacal effigies in whose neighbourhood the action of the branch takes place. The inexplicable theme traced on our land in stone circles and earthwork effigies had been reflected in *Perlesvaus*; but who was the French writer? What did he know of Glastonbury and how did he come to know it?

11 Decline of Knighthood

Layamon's *Brute* was the first poem on the Arthurian story to be written in the vernacular. From the middle of the twelfth century, as Anglo-Saxon gave way to Middle English, people went on telling the story. The English versions are usually taken from themes in the Vulgate Cycle, and they are frequently vapid and dull, but they often give off gleams in their pictures of scenery and character. The late thirteenth-century *Arthour and Merlin*, written to be recited, a tale of the military exploits by which Arthur, aided by Merlin, subdues the north, opens with a lovely impression of landscape:

> Now He that madeth with His hand
> Wind, wood, water and land,
> Give them all good ending
> That listeneth to my talking!

Arthur is fighting to defend the lands of his ally King Leodogrance against King Ryence of North Wales. Leodogrance is the father of the matchless beauty Guinevere, whose Roman origin, as stated by Geoffrey of Monmouth, has now been suppressed. Leodogrance has another daughter, also called Guinevere, whom he begot on his steward's wife one day when the Queen was at church. The half-sisters are extremely like each other and the story repeats yet again the strange theme of the double Guinevere. This is so mysterious and so persistent, it seems to arise like some image of the subconscious. Saklatvala[3] suggests a possible factual origin. Arthur, he thinks, may, as part of a peace treaty, have contracted a marriage with a Saxon princess, possibly called Wenever or Winiver, and when hostilities broke out again, he may have returned her to her own people. Saklatvala points out that, in Caradoc's *Life of St Gildas*, Arthur is besieging Glastonbury because Melvas, King of the Summer Country, has abducted Arthur's wife. The story is of course quite different from the one postulated, but the fact of separation is common to both. In the *Life*, Guinevere is restored to Arthur. A reconciliation, or a re-affirmation of the marriage, might have given grounds for the legend of two successive marriages to wives each called Guinevere, or to the most metaphysical form of it which is sometimes found, in which the King is confronted with a true and a false Guinevere and has to make his choice of them. The interesting feature of the idea is its extraordinary quality of survival, for it occurs in contexts where it adds nothing to the effect of the narrative.

Its appearance in *Arthour and Merlin* is a case in point; the presence of the illegitimate half-sister contributes nothing, but the details of social life in the castle, where Arthur and Guinevere are betrothed, are of fascinating interest. When Arthur and his companions return, war-stained, there is a charming, luxurious scene in which Guinevere and other young ladies wash them in 'rich baths'. Guinevere herself washes Arthur:

> And before every gentleman was
> Maidens to serve, with great solas.

The idea that the strictest propriety was at all infringed by people of the opposite sex appearing naked in front of each other, was of later date than the thirteenth century. Iseult was in Tristan's chamber while he was in his bath, when she saw the notch in his sword that fitted the piece of steel found in her uncle Morholt's brain after Tristan had killed him. Many pictures of the thirteenth and fourteenth centuries show knights in their baths attended by ladies; sometimes a knight and a lady are in the bath together.

Another verse of *Arthour and Merlin*, describing Guinevere's arming of Arthur,
shows the recognized influence of sexual emotion on fighting courage:

> That same day, par amour,
> Guinevere armed King Arthour . . .
> At that arming the geste sayeth this –
> Arthour the maiden gan kiss –
> Merlin bade Arthour the King
> Think on that ilke kissing,
> When he came into bataile.

Arthur's image continued, not only to interest the listener who wanted to hear
a story, but as an inspiration to kings. In 1344, Froissart, writing the chronicles
of the Hundred Years War from both the French and English standpoints, says
that Edward III vowed to establish a Round Table at Windsor, 'as Arthur had
left it, for three hundred knights'. Froissart had heard, and taken it for true, that
Windsor Castle had been built by Arthur. Edward III began to erect a circular
building, 200 feet in diameter, to house the sittings of this Round Table, but it was
never finished. One feast was held for it, in 1345. Four years later the King founded
the Order of the Blue Garter, which has remained ever since. It is suggested that
he abandoned the idea of a Round Table, because the French King had founded
one to prevent the chivalry of Italy and Germany from resorting to England.
Froissart does not say that the garter, of which Edward observed '*Honte y soit
qui mal y pense*', belonged to Lady Salisbury, but he gives a poignant description
of Edward's staying in her husband's castle at Durham, of his passionate longing
for her and of her gentle repulse. Though the outcome was altogether different,
the King's painful yearning, his inability to take his eyes off her or to speak to
anyone else when she was there, reminds the reader of Geoffrey of Monmouth's
description of Uther Pendragon, smitten with the beauty of Igerne: 'When the
King spied her among the others, he did suddenly wax so fain of her love, that
paying no heed unto none of the others he turned his attention only upon her.'
This was in 1341 at the beginning of the Hundred Years War. Odious and
criminal as this enterprise strikes us now, with the hideous devastation of France
and the appalling waste of English energy and wealth, it showed Edward III and
his son the Black Prince as military commanders of very high capacity. Edward
finally lost all the English territory in France except Bayonne and Bordeaux,
though he gained Calais, which the English prized extremely as giving them
control of part of the Channel, but in the last resort the most significant fact of this
era of the war was that the Battle of Crécy, in 1346, was not won by English
mounted knights but by English archers. The development of the use of archery
was the great change in the military tactics of the fourteenth century. The English,
it is said, learned the use of the long bow from the Welsh. This weapon could fire
six arrows a minute, and could split an oyster shell at 100 yards. Edward I had used
archers in his victory over Wallace at Falkirk, but it was at Crécy that their deadly

Worn by the Black Prince: chain and plate mail combined, giving greater protection than earlier suits of chain mail only

power was demonstrated to Europe. The English archers, Froissart said, fired so rapidly, their arrows flew as thick as snow. The Genoese crossbowmen, hired by the French, fired so slowly by comparison, the French King became mad with rage and ordered the French to fall on them and kill them. The fearful exhibition at Crécy in 1346, and at Poitiers in 1356, ushered in a new era of military history. It gave rise to the saying, current in England for many generations, that no one may take the law of a grey goose, as these birds supplied the English arrows with their feathers. Crécy marked the beginning of the decay, though long and slow, of the power and prestige of the knightly order.

Froissart's accounts of the engagements of the French War and the courageous debonair character of Edward III – sometimes darkened by an access of rage, as when he threatened to hang the burghers of Calais – give the illusion that the chronicles of Edward, and those of Arthur, are of the same weaving. A fourteenth-century English poem called the Thornton *Morte Arthur*, from the name of the transcriber, Robert Thornton, follows the familiar lines of Arthur's departure from England to conquer France and Rome, of his prophetic dream and his recall to deal with the treachery of Modred, but the description of Arthur's embarkation is far fuller and more vivid than any previous one, and might stand for that of Edward III when setting out for Sluys in 1340.

'The sailors make ready barges, in which they bring on board horses, and stately helms, tents, cloak-bags, coffers, and rich shields. Horses, hackneys and chargers they stow on board, the properties of stern, bold knights. When everything was shipped that had to go, they delayed no longer but untied the hawsers quickly, as the tide was running. Sea men on the prow coiled up the cables. They pull the sails to the top of the rigging and turn to windward. Standing on the starboard, they break out into lusty singing. The ships draw their full depth, and fare forth with spread sail. The shipmen quickly shut the port holes and throw plumblines on the sea to take soundings. When the light fails, they skilfully plot their course by compass and loadstone, on the night tide.'

When Arthur arms himself to attack the cannibal giant on St Michael's Mount, he puts on chain mail over a jacket, a helmet of burnished silver and metal gloves, gilded and set with small gems. By the last quarter of the fourteenth century, when the poem was written, he might well have been wearing chain mail reinforced at shoulders, elbows, thighs and legs with plate. The Black Prince died of malaria in 1376. The beautiful effigy on his tomb in Canterbury Cathedral is all in plate armour except for the chain mail coif worn under the helmet, a close-fitting steel cap known as a basinet. According to the instructions in his will, made the day before he died, his head rests, as on a pillow, on a great helmet, 'our helmet of the Leopard'. The latter was a crest, the model of a leopard made in gilded leather, of which the tail hung down at the back of the wearer's neck. The actual helmet, of which the one on the tomb is a copy, shows the dints and scars of blows.

The Thornton *Morte Arthur* carries another reminiscence of the reign of Edward III; in the description of the victory Arthur is supposed to have gained

over the Emperor at Soissons, the success is ascribed to the King's archers: 'With flighted arrows they shoot full strongly, piercing with feathers the fine mail; such shooting is grievous; the flesh is injured; they fly from a distance, in flanks of horses. The bolts pierce them so swiftly, they shrink from the sharp arrows, the whole troop shudders.'

An Arthurian poem of about 1400, a translation of the Vulgate *Morte Artu*, is the first English version of Lancelot and the Maid of Astolat, whose story is a uniquely successful feat of adolescent self-dramatization. When Lancelot rejects the offer of herself, she brings on her death by neither eating nor sleeping. When she is dead her father carries out the deeply satisfying presentation she has devised; in her richest clothes she is laid in a black-draped barge, and with her letter to Lancelot 'in a rich purse', she is rowed downstream to Westminster. In this poem the verse is not of a high order but it is full of insight. Lancelot has seen that the girl is sick with love for him; he calls her brother and together they go to her room where she is lying on her bed weeping.

> He sat him down for the maiden's sake
> Upon her bed thereas she lay,
> Courteously to her he spake
> For to comfort that fair may.

She sat up and took him in her arms, begging for his love, and he gently refused her, trying to perform the impossible task of making her see reason. His consent to wear her favour at the Winchester jousts accords with his plan of appearing there incognito. He approaches Winchester, having disguised himself as an old man, and King Arthur, who is standing on a tower with Sir Erwayne, watching arrivals, says: 'Who can that be?' Erwayne answers:

> Sir, it is some olde knight
> Come to see the young knights ride.

But as they watch, the horse stumbles, and the immediate, instinctive adjustment of the rider's limbs defeats his disguise in an instant:

> As he the bridle up gan take
> Thereby wist they both anon
> That it was Lancelot du Lake.

When the miserable denouement is reached, and Lancelot, having rescued Guinevere from burning, carries her off to Joyous Garde, a pitched battle is fought by his forces and the King's. One of the most piercing moments in the whole Arthurian cycle is when Lancelot, finding the King with his horse killed under him, puts up Arthur on his own mount, exclaiming that he never can forget who made him knight.

None of these verse tales, however, can compare for power and brilliance with the poem of about 1400, *Sir Gawaine and the Green Knight*, a purely English work owing nothing to foreign origins, an exhibition of alarming poetic genius. The story is one of those in which the hero is attached to Arthur's court, but his adventures carry him away from it. On New Year's Day, when the King and Queen and court are assembled for dinner, a knight of unusual size rides his horse into the hall, demanding that some knight shall give him a blow on the neck with the axe he carries, and come to the Green Chapel next New Year's Day, to suffer a return blow.

> Amazed at the hue of him
> A foe of furious mein,
> Men gaped, for the giant grim
> Was coloured a gorgeous green.

So was his horse, and the knight's clothes and accoutrements, and the horse's trappings, were all green. The gold and the steel were stained green, the harness

'glimmered and glinted with green stones', and gold threads were twined in the 123
horse's green mane.

Arthur immediately offers himself to the knight's challenge, but Gawaine
interposes and takes it on himself. With one blow of the axe he cuts off the Green
Knight's head, which rolls along the floor, blood spurting against the green flesh.
The Green Knight picks it up. It lifts its eyelids and 'looks glaringly'; then it
charges Sir Gawaine to keep tryst at the Green Chapel a year from that day.
Holding it by the green hair, its owner sets his horse at a gallop and charges out
of the hall.

The tale of Gawaine's journey through the Wirral in dead winter, at the end of
the year, to keep his vow; his adventures at the castle of Sir Bertilak, a genial and
generous host of handsome appearance and normal colouring in whom Gawaine
does not recognize the Green Knight, have nothing to do with Arthur. It is a tale
of old magic whose meanings are disputed but related with such visual brilliance
and emotional force, reading it is like experiencing some thrilling nightmare. Its
leading feature is description. Gawaine's armour, which he puts on in readiness
for his adventure, shows how, by 1400, plate armour was reinforcing mail:

> Then they set the steel shoes on the strong man's feet,
> Lapped his legs in steel with lovely greaves
> Complete with knee pieces polished bright
> And connecting at the knee with gold-knobbed hinges –
> Then came the cuisses which cunningly enclosed
> His thighs, thick of thew, and which thongs secured.
> Next the hauberk, interlinked with argent steel rings,
> And resting on rich material, wrapped the warrior round.
> He had polished armour on arms and elbows,
> Glinting and gay, and gloves of metal.

In this heavy and ice-cold covering,

> Half slain by the sleet he slept in his armour
> Night after night among the naked rocks,
> Where the cold streams ran clattering from the crests above
> And hung high over his head in hard icicles.

After this duress, to which his armour added as much suffering as did that of
Cœur de Lion's knights in the burning sand, he sees, through oak woods in a
valley, Sir Bertilak's castle, shining and surrounded by a moat; its description
sounds as if it had been built by Edward I:

> Into the water the wall went, wondrous deep,
> And then to a huge height upward it reared,
> In hard-hewn stone up to the cornice
> Which was buttressed under battlements in the best style.

The towers and turrets were all tipped with crenelations.

aymude is mukil on þt Vil me ne(on)gt amend
Sum tune V as trech eas tton þ froth aine cowpe hue dfend

Here Gawaine in his exhausted state is received with lavish hospitality; wrapped in an ermine-lined mantle, he is seated beside a hearth glowing with charcoal. A trestle table is put up, covered with a shining clean white cloth, silver spoons, salt-cellars and napkins, and a delicious dinner is served to him, beginning with several rich soups. The servants apologize for the rest of the dinner's being only fish – it is the fast of Christmas Eve – but the different kinds of fish are exquisitely cooked and sauced.

When Sir Bertilak returns to his castle after hunting, he receives the guest with cordial courtesy and arranges with him that he, the host, shall give Gawaine the spoils of his hunting every day on his return home, and Gawaine shall give him anything that he may have received while he remained in the castle. Gawaine has now to withstand the advances of Sir Bertilak's beautiful wife, who visits him in the mornings before he is out of bed. This he does for two days, accepting only kisses which he passes on to Sir Bertilak in the evening, in return for the spoils of the chase; but on the third morning, when the lady offers him a green lace which will protect him from any wound, fear of his coming ordeal makes him accept it and conceal the fact from his host.

When New Year's Day comes, and he must keep his tryst, he rides out to find the Green Chapel, which he is told is not distant. He comes to a deserted ravine, where rocks shoot up into the sky; a mound beside a stream, all overgrown with green grass, proves to be hollow, and he is wondering if this can be the place, when in the eerie silence he hears the sound of an axe being whetted:

> What! it clattered amid the cliffs, fit to cleave them apart,
> As if a great scythe were being ground on a grindstone there,
> What! It whirred and it whetted, like water in a mill
> What! It made a rushing, ringing din, rueful to hear.

The Green Knight appears and prepares to return Gawaine's blow. If he had not accepted the green lace, the axe would have fallen on him harmlessly. As it is, it grazes his neck and his blood falls shimmering on to the snow. It is now revealed that the Green Knight is none other than Sir Bertilak, who had been enchanted by Arthur's sister Morgan le Fay:

'I was entirely transformed and made terrible of hue' – to work as much mischief as possible to Arthur's court because she hated Guinevere. After the exchange of many courtesies, they part, and Gawaine returns to Arthur, to whom he confesses how he has fallen short. Everyone, from the King downwards, welcomes, consoles and cheers him, and they decide to form a brotherhood whose device shall be a green baldric, an echo perhaps of Edward III's founding of the Order of the Garter.

The knights of Arthur's court are striking figures of romance; the Green Knight is a terrifying apparition; but if one wants to see what a knight looked like, riding along the road in real life in the 1380s, the master of realism has shown one.

Chaucer's collection of *Canterbury Tales* includes some stories of romance and magic, but unlike his contemporaries he shows no interest in Arthur.

The Wife of Bath tells a tale of which the unnamed hero is a knight of Arthur's court and she begins it with lines that, from her, are unexpectedly charming:

> In th' olde dayes of the King Arthoure
> Of which that Britons speaken great honour,
> Al was this land fulfilled of fayerye . . .

but the Knight, who is one of the company of twenty-nine, is a figure of straight-cut professional distinction. The Crusades were over, but he had fought in fifteen great battles against Turks and Moors. On three occasions he had taken part in a *pas d'armes*, fought in the lists to decide the issue between opposing forces, and each time he had killed his man. He is the typical professional soldier, whose type has

In Lincoln Cathedral, on a fourteenth-
century misericord: an Arthurian knight
falling from his horse

DECLINE OF KNIGHTHOOD

127

not altered, with his high courage, his formidable skill, his great reputation, his modest, unassertive bearing, his simple courtesy to everyone. He is riding on the pilgrimage in the rust-marked coat he had worn under his mail; his turnout is quiet, except that his horse is such a fine animal. He shows his plain sense when he checks the monk's lugubrious recital of the reverses that have overtaken famous men. Don't let us hear any more of this sort of thing, he says at last. Tales like this are very distressing. What I like to hear about is how men, from humble beginnings, arrive at good fortune and success:

> Swich thing is gladsome, as hit thinketh me!

The tale he himself tells is, naturally enough, a romance about two young knights who are both in love with Emily, a girl with a chaplet of flowers on her head and a yard of gold hair in a plait down her back. The climax is a tournament; the knight's account of this is professional, and does not omit to state that the jousters were to fight with maces and swords only, and no other offensive weapons of any kind were to be brought on to the ground by anyone: the sort of prohibition it is attempted to enforce at football matches today. The knight and his colleagues understood how to get it carried out.

At his own wish, the Green Knight beheaded
by Gawaine in the presence of Arthur and
Guinevere

12 The Background to Malory's Arthur

The greatest of all versions of Arthur's story, Thomas Malory's *Morte D'Arthur*,
was finished, so he said, 'in the ninth year of the reign of King Edward IV', that is,
between 1469 and 1470. The work itself is wonderful and its immense popular
success shows once again that the story-receiving public, with all their fondness
for love affairs and supernatural happenings, were also much engaged by tales
about a king who was a soldier.

Richard I, Edward I, Edward III and the Black Prince had made it possible for
them to identify the imposing figure who was the disposer of their fates with the
King in the British story. The spell's continuity had been broken by Edward II
and Richard II; Henry IV, though strong and authoritative, was lacking in charisma.
With Henry V, however, the idea of the martial king was re-created and brought
to a burnished success. The King's physical courage, his technical skill as a
fighting man, were matched by his genius for army administration, his grasp of the
problems of transport and commissariat. When the English army had marched
60 miles inland from Caux, looking for a place to cross the Somme, their scouts
found two fords, but they were marshy. Henry spent a day having the causeways
strengthened; then he himself supervised the crossing of the soldiers at one ford,
while two of his generals saw the horses and baggage across the other. His prowess
as a fighting man was spectacular. The armour of the fifteenth century was now
entirely of articulated plate; the shaping to the exact contour of the limbs was
masterly, and the overlapping pieces, held together inside by leather straps,
allowed a certain degree of flexibility, but the weight of the whole suit was formidable. It was said of Henry V that he wore his armour 'as if it were a light cloak'.
This trait was picked up by Shakespeare,[21] when he makes Richard Vernon
describe Prince Hal in full armour mounting his horse, not laboriously hoisting
himself into the saddle, but getting up with a spring that makes him

> Rise from the ground like feathered Mercury . . .

At the Battle of Agincourt Henry wore round his helmet a circlet of gold containing,
among other jewels, the Black Prince's ruby, given to the latter by Pedro the Cruel.
This gleaming wine-red stone, the size of a small hen's egg, may now, by the
purest luck, be seen in one of the State Crowns. A blow from a French sword on
the King's casque split the circlet and a piece of it fell to the ground, but not the
piece containing his great-uncle's gem. The episode is reminiscent of Chrétien de

Troyes's saying, in *Érec et Énide*, that Érec and his assailants were 'knocking the
jewels out of the helmets and dealing each other fearful blows'.

The image of the armed knight of the era when the vision of Arthur became
fixed once and for ever in the public mind, is represented by the effigy of Richard
Beauchamp, Earl of Warwick, on his tomb in Warwick parish church. The elegance
of late-fifteenth-century plate armour, emphasizing wide shoulders, narrow waist
and long legs and the exquisite curved and pointed shapes of the overlapping plates
is seen at a glance. The Earl's head is resting on his helmet, wearing only his
beautifully sculpted waving hair. Instead of being clasped in a conventional pose,
his hands are spread apart in a gesture of rapture and astonishment at the prospect
of heaven above him.

The Earl is also delineated in a series of superbly vivid and graceful drawings –
*The Pageant of the Birth, Life and Death of Richard Beauchamp, Earl of Warwick,
K.G.* – which display him jousting at the wedding festivities of Henry IV, fighting
for Henry against Owen Glendower at the Battle of Shrewsbury, dining with the
King of France on an embassy, received by the Pope, fighting on foot in the lists
at Verona, welcomed by the Doge of Venice and the Patriarch of Jerusalem and
returning home by way of Russia, Lithuania, Poland and Westphalia. These far-
flung travels would not surprise his contemporaries; if people did not make them,
they were accustomed to hear about them; Sir John Mandeville, writing his
Travels in 1356, heads his opening chapter: 'To teach you the Way out of England
to Constantinople'.

Warwick on his return was appointed by Henry V Captain of Calais; he took
a notable part in the siege of Rouen, and Plate XXXVIII of the *Pageant* shows a
prospect of Rouen, walls, towers and a drawbridge, across the river; in the foreground, within a wooden palisade, is the English encampment. Between two
circular tents, richly ornamented, Henry V is standing, fully armed with a crown
round his helmet; the Earl, also armed, kneels before him. These drawings have
a special interest; one of the followers in the Earl's train, who took part in the
siege of Calais in 1436, was the Warwickshire squire, Sir Thomas Malory.

The whole of his career was spanned by a period of continuous or intermittent
warfare. The death of Henry V ushered in the long-drawn-out defeat of the
English in France; by 1453 they had lost control of everything in France except
Calais. Meantime the marriage of the simple, good but mentally unstable Henry VI
with Margaret of Anjou, a beautiful, savage girl of fifteen, which was intended to
keep Anjou and Maine for the English, failed of its object, and, since Margaret was
wholly intractable and felt that she must act for two, precipitated the Wars of the
Roses.

These broke out in 1455; the powerful, arrogant Duke of York asserted that his
claim to the throne was better than the King's, since Henry VI was descended from
John of Gaunt, Duke of Lancaster, the third son of Edward III, but York was
descended, through his mother, from Edward III's second son, Lionel Duke of
Clarence. Such a claim would not have been brought forward with a king of the

calibre of Henry v; with one of Henry vi's incapacity, the prospect it held out was too tempting to resist.

Margaret of Anjou defeated the Duke of York at the Battle of Wakefield in 1460. She had his head cut off, crowned with a paper crown and stuck up over one of the gates of the city of York. Her seven-year-old son, Edward Prince of Wales, was with her and she made him pronounce sentence of death on other prisoners, who were executed in his presence, but the next year York's son Edward, when he defeated the Lancastrian forces at Mortimer's Cross in Hereford, showed the promptness, energy and military skill that stood him in good stead in maintaining his crown as Edward iv.

Richard Neville, created Earl of Warwick when he married the Beauchamp heiress, had thrown in his lot with the Yorkists and saw Edward iv crowned in 1461. The King's height and fairness, his splendid physique created a confidence in his power to rule. He was gay and debonair but capable of an astute secretiveness. He showed this in 1464, when he checked the negotiations Warwick was making, to marry him to a French princess, by explaining that he had already married Elizabeth Woodville, the impecunious widow of a Lancastrian knight, Sir Edward Grey, with two sons, and five years older than the King himself. The total unsuitability of the match shows how potent her fascination must have been. Unlike Margaret of Anjou, who had the fierceness of a starving tigress, Elizabeth Woodville was gentle and caressing in manner, pale and slight with long gold hair. Her mother had had the good fortune to captivate Henry v's brother John, the late Duke of Bedford. The Duchess of Bedford had been spoken of in connection with witchcraft; the same accusation was freely bandied about her daughter, to account for her more astonishing success.

Once acknowledged as Queen, Elizabeth revealed an unquenchable appetite for the advancement of her relatives; the Woodvilles were given peerages and offices; four of her sisters were married to unenthusiastic peers; the eighty-year-old Duchess of Norfolk, of enormous possessions, was forcibly bestowed on the Queen's brother John, a youth of twenty who was told to shut his eyes and open his mouth, and see what the Queen would send him. The King supported these arrangements as he wanted a party of his own which would be independent of Warwick. The latter, furious at the turn of events, joined Margaret of Anjou in France; Louis xi offered to support an invasion of England headed by the two of them, because he wanted an English alliance against the Burgundians.

This invasion was mounted in 1470; Edward, surprised, escaped in the night. Elizabeth Woodville, who had borne him three daughters, was again pregnant, and Edward had left her in the Tower for safety. She was therefore in the same fortress with the unhappy, unseen Henry vi. She showed considerable energy in getting the stronghold victualled for a siege, but when Warwick advanced on London she became terrified and had herself rowed by barge upstream to Westminster, where she took refuge in a stone-walled, stone-floored building, standing between St Margaret's Church and the Abbey, and known as the Sanctuary. Here,

Sir Richard ꝑenell a noble knyght by hys fader and moder Onƙer

in almost destitute conditions, she gave birth to the Prince Edward, elder of the two ill-fated children known as the Princes in the Tower.

The return of Edward IV at the head of another invading army in 1471 ended in the crushing defeat of the Lancastrians at Barnet, where Warwick was slain, and at Tewkesbury, where Margaret's son Prince Edward was murdered after the battle, it was said in the very presence of Edward IV. On the night of the latter's triumphant return to London, Henry VI on his orders was put to death in the Tower.

The rigorous conditions she had endured in the unfurnished stone-built Sanctuary made her return to life in a palace the more delicious to Elizabeth Woodville. Edward IV in his flight from Warwick's army had been beholden to the Lord of Grauthuse, the Governor of Holland, and the King repaid this hospitality in 1472, when the Lord of Grauthuse was astonished at the luxury and brilliance of life in Windsor Castle. A suite had been prepared for him, all hung with white silk and white linen. His bed had a counterpane of cloth of gold, trimmed with ermine, the canopy was cloth of gold, the curtains white silk. In another chamber were two baths placed under tents of white cloth. Lord Hastings, the King's Chamberlain, undressed the guest, and they took their baths side by side; when they had been in the baths as long as they wished, servants brought them green ginger, syrups of different kinds, comfits and sweet wine.

Such were the conditions of court life that formed the unspoken background to Malory's presentation of Arthur. The latest research into his own way of living has revealed that he was charged with a series of offences: lying in wait to murder, robbery, rape, cattle-stealing, extorting money by threats. These deeds are sometimes extenuated, sometimes denied outright, but if they were all proved true, Malory would not be the only man of great literary gifts whose conduct has been highly anti-social.

It is generally accepted that he was a Yorkist knight who served as a young man under Richard Beauchamp, Earl of Warwick; who, for some misdoing, real or alleged, served a term of imprisonment before 1462; that in that year he accompanied Warwick the Kingmaker on an expedition against the army which Margaret of Anjou had recruited in Scotland and brought down through England, pillaging as they came. Since Warwick turned his coat and gave his allegiance to the Lancastrian side, fighting against Edward IV's army at Barnet, it is assumed that Malory changed sides also; this, if true, would explain why, when Edward IV in 1468 issued two pardons to knights who had fought with the Lancastrians, Malory was excluded from both of them. It would also add point to his outburst against 'new fangledness', change for change's sake. He says, speaking of the knights who abandoned Arthur's cause for that of Modred: 'Lo, all ye Englishmen, see ye not what a mischief here was! For he that was the most king and knight of the world, and most loved the fellowship of noble knights, and by him were they all upholden, now might not these Englishmen hold them content with him. . . . Alas, this is a great default of us Englishmen, for there may no thing please us no term.'[22]

He was presumably in prison on 1468, and it is thought he may have died there, because he was buried in the Grey Friars Church beside Newgate gaol. He was certainly in prison at the time of finishing his book, for he says in his last end-piece: 'I pray you all, gentlemen and gentlewomen that readeth this book of Arthur and his knights, from the beginning to the ending, pray for me while I am alive, that God send me good deliverance, and when I am dead, I pray you all, pray for my soul.'

The conditions of Malory's imprisonment must have been, at best, irksome, but whatever they were, they allowed him to write one of the great works of the English language. It is partly a translation, partly an adaptation from a wide collection of sources, which include English metrical versions of the Arthurian story: the Thornton *Morte Arthur, Arthour and Merlin*, the stanzaic version of *Le Morte Artu*; but the chief source is the five immensely lengthy stories of the French Vulgate Cycle. He very frequently refers a passage to these, saying: 'As the French book maketh mention'. Some parts of the work for which no originals have been found are assumed to be his own. It remains mysterious as to how, in Newgate, he could have laid his hands on the library of books he was using; that he was able to get them suggests that his imprisonment, however wearing to his spirits, was of a tolerably lenient kind.

The form in which, up to forty years ago, we possessed this masterpiece is now seen to be, structurally, quite different from what it was as Malory arranged it: it was then realized for the first time how much editing of the text had been done by the printer.

William Caxton, who began life as a draper, had risen by natural ability to the position of governor of the English merchants in the Low Countries. While he was in Cologne he saw the new art of printing being practised and he learned it himself. In 1474 he set up the first English printing press. The great churches of Westminster Abbey and St Paul's were used for numerous lay occupations, chiefly those of buying and selling. Merchants had a recognized meeting place in the central aisle of St Paul's; Caxton was allowed to set up his press in one of the side chapels of Westminster Abbey, and an association of printers is called a 'chapel' still.

Caxton's commercial intelligence made him choose to print the books he was sure people would want to read; he included in his earliest publications some of the great stories of the world: *The Receuil of the Histories of Troy, The Subtle Histories and Fables of Aesop*, the collection of stories about saints called *The Golden Legend*, Ovid's *Metamorphoses*. Then, he said, 'Many noble and divers gentlemen of this realm of England' asked him, over and over again, why he did not print 'the noble history of the Saint Greal and of the most renowned Christian king . . . King Arthur, which ought to be remembered among us Englishmen, to fore all Christian kings.' Caxton had answered that some men said, 'There was no such Arthur.' One of the gentlemen replied that to say so was nonsense, and cited the various relics to be seen of Arthur and his knights, his tomb at Glastonbury, the accounts of him in various learned books. In Westminster Abbey, in the shrine

134

of St Edward the Confessor, there was to be seen 'the print of his seal in red wax, closed in a beryl'; in Dover Castle, Gawaine's skull was on view; in Winchester there was the Round Table; 'in other places, Lancelot's sword and many other things'. The tomb at Glastonbury, whosesoever it might be, was of course to be seen in the 1480s. The Round Table still hangs on the wall of the Great Hall of Winchester Castle. It is supposed that it may have been used at one of the jousts of the Mensa Rotunda; its present painting, in green and white with Tudor Roses in the centre, was done by order of Henry VIII. The impression of the seal, said to be Arthur's, since it was enclosed in an aquamarine, was probably stolen from the

Confessor's shrine at the Reformation. Caxton's patron also mentioned, as evidence of Arthur's existence, the town of Camelot in Wales, where there are 'great stones and marvellous works of iron lying under the ground, and royal vaults which divers, living now, have seen'. This seems to be a reference to the Roman remains at Caerleon; Geoffrey of Monmouth had described Caerleon as Arthur's capital; Caxton transfers to it the name Camelot, though Malory himself says more than once that Camelot is now called Winchester. At all events, the arguments and persuasions of the gentlemen, and Caxton's acting upon them, showed a genuine popular belief in Arthur as a historical personage and a strong wish to hear about him.

Therefore, Caxton says, he undertook the printing of a book of 'the whole history of King Arthur and of certain of his knights', and he set it up from 'a copy unto me delivered'. This copy, he said, 'Sir Thomas Malory did take out of certain books of French and reduced into English'. Caxton dedicates the work to 'all noble princes, lords and ladies, gentlemen or gentlewomen that desire to read, or hear read, of the noble and joyous history of the great conqueror and excellent king, King Arthur, sometimes king of this noble realm called Britain'.

Though it appears that several copies of Malory's text had been made, none of them had been seen after Caxton had made his version, and the script Caxton had used had disappeared also. It was only when a manuscript copy of Malory's work was discovered in the Fellows' Library at Winchester College, in 1934, that it was seen, as demonstrated by Professor Vinaver, how much editing of Malory's text Caxton had done.

Caxton said himself that he had divided the work into twenty-one books, 'every book chaptered, as, hereinafter, of God's grace shall follow'. He had done more; he had disguised the fact that Malory had written eight separate, independent tales. Caxton altered the order in which Malory had arranged them and omitted all Malory's end-pieces except the last, with the aim of making the book appear, not a collection of stories but a homogeneous whole.

The outstanding features of the Vulgate Cycle and particularly of its *Lancelot* are inordinate prolixity and length and a series of the most elaborate inter-communications between the different strands of the narrative. Malory, with the combined instincts of a great storyteller and a man of action, separated out from this closely woven background the individual stories he chose to tell, shortening, simplifying and so greatly increasing narrative effect. He arouses both admiration and sympathy when he says: 'And so I leave here of this tale, and over-skip great books of Sir Lancelot du Lake, what great adventures he did when he was called Le Chevalier du Chariot.'[23] The copy of the Vulgate Cycle he was using in Newgate gaol must have been in separate volumes, perhaps indeed a separate volume had become unbound, because he adds: 'And because I have lost the very matter of Le Chevalier du Chariot, I depart from this tale of Sir Lancelot and here I go unto the Morte of King Arthur.' Thus Malory's object and Caxton's were essentially opposite. Caxton's experience as a publisher, his flair for knowing what would take, must have led him to believe that the book would sell better as a single work than as a collection of tales; to confirm the impression that it was one book, he gave it the title *Le Morte D'Arthur*, though he admits in the final colophon that it treats of 'the birth, life and acts of the said King Arthur and of his noble knights of the Round Table, their marvellous enquests and adventures'.

He says nothing at all of how the manuscript came into his possession, fifteen years after the writer's death. That it did so come into the hands of a printer ensured that this version of the stories of Arthur and his knights should be established as one of the most famous works in the English language.

Uther Pendragon and Igraine (together on
right) before her magical seduction by him
in the form of her husband the Duke of
Cornwall

136

The fyzst boke.

¶Here begynneth the fyzst
boke of the mooſt noble and
wozthy pzince kyng Arthur
ſomtyme kyng of grete Bzy
tayne/now called Englande
whiche treateth of his noble
actes and feates of armes ⁊
chyualrye/and of his noble
knyghtes of the table roũde
and this volume is deuyded
in to .rri. bokes.

¶How Utherpendzagon ſente foz the
Duke of Coznewayle and Jgrayne his
wyfe/and of theyz ſodayn departynge
agayne.   Capitu.j.

T befell in the days
of ꝑ noble Utherpen
dzagon whã he was
kynge of Englande
and ſo regned/there
was a myghty and
a noble Duke in Coz
neWayle that helde longe tyme Warre
agaynſt hym. And ꝑ Duke was named
the Duke of Tyntagyll/⁊ ſo by meanes
kynge Uther ſente foz this Duke/char
gynge hym to bzynge his wyfe w hym
foz ſhe was called a ryght fayze lady/⁊
a paſſynge wyſe/⁊ Jgrayne was her
name. So whan the Duke ⁊ his wyfe
Were comen to ꝑ kynge/by the meanes
of grete lozdes they Were bothe accoz
ded/⁊ the kyng lyked ⁊ loued this lady
Well/and made her grete chere out of

a

13 Malory: The Legend Immortalized

Newgate was one of the Roman entrances to the City of London. It stood on a north-west reach of the city wall, whose lower levels were still Roman brick, above which medieval stonework rose into battlements. At Newgate, the gatehouse over the portcullis, a tower on each side of it and buildings inside the wall, were used as one of the city gaols for prisoners less important than those lodged in the Tower. Fields came up to the city walls, but when the wind was in the wrong quarter, the air of Newgate must have been mephitic, for immediately inside the gate was the Newgate meat market and, leading off it, the shambles; a little street in the neighbourhood was called Stinking Lane.

Some care had been taken for the prisoners; the gaol had been rebuilt with money left for the purpose in the will of the Lord Mayor Dick Whittington, and another benefactor had arranged for water from a nearby conduit to be piped to it. Whittington had also made a benefaction in the neighbourhood which, it is possible, may have been of the greatest use to the imprisoned Thomas Malory. The preaching order of Grey Friars, who received a great deal of money in subscriptions, had built their imposing church, Christ Church, on the north side of the meat market. In 1423, Dick Whittington built the community a library. It was rectangular, 129 feet long by 30 feet wide, and it contained twenty-eight reading desks and eight double settles. He also gave them £400 worth of books.

It is allowable to wonder what these may have been and if they included Arthurian stories in French prose and English verse; if the collection were the Lord Mayor's personal library, they may well have done so. Had a good-hearted governor of Newgate gaol arranged for some of these volumes to be lent to his prisoner, it would have been a matter of only a few minutes' walk to bring them; but if such loans were made, they could hardly have accounted for all the books that Malory used. Since he said himself that he had lost part of the matter of *Le Chevalier du Chariot*, it does not sound as if the copy he used of the Vulgate *Lancelot*, at least, had been a precious book lent to him as a favour.

If a remedy could be found to soothe the gnawing misery of an indefinite prison sentence, Malory must have found it in his absorbing task.

He made his first book *The Noble Tale of King Arthur and the Emperor Lucius*, in which he closely followed the Thornton *Morte Arthur*, except that he altered Arthur's route across Gaul to correspond with Henry v's march from Caux up the Somme. The second book, for which he used a French original, the Vulgate *Suite*

BELOW Arthur, troubled by Merlin's
prophecy, setting adrift a boatload of
children born on May Day, and OPPOSITE
drawing the sword from the stone, as the feat
that would prove him the rightful King

138

de Merlin, he called *The Tale of King Arthur*. There was of course no chronological
order between the two. The most important parts of *The Tale of King Arthur* are
the account of Arthur's begetting by Uther Pendragon, his proving his right to the
crown of Britain by pulling a sword out of a stone, his receiving the sword
Excalibur from the Lady of the Lake, and the birth of Modred, of whom Malory
does not say, at this point, that he was Arthur's son begotten, in ignorance, on his
sister; he says only that Merlin had told Arthur that he should be slain by one born
on May Day, and therefore Arthur had ordered all the babies born on May Day,
begotten of lords and born of ladies ('some were four weeks old, some less'), to be
put into a ship and driven out to sea; that the ship was wrecked and all the babies
drowned except Modred, who was washed ashore and found by a good man, who
took care of him. Then there is the morbid tale of Balin and Balan, the brothers
who kill each other not knowing whom they are fighting; Arthur's marriage to
Guinevere, the establishment of the Round Table and the story of Merlin fatally
besotted on Nimue, one of the Ladies of the Lake, who became so wearied by his

et lors aporta lespee toute nue en
tre ses mains si le menerent alau
tel et si le mit sus·

T quantil liot mise si le sacre
rent et enoynssent et enfisset
toutes iceles coses que ondoit

importunities that she caused him to go down under a great stone 'to let her wit of the marvels there', and 'so wrought for him there, that he came never out, for all the craft he could do'. Vinaver shows that, when Malory had finished *The Tale of King Arthur*, he cannot at that time have had the rest of the Vulgate Cycle beside him, because he says: 'Who that will make any more, let him seek other books of King Arthur.'

The next book is *The Noble Tale of Sir Lancelot du Lake*, for which Malory made his drastic and effective cutting of the Vulgate *Lancelot*. *The Book of Gareth*, which follows it, is one for which no original has been found, though it is supposed to have one in a lost French source. Apart from the great stories of Arthur, Tristan and Lancelot, it is one of the very best in Malory's collection. The hero Gareth is a young man of large physique and exceptional strength. He comes to court, where he is unrecognized by either his uncle, King Arthur, or his brother Gawaine. For some perverse reason he enlists as a scullion in Arthur's kitchen, where Sir Kay the steward treats him badly and, because his hands are very large, gives him the ironic nickname of Beaumains. Everyone laughs at him except Lancelot, who is kind to him from the very first. The boy is passionately interested in knighthood and, though performing his scullion's duties, makes a point of watching every exhibition of the knights' skill. At last he puts a term to his own servitude, dons the armour that his mother had originally provided for him, and challenges Lancelot. The latter is astounded at his strength: 'he fought more like a giant than a knight', and it is all Lancelot can do to keep himself from being overthrown. He cries at last: 'Fight not so sore, your quarrel and mine is not so great but we may leave off.' 'Truly,' said Beaumains, 'but it doth me good to feel your might!'

The young man's gentleness and forbearance, such as are sometimes found with a large and powerful frame, is taxed by the haughty girl Linet, who disdains to have him appointed to her by Arthur for the rescue of her beleaguered sister Dame Lionesse, for she thinks him a mere kitchen knave. Her behaviour is irrationally ungrateful and unkind, until her abuse and scorn are at last checked by his continued successes against her sister's adversaries. 'Alas, she said, fair Beaumains, forgive me all that I have mis-said or done against thee. With all my heart said he, I forgive it you, for ye did nothing but as ye should do, for all your evil words pleased me . . . and since it liketh you to say thus fair unto me, wit ye well . . . there is no knight living but I am able enough for him.'

It is not, however, Linet with whom he falls in love, but her sister Dame Lionesse; he brings her to Arthur's court and their delightfully happy mutual passion is crowned by marriage, and Linet, now cured of her pathological disagreeableness, is married to another knight. Gareth had been parted from Gawaine for so long that he now got to know his brother's character for the first time. His glowing affection for Lancelot, which the great knight inspired to a touching extent in so many people, remains and increases: 'Lord! The great cheer that Sir Lancelot made of Sir Gareth, and he of him, for there was never no knight that Sir Gareth loved as he did Sir Lancelot.' But he withdraws himself from his brother, for Sir Gawaine was vindictive, 'and where he hated he would be avenged with murder, and that hated Sir Gareth'. Though Malory is now seen to have written his stories as separate entities and independent of chronology, this passage must have left its mark on his mind as a shadow on the path when he wrote his last one.

Malory's indescribable magic is at its strongest in the last two books, *The Tale of Sir Lancelot and Queen Guinevere* and *The Tale of the Death of King Arthur*, but he exerts it in fits and starts all the way through. He accomplishes the extraordinary feat of writing in a passionate and stately vein and yet sounding as if he were not writing but speaking. His dialogue is always living, sometimes it blazes with immediacy.

'That is truth, said Sir Gareth, an I have not you and wield not you as my wife, there shall never lady nor gentlewoman rejoice me. What, nephew, said the King, is the wind in that door?' When Lancelot has come to rescue the Queen from Sir Meliagraunce, who has abducted her, he is angry to find she has appeared to compromise with this evil knight; as for him, no one living except King Arthur or herself should restrain him from striking Meliagraunce stone dead.

'That wot I well, said the Queen, but what will ye more? Ye shall have all thing ruled as ye list to have it.'

He does not dwell on the impressions of eye and ear; he records them briefly, and they give their effect like the plucked string of a harp. Sometimes it is only a phrase: 'They turned their horses and rode over waters and through woods.' Sometimes the visual scene is presented like one in an illumination, but more realistic and more beautiful: 'When Sir Lancelot came to the castle he alighted and tied his horse to a ring in the wall and then he saw a fair green court and thither he dressed him, for there, him thought, was a fair place to fight in. So he looked about and saw much people in doors and windows that said: fair knight, thou art unhappy!'[24] There is the ominous little picture of Balin's saying to the distraught knight who cannot find his lady, 'I will into the castle and look if she be there. So he went in and searched from chamber to chamber and found her bed but she was not there. Then Balin looked into a fair little garden and under a laurel tree he saw her lie upon a quilt of green samite and a knight in her arms, fast embracing each other, and under their heads grass and herbs.'[25] It might be argued that some of his detail is enchanting to us only because it is a detail of period, but had it not possessed intrinsic effectiveness, Malory would not have used it. It is of course interesting to us to be reminded, for instance, that in the fifteenth century, once people were out of a chamber that was illuminated with standing lights, their only light was carried in the hand; but his own audience would see the force of the passage in *The Book of Gareth*, when Gareth, benighted in a lashing storm, comes to a castle and hears the watchmen talking on the walls. He is at first refused admittance, but when the duchess whose castle it is hears of the suppliant knight, she wants to have a look at him, 'so she went up into a tower over the gate, with great torchlight'.

Guinevere sending her ring as a love token
to Lancelot

His mention of sound is even more evocative. When Arthur, at the beginning
of his reign, is fighting eleven kings for the preservation of his realm, he is aided by
King Ban, and in one encounter 'King Ban came in so fiercely that the strokes
resounded again from the wood and the water.'[26] Sir Bors, after a daunting
experience of the devil's tempting him in the likeness of a rich, beautiful woman,
whom he withstands and who thereupon vanishes with all her gentlewomen and
the tower on which they had been standing, rides on his way somewhat shaken.
'Then he heard a clock smite on his right hand, and thither he came to an abbey . . .
closed with high walls, and there was let in.'[27]

The knights were so dependent on their horses, it is natural to be told, often,
how the horses were watered, how they were turned loose to graze, how they had
to be rested as well as their riders, how they, too, were sometimes hideously
wounded. Malory is conscious all the time of the impression of their presence.
When Lancelot goes in search of King Bagdemagus, he rides into an abbey yard,
and 'the daughter of King Bagdemagus heard a great horse go upon the pavement.
And then she arose and went to the window, and there she saw Sir Lancelot.'[28]

It is the great story of the loves of Lancelot and Guinevere, and how they ended
by wrecking the Fellowship of the Round Table, that shows Malory's powers as
a narrator at their best. The superbly effective story of Elaine le Blank, the Fair

Maid of Astolat, comes from the Vulgate *Morte Artu*, and Malory must also have
read it in the English metrical version because one of his most haunting lines in *The
Tale of the Death of King Arthur* is a quotation from the latter; but, in spite of his
having had not one original only but two, his version is a piece of indigenous
English storytelling.

Lancelot has been called the first hero of the modern novel. He is a man of great
professional and private virtues, who has not the strength to resist a passion which
he for a long time half believes, and at last wholly believes, is wrong. This in itself
is a combination of great human interest, but he is also quite extraordinarily
lovable. He has his enemies, some of whom are jealous of him and some who are
indignant at his liaison with the Queen, which becomes more and more widely
known, though not to the King (it is the refusal of a number of these knights to
accept the position any longer, which causes the outbreak of the civil war). But,
apart from some few who are ill disposed towards him, to know him is to love him.
Not only does Guinevere love him, Arthur loves him with all his heart; not only
the Maid of Astolat but her brother Lavaine; the knights who are devoted to him
feel an admiration for his professional powers and virtues, his skill, courage and
magnanimity, and a strong personal affection for a highly attractive man. He
might claim to be the most fascinating character in fiction.

MALORY:
THE LEGEND IMMORTALIZED

Merlin the magician, Arthur's tutor, who
foretold the passion of Lancelot and the
Queen

144

He was not allowed the full vision of the Holy Graal because of his adulterous love, but in the episode of the healing of Sir Urre, he appears so inexpressibly humble and noble that his character would challenge comparison with those of unswerving chastity. Sir Urre cannot be whole of his wounds and is brought to Arthur's court in a litter, to see if anyone there can exert the healing touch. Beginning with Arthur himself, a body of knights, whose names fill an entire chapter, attempt the cure but the wounds bled still. At last Lancelot is seen riding in the distance. When he presents himself Arthur explains the matter and says he must now make the assay. 'Jesu defend me, said Sir Lancelot, when so many kings and knights have assayed and failed, that I should presume upon me to enchieve · all that ye, my lords, might not enchieve. . . . Ye take it wrong, said King Arthur, ye shall not do it for no presumption, but to bear us fellowship, insomuch ye be a fellow of the Table Round.' Lancelot unwillingly kneels down by the wounded knight, 'saying secretly to himself, Thou blessed Father, Son and Holy Ghost, I beseech Thee of Thy mercy . . . Thou mayst give power to heal this sick knight by Thy great virtue . . . but, good Lord, never of myself.' Then he asks the knight to let him see the wounds; he searches them, and after they have bled a little, they are as whole as if they had been healed for seven years.

'Then King Arthur and all the kings and knights kneeled down and gave thanks and praises unto God and to His Blessed Mother. And ever Sir Lancelot wept as he had been a child that had been beaten.'

The liaison is rent by frequent quarrels: 'What aileth ye, said the King, that ye cannot keep Sir Lancelot upon your side?' They arise because the woman cannot bear the strain of the passion with the stringent necessity for self-control. The situation between Lancelot and Guinevere is like that of Vronsky and Anna Karenina. The quarrel which leads to the episode of the Maid of Astolat arose because Lancelot, realizing that the affair was becoming dangerously public, had been encouraging the conversation of other ladies, a precautionary measure which gave the Queen jealous pangs. Arthur goes to Winchester to preside at a great tournament; the Queen says she is not well enough to go, and Lancelot also stays behind to have her company. She upbraids him for it, saying it will cause them to be slandered. 'Madam, said Sir Lancelot, I allow your wit. It is of late come since ye were wise.' He departs to Winchester but, having given out that he would not be there, he feels obliged to appear in the lists incognito. This causes him to accept Elaine's token, a red sleeve embroidered with pearls, to wear on his helmet. Since he is known never to wear any woman's favour except the Queen's, this will render his disguise complete. He borrows a shield from one of Elaine's brothers, a young unknown knight laid up with wounds, and leaves his own in her keeping. Victorious in the lists at Winchester but badly wounded, he is taken away by Elaine's brother Sir Lavaine, who says of his sister's passion, 'She doth as I do, for since I first saw my lord Sir Lancelot, I could never depart from him.' He leads Lancelot, bleeding heavily and unable to sit his horse upright, to the hermitage of a skilful old leech, in a wood outside Winchester, who puts him to bed and sets about curing him.

Arthur depicted on a fifteenth-century
tapestry as one of the Nine Worthies, who
also included Charlemagne

MALORY:
THE LEGEND IMMORTALIZED

145

Meanwhile Arthur, who alone had recognized him, sends Gawaine to find him out. Gawaine traces him to the house of old Sir Bernard of Astolat, and asks Elaine if she knows the name of the mysterious knight.

'Nay truly, said the damosel, I know not his name nor from whence he cometh, but to say that I love him, I promise you and God that I love him.' She tells Gawaine that she has the knight's shield, and Gawaine at once recognizes it. He returns to the court and tells everyone that the unknown knight was Lancelot. The Queen is frantic with anger, but Bors, who had wounded him, in intense anxiety and contrition goes to seek him. He finds him, still very weak, in his bed at the hermitage, and Elaine nursing him night and day. She had gained her father's permission for this, saying that if she be not allowed, 'I wot well I shall go out of my mind.' Bors, sitting by Lancelot's bed, tells him of the Queen's anger over the Maid of Astolat.

'But is this she, said Sir Bors, that is so busy about you? She it is, said Sir Lancelot . . . I cannot put her from me. Why should ye put her from you? said Sir Bors. She is a passing fair damosel and a well-beseen and a well taught . . . and I see by her diligence about you that she loveth you entirely.' The reply is ominous. 'That me repenteth, said Sir Lancelot.'

When he is cured and about to take leave of Sir Bernard, the girl says: 'Now fair and courteous knight, have mercy upon me and suffer me not to die for thy love. What would you that I did? said Sir Lancelot. I would have you for my husband, said Elaine. Fair damosel, I thank you, said Sir Lancelot, but truly, said he, I cast me never to be wedded man. Then fair knight, said she, will ye be my paramour? Jesu defend me, said Sir Lancelot, for then I rewarded your father and your brother full evil for their great goodness. Alas, said she, then must I die for your love. Ye shall not so, said Sir Lancelot,' and he promises that, for her great kindness to him, he will bestow the very great dower of one thousand pounds a year on her and whatever knight she may choose to marry. She refuses anything of the kind; she wants only to be his wife or his mistress.

'Fair damosel, said Sir Lancelot, of these two things ye must pardon me. Then she shrieked shrilly and fell down in a swoon.'

For nine days she maintains her refusal to eat, drink or sleep; and having got her father's consent to the astounding feat of self-projection she has devised, on the tenth day she dies. The letter she has caused to be written to Lancelot is fastened in her hand, and her corpse, in all her richest clothes, is laid in a black-draped barge and rowed downstream to Westminster.

Guinevere has refused to allow Lancelot into her presence. She and the King are standing in a window of the Palace of Westminster when they see the barge on the water beneath their eyes. The King goes down to see what is to do, 'and there he saw the fairest woman lie in a rich bed, covered unto her middle with many rich clothes, and all was cloth of gold, and she lay as though she had smiled'. The King orders the letter in her hand to be read aloud to the assembled court. It says: 'Most noble knight, Sir Lancelot, now hath death made us two at debate for your love. I was your lover that men called the Fair Maid of Astolat, therefor unto all ladies I make my moan; yet pray for my soul and bury me at least. This is my last request. And a clean maiden I died, as I take God to witness. Pray for my soul, Sir Lancelot, as thou art peerless.' This spectacular justification of Lancelot in the Queen's eyes fills Guinevere with compunction. She says: 'Ye might have showed her some bounty and gentleness that might have preserved her life.' Lancelot says what he had tried to do, and that he could have done no more. 'For Madam, said Sir Lancelot, I love not to be constrained to love, for love must arise of the heart and not by no constraint.' It is the King who replies: 'That is truth and many knights' love is free in himself and never will be bounden, for where he is bounden, he looseth himself.' The Queen sends for Lancelot privately and asks his pardon. 'This is not the first time, said Sir Lancelot, that ye have been displeased with me causeless, but Madame, ever I must suffer you, but what sorrow I endure, ye take no force.' The episode, with its brilliant spectacle and its keen suffering, recedes into the past. 'So passed on all that winter with all manner of hunting and hawking, and jousts and tournaments were many, between great lords.'

Malory's writing his book in Newgate gaol gives poignancy to his outburst on the beauty of May with which he ends Book XVIII. 'It giveth to all lovers courage, that lusty month of May.' This introduces the next book, in which 'it befel that in the month of May, that Queen Guinever called unto her knights of the Table Round, and she gave them warning that early upon the morrow she would ride a-maying into woods and fields beside Westminster.' This she could well do, for west of the city, on the curve of the river at which Westminster stood, there were, in a row upon the Strand, the Palace of Westminster, St Stephen's Chapel, Westminster Hall and, at a slight angle turning northwards, Westminster Abbey. Behind these buildings were fields, thickets, woods, stretching to the horizon.

The expedition ends in disaster. It repeats in firm outline the shadowy incident in Caradoc of Lancafarn's *Life of Gildas*, when Melwas, King of the Summer Country, seized Guinevere and held her captive on the Glass Island. The world has changed since then; it is the rich, sophisticated era of the 1460s; Guinevere, now a Queen renowned throughout Christendom, has ridden out, accompanied by ladies and by ten knights, all dressed in green, in the light of a May morning. In the wet fields round Westminster, where the land had once been a marsh, they have picked herbs, mosses and flowers and stuck themselves all over with them, when the evil knight Meliagraunce starts out of a wood with a hundred and sixty armed men at his back, and telling the Queen that he has long lusted for her, over-powers her few knights and carries them all off to his castle south of the Thames. The Queen manages to send a child with a message to Lancelot, who tears off in pursuit. 'The book saith he took the water at Westminster Bridge and made his horse to swim over Thames to Lambeth.' On the opposite shore, his horse is riddled with arrows by Meliagraunce's archers, and Lancelot jumps into a carter's wain, a much more credible version of the original Knight of the Cart. Pathetically his horse follows him, stumbling, with its guts hanging out; 'and ever he trod his guts and his paunch under feet', a reminder of what happened at Crécy, Poitiers and Agincourt. When Lancelot makes his way into the castle, Guinevere has not been raped because she has told her companions not to leave her for a moment. Meliagraunce, who had planned the abduction because Lancelot was away, is terrified at his appearance on the scene; he persuades Guinevere to intercede for him. When she does, this brings on another lovers' quarrel.

'Ah, Madam, said Sir Lancelot, an I had wist ye had so soon been accorded with him, I would not have made such haste unto you. Why say ye so? said the Queen. Do ye repent yourself of your good deeds? . . . I accorded never unto him for favour nor love I had unto him, but to lay down shameful noise.' Lancelot replies that he has always disliked shameful noise himself, but that nothing should have induced him to compromise with Meliagraunce. She knew that, the Queen said, but what did he want now? Everything should be done as he wished it to be. 'Right so, the Queen took Sir Lancelot by the bare hand, for he had put off his gauntlet, and so she went with him to her chamber and there she commanded him to be unarmed.' On the fourteenth-century Arundel tomb in Chichester Cathedral the Earl holds his right gauntlet in his mailed left hand; his bare right hand holds his wife's.

The story now follows, through the Vulgate *Lancelot*, the plan originally laid down by Chrétien de Troyes, but Malory's telling has a conviction of its own. The party are all lodged in Meliagraunce's castle, the wounded knights in a chamber next to Guinevere's, so that she could take care of them. Lancelot makes an assignation with her for that night and after dark he goes to a place in the garden where he has seen a ladder. He takes his sword in one hand and the ladder under his arm, and sets it up against the Queen's window, 'and there anon the Queen was ready to meet him'. He tears the bars out of their sockets and gets into the chamber, where he spends the night, leaving the Queen's bed marked with the blood from his torn hands. When Meliagraunce next day declares that one of the wounded knights must have lain with her, Lancelot appears in the middle of the fracas and challenges him to single combat at Arthur's court. In this fight Lancelot kills him, and this is accepted as tantamount to a revelation that he had slandered the Queen. 'And the King and Queen made more of Sir Lancelot du Lake and more was he cherished than he was aforetime.'

But the knowledge of the liaison has got to the point at which it can no longer be ignored. Modred, cowardly and vicious, and his brother Agravaine, keep watch and at last they and a posse of their supporters discover Lancelot, unarmed, in the Queen's bedchamber. Lancelot kills the first man who enters and manages to hold the door while he puts on some of the dead man's armour; then he fights his way out. He offers to take Guinevere with him but she refuses, saying if she is brought to the fire, he can rescue her if he thinks fit. He says: 'Have ye no doubt, if I am living, I shall rescue you.'

He performs the rescue outside the walls of Carlisle when Guinevere, already stripped to her smock, is about to be led to the stake. Fighting his way through the mêlée, he unknowingly kills not only Sir Gaheris but his brother, Lancelot's beloved friend Sir Gareth, the brothers of the vengeful Sir Gawaine. He makes the bystanders put clothes on the Queen and takes her up behind him, coursing away to his castle of Joyous Garde, of which Malory says: 'Some say that it was Alnwick and some say that it was Bamborough.' Arthur, Gawaine and a great army come up to Joyous Garde and begin a lengthy siege. 'Then it befell on a day in harvest time that Sir Lancelot looked over the walls and spoke on high to King Arthur and Sir Gawaine.' Arthur accuses him of vile treachery and Lancelot denies the charge in a stately, impressive and touching manner, though Malory has described vividly one occasion of his adultery within the last few pages. The situation is resolved by the Pope's ordering Arthur to take his queen to himself again. Lancelot brings her out of the castle, and they kneel before the King. 'The King sat still and said no word, and when Sir Lancelot saw his countenance, he arose and pulled up the Queen with him.' He begins to say that, when he was ambushed in the Queen's chamber, Sir Agravaine and Sir Modred called him traitor and recreant knight.

'They called thee right, said Sir Gawaine. My lord Sir Gawaine, said Sir Lancelot, in their quarrel they proved themselves not in the right.' As Lancelot had vanquished his accusers in trial by combat, it was supposed that he had established the truth of his denial. Arthur's love for Lancelot is so great, he would be reconciled to him, but Gawaine will not forgive the dreadful accidental killing of his brothers and overbears the King. Lancelot is banished and goes with his companions into France, to the kingdom of his father, King Ban of Benoic, where Arthur follows him to make war *à outrance*. It is announced that Lancelot and Gawaine shall decide the issue in single combat; and here, in a scene of the arms and customs of the fifteenth century, is a vestige of something centuries older. Gawaine has the trait that he gains physical strength from undern (the hours between nine and twelve a.m.) until high noon. Malory says he had this gift from a holy man, but it is clear, as Loomis says, that Gawaine was originally a sun-god, whose power increased till noon and declined after it. Despite this asset, Lancelot gets the better of him by enduring, merely, the hours of Gawaine's strength and, when these have declined, striking him to the earth. Twice this supernatural contest is fought, and each time that Gawaine is laid along the ground, he calls to Lancelot to come near again and continue the fight. Lancelot replies that he will fight him again when Gawaine is on his feet, 'but to smite a wounded man that may not stand, God defend me from such shame.'

Arthur has left Modred regent of England in his absence, and Modred determines to seize Guinevere and marry her by force, though she is his father-uncle's wife. In 1485, Richard III, on the death of his wife Anne Neville, considered marrying his niece, Edward IV's daughter, Elizabeth of York. The idea was so shocking to his supporters, that he was obliged to make a public declaration that he did not intend it. Guinevere, helpless in Arthur's absence, could only pretend consent to Modred's design, but under pretext of providing for the wedding, she

The vengeful Gawaine parting from Arthur
and Guinevere to set out on a mission of
valour

MALORY:
THE LEGEND IMMORTALIZED

149

went to London and shut herself up in the Tower, which she victualled for a siege
as Elizabeth Woodville had done.

Arthur returns to England, where, as Malory says, Modred waited, to try to
prevent his own father from landing on the realm of which he was king. The fatal
battle between the father and son is not named, but Malory, following the Vulgate
Morte Artu, sites it on Salisbury Plain. The account of a widespread carnage is
concluded in a pictorial climax of monumental grimness: 'King Arthur was ware
where Sir Modred leaned upon his sword among a great heap of dead men.' The
King runs upon him and thrusts him through with his spear, 'and right so he
smote his father Arthur with his sword holden with both his hands, on the side
of the head.' Modred falls dead and Arthur lies fainting on the ground.

It is now moonlight and robbers creep over the battlefield, stealing their jewels
from the dead. Sir Lucan, who with Sir Bedivere is one of the two of Arthur's
followers left alive, says they must get the King into some town. 'I would it were so,
said the King, but I may not stand, my head works so.' They begin to carry the
King between them, but in the attempt Sir Lucan falls dead. Arthur, alone with
Sir Bedivere, charges him to take the sword Excalibur to 'yonder water-side', and
to throw it in, 'and come again and tell me what thou seest'. Several rivers cross
Salisbury Plain, the Wylye, the Avon, the Bourne, the Nadder; Malory speaks
only of the waterside, the water's edge, but he seems to have in mind a wide

Arthur, mortally wounded, sitting in sorrow
as the sword Excalibur, hurled by Bedivere,
is retrieved by the Lady of the Lake

stretch of water, such as is formed by a confluence of the Avon, the Bourne and the Nadder, now within the town of Salisbury, perhaps then on open land.

Bedivere takes the sword and makes for the water, 'but by the way he beheld that noble sword, that the pommel and the haft was all of precious stones', and he feels he cannot sacrifice it. Twice he does this and his disobedience is exposed when he tells Arthur, the first time, that he saw only 'the waves wap and the waters wan'. The magical line comes from the stanzaic *Morte Arthur*. It could be taken to mean that he saw the waves ripple, and either the pale waters or the waters turning pale; Hamlet uses the word as a verb when he says of the First Player: 'All his visage wanned.' Malory has already said that it is moonlight, and the image of the moonlit waves is before the eye. When, the third time, Bedivere did the King's bidding and threw the sword as far across the water as he could, 'there came an arm and an hand above the water and met it and caught it, and so shook it thrice and brandished, and then vanished away the hand with the sword.' The task fulfilled, he carries the King on his back to the water's edge, and there 'a little barge hove, with many fair ladies in it, and one of them a queen, all in black hoods and they all wept and shrieked when they saw King Arthur.' The King is laid in the barge with his head on one of their laps; then the queen says: 'Ah, dear brother, why have ye tarried so long from me? alas, this wound on your head hath caught overmuch cold.' Bedivere cries: 'Ah, my lord Arthur, what shall become of me? . . . Comfort thyself, said the King, and do as well as thou mayest; in me there is no trust to trust in; for I will into the vale of Avilion, to heal me of my grievous wound; and if thou never hear more of me, pray for my soul.'

Wherever the Battle of Camlann was actually fought, Arthur's story could not end in a more appropriate place, by the light of the moon, in the neighbourhood of Stonehenge, the great temple to the religion of our mysterious past.

Bedivere in his distress takes to the forest, where he finds a hermitage and in it a chapel, where is a new-made grave. It is the grave of Arthur, who has been brought there by three queens. Only one of them had been recognized in the barge, Arthur's sister Morgan le Fay; the other two are now said to be the Queen of Northgalis and the Queen of the Wastelands. Malory says: 'Yet men say in many parts of England that King Arthur is not dead, but had by the will of our Lord Jesus into another place, and men say that he shall come again . . . I will not say it shall be so, but rather will I say that here in this world he changed his life. But many men say there is written upon his tomb this verse: *Hic jacet Arturus, Rex quondam, Rexque futurus.*'

Malory's supreme achievement in his final book is that the story of Lancelot and Guinevere reaches its harrowing climax and yet is overtopped by Arthur's destruction and death. Lancelot finds her, taking refuge in a nunnery at Almesbury; she faints at the sight of him, and when she comes to, she says: 'Through this man and me hath all this war been wrought, and the death of the most noblest knights of the world, for through our love that we have loved together, is my most noble lord slain . . . therefore Sir Lancelot, I require thee and beseech thee heartily, for

vant gyfles voit que
faire li couient. sire
uient arriere la oule
re estoit si la p̃ent ẽ la rça m

all the love that ever was betwixt us, that thou never see me more . . . for well as I have loved thee, mine heart will not serve me to see thee, for through thee and me is the flower of kings and knights destroyed.' Let him, she says, go to his own realm and take a wife there, to live with in joy and bliss; 'and I pray thee, heartily pray for me to our Lord that I may amend my living'. Lancelot says that, return to the world and marry he never will. 'I take record of God, in you I have had mine earthly joy, and if I had found you so disposed, I had cast me to have had you into mine own realm.' But since she is determined to enter an order, he will enter one too. 'Wherefor Madam, I pray you, kiss me and never no more. Nay, said the Queen, that shall I never do, but abstain you from such works.'

Lancelot finds refuge in the hermitage where Arthur's tomb is made. Within half a year he is joined there by seven more of Arthur's knights; they are all received as priests, 'and so their horses went where they would, for they took no regard of no worldly riches'. After six years of solemn religious life, Lancelot has a clairvoyant dream that Guinevere is dead and that he and his fellows must go to fetch her corpse and to bury it beside King Arthur's. When he arrives with the cortège at Almesbury, he finds that the Queen has died within the last half hour and hears that she also had had a dream, that Lancelot was a priest 'and hither he cometh as fast as he may to fetch my corpse and beside my lord King Arthur shall he bury me'. One of the world's greatest love stories has its crowning when the dying Guinevere exclaims: 'I beseech Almighty God that I may never have power to see Sir Lancelot with my worldly eyes.'

Lancelot and his companions bring the Queen's funeral procession, with incense and torches, on foot from Almesbury to Glastonbury. When she has been interred beside Arthur, Lancelot falls down senseless over the tomb. Rebuked by the hermit for so much grieving, he replies: 'My sorrow may never have end, for when I remember of her beauty and her noblesse, that was both with the king and her, so when I saw his corpse and her corpse so lie together, truly my heart would not serve to sustain my careful body. Also when I remember me how, by my default . . . they were both laid full low . . . wit you well, said Sir Lancelot, this remembered of their kindness and mine unkindness . . . I might not sustain myself.'

After this Lancelot falls into a decline and dwines away. One night the hermit wakes up, laughing for joy, so that the others are wakened by him. He tells them he has had a dream: 'Here was Sir Lancelot with me, with more angels than I ever saw men in one day. And I saw the angels heave up Sir Lancelot into heaven, and the gates of heaven were opened against him.' The others say the dream means nothing, but they go to look at Sir Lancelot to reassure themselves; they find him stark dead, 'and he lay as he had smiled, and the sweetest savour about him that ever they felt'.

The three persons had an extraordinary love for each other, and the love the reader feels for all three of them is the tribute commanded by this version of one of the greatest stories in the world.

Set for ever in Malory's language, the visual image, unalterable, of Arthur and his knights is that of the men who fought the battles of the Wars of the Roses. The sense of insecurity, that an existing order of society was being destroyed, is echoed in the elegiac tone of Malory's work. He says he finished it in the ninth year of the reign of King Edward IV. It is with a sense almost of clairvoyance that one stands in the north transept of Canterbury Cathedral, looking up at the great portrait-window, executed by the King's glazier William Neve about 1480. In the centre lights the King and Queen, crowned, kneel facing each other. Behind the King kneel, one behind the other, Prince Edward and Prince Richard, the Princes in the Tower. Behind the Queen, in single file, kneel the five Princesses, their hair a stream of gold poured down their backs, crowned with chaplets of the white roses of York. At the time Malory was writing, this was how people saw a king and a queen, and young nobles, *damoiseaux* and *damoiselles*. The picture of the Queen is Elizabeth Woodville's best portrait; in it is clearly seen what, for a time at least, enchanted the robust and sensual king; wearing a heavy, jewelled crown of alternate crosses and fleurs-de-lis, with joined hands and downcast eyelids, slender, pale, graceful, inscrutable, she might have sat for one of the queens who came to bear away Arthur.

In full plate armour, the Red Cross Knight
from Spenser's *Faerie Queene*

14 The Tudors

Bosworth Field, the victory of Henry VII's forces over those of Richard III, was the last great battle fought in England with the armour Malory knew and in which he invested Arthur's image for all time, the plate that rang from sword blows with a din that echoed over wood and water. The complete suit of plate armour remained in use for parades and tournaments for another hundred years, but the sixteenth-century development of the use of black powder, or gun powder, altered the type of armour used in the field. It became necessary to have a breastplate thick enough to withstand shot, and this was so heavy that everything except the helmet was sacrificed to it. Thigh-pieces could still be worn if the soldier wished, and the death of Philip Sidney in 1586 was caused by his going into action at Zutphen without them and receiving a wound in the thigh from which he died of gangrene three weeks later, but the usual picture of the soldier of the sixteenth century shows a man in substantial leather doublet, hose and thigh boots with a metal corselet and helmet.

The policy of Henry VII put an end to battles on English soil, a quietude which lasted till the Civil War, and it would have seemed natural that the myth of King Arthur should now wane in its power over the national imagination, but such was its unquenchable vitality, it took out a new lease of life.

Henry VII claimed the English throne by right of conquest as it was allowable to do, if the person concerned were within the circle of those who had a lineal right. Henry VII's lineal claim was that his mother, the Lady Margaret Beaufort, was the great-granddaughter of John of Gaunt; but the Beauforts, Gaunt's illegitimate children by Catherine Swinford, though legitimized by Parliament as an act of courtesy to their father, had at the same time been declared incapable of the succession. Henry strengthened his dubious lineal claim by marrying Elizabeth Plantagenet, the eldest daughter of Edward IV, who since the murder of her brothers had become the Yorkist claimant of the crown.

The beautiful wheel window he put up in York Minster, where the Royal Arms are encircled by a mass of red and white roses, is a translucent, glowing statement, high above men's heads, of the policy of unity and reconciliation; but Henry disdained to admit that he was King even partly in right of his wife and he did not have her crowned until two years after his accession. Some additional potency to infuse into his own claim was very desirable. Edward I had claimed the overlordship of Scotland on the ground that he was descended from Arthur; Henry VII claimed that, *inter alia*, his descent from Arthur made him the rightful King of Britain.

Geoffrey of Monmouth had said that Cadwallader, the last British king, who had fled from the Saxons to Brittany, was told by an angel's voice that he should not return to Britain 'for God had willed that the Britons should no longer reign in Britain, before the time did come which Merlin had prophesied to Arthur'. This time, it seemed, had come now. Henry VII had been kept in Pembroke Castle till he was four, with an opportunity to hear British legends in those impressionable years. He had marched to Bosworth with a banner displaying a dragon, the creature that Uther Pendragon was said to have borne on his helm in gold, and he had been victorious. His Welsh descent was regarded by him as an asset. His grandfather Owen Tudor, who had captivated and secretly married Catherine de Valois, the widow of Henry V, was, apart from being very handsome, of no personal account; he had been one of the Queen Dowager's household officers, but her sons by him, Jasper and Edmund, had distinguished themselves, and Edmund had married the important little twelve-year-old Margaret Beaufort. It was not, however, his eligible father and uncle who interested the King, but the fact that his grandfather Owen Tudor claimed to be related to Owen Glendower. Henry appointed a commission to inquire into Glendower's ancestry; they consulted British and Welsh books of pedigrees and were able, as might be supposed, to supply the King with 'his perfect genealogy from the ancient kings of Britain'.

Whether so intellectual and astute a man as Henry VII believed their findings, remains an enigma, but the work had been done. When the King's eldest son was born Henry had him christened Arthur. Hall in his *Chronicle of the Noble and Illustre Families of Lancaster and York* says: '. . . of which name Englishmen no more rejoiced than outward nations and foreign princes trembled and quaked, so much was that name to all nations terrible and formidable'. Bacon, more moderately, says in his *History of Henry VII* that the child was christened Arthur, 'according to the name of that ancient, worthy king of the Britons, in whose acts there is truth enough to make him famous, besides that which is fabulous'. When the young Prince was married to Catherine of Aragon, among the elaborate pageants in the streets of London was one at Soper Lane, 'in a manner of a heaven, wherein was painted the twelve signs and over them was Arthur, fully armed, in his golden chair'.[29] Bacon says: 'In all the triumphs of this marriage, there was a great deal of astronomy, the lady being resembled to Hesperus, and the Prince to Arcturus'; but, he adds, 'it should seem, it is not good to fetch fortunes from the stars,' as the Prince died a few months after his wedding.

Considering his intellectual and practical cast of mind, it was a sign of Henry's genius for kingship that he saw the value of the legendary ancestry he claimed. Henry VIII, who profited so greatly by the achievements of his father, inherited also the glamour of Arthurian descent. He had the Round Table hanging up in Winchester Castle repaired and painted. At the Field of the Cloth of Gold his banqueting house at Calais had among its decorations a figure of King Arthur. Henry VIII in his prime had the physique which made natural his association with Arthur; in the troubled political situation of 1533, when the King had repudiated Catherine of Aragon to marry Anne Boleyn, the Ambassador Chapuys wrote to Charles V: 'All that know the King have great pity at his misordering, considering his great nobleness and fame, which is greater than that of any prince since King Arthur.'

The Matter of Arthur had always inspired a passionate conviction; in the twelfth century, the Bretons had been ready to fall upon anyone who denied his existence; the fund-raising French canons visiting Bodmin had been attacked by the populace when one of them made an incautious remark about the King. In the sixteenth century the bitterness was as keen but it now inspired the work of scholars and antiquarians.

John Leland, who left the striking first-hand description of Cadbury, had visited the hill fortress in the course of his *Itinerary*, which he made between 1534 and 1543. The first English antiquary, he formed a great collection of Latin notes on an antiquarian tour throughout England. An absorbing interest and a passionate love inspired his travels and researches; his accounts of what he saw are invaluable, but he believed that, as the truths of history are handed down from generation to generation, if our predecessors believed a thing, we are justified in believing it. The emotion with which Leland makes this assertion is very interesting in a study of the growth of legend. It makes him, of course, unreliable as a judge of historical fact. His indignation was roused by the mildly sceptical comments of Polydore Vergil, a cultivated Italian cleric who had been sent over to England by the Pope to collect the tax known as Peter's Pence and, finding himself very comfortable here, had remained ever since, occupying a stall in Wells Cathedral from 1508 until his death in 1544. In his *Historia Anglia*, Polydore Vergil had said: 'The common people is at this present so affectioned, that with wondrous admiration they extol Arthur unto the Heavens. . . . Not many years since in the Abbey of Glastonbury was extructed a magnificent sepulchre, that posterity might gather how worthy he was of all monument, whereas in the days of Arthur, this abbey was not builded.'

This was too much for a native Englishman to bear with any patience. In 1544, Leland published his *Assertion of the Most Noble Arthur*, in which, in his sensitive but unhistorical manner, he defended the value of tradition and added, as tangible evidence of Arthur's existence, that he had seen the King's seal at the shrine of the Confessor. He wished all unbelieving persons might see it, 'so great is both the majesty and the antiquity of the thing'. Since the continuous process of handing on evidence is so important, he wished that we might have had, as a link in the chain, 'some notable testimony of Polidorus the Italian', but the latter was so faint-hearted, so lukewarm, Leland said that sometimes he himself was inclined to laugh and sometimes made positively angry by his remarks, untrue, and filled 'with Italian bitterness'.

When a translation of Leland's *Assertion of Arthur* was made by Ralph Robinson, and published posthumously in 1582, it was dedicated to 'The Society of Archers in London, yearly celebrating the magnificence of Prince Arthur'.

The next wave of interest in the idea of the British King came in the reign of Elizabeth. Like her grandfather, the Queen was conscious of the Welsh strain in her ancestry. To it might perhaps be ascribed, though her brother and sister had been without it, that touch of magic in her personality to which even her enemies bore witness. In Mary Tudor's reign the Spanish Ambassador had warned his master Charles v: 'The Princess Elizabeth is very dangerous; she has a spirit full of incantation.' Her great minister William Cecil was of Welsh origin and one of his connections was her oldest attendant; Blanche Parry said that she had seen the Queen rocked in her cradle. On her accession, Elizabeth made her the Keeper of the Queen's Books in Windsor Castle. It was, it is supposed, from this old and learned lady that the great-great-granddaughter of Owen Tudor learned to speak Welsh.

The house party Lord Leicester gave for the Queen at Kenilworth in 1575 was one of the most splendid occasions that marked the period of her reign's established, brilliant success. The Queen and her retinue arrived at the castle on the beautiful evening of July 9. The porters guarding the entry had been built up with buckram so as to appear larger than life and furnished with clubs of gigantic size, because it was said that in King Arthur's time the land was peopled with giants. The programme Lord Leicester had arranged for the Queen's entertainment included masques, plays, dances, hunting, fireworks; in all its richness and variety, he yet thought it suitable that on the Queen's first entry into the castle, the greetings should speak to her of Arthur. The Arthurian giants stood at the gateway which the Queen and her train approached over a bridge that spanned an ornamental water beside the curtain wall. As the Queen rode on to the bridge a raft sparkling with lights floated across the mere. On it was a nymph in silk robes who, in a boy's high voice, addressed a speech to her beginning:

> I am the Lady of this pleasant lake
> Who, since the time of great King Arthur's reign
> That here with royal court abode did make,
> Have led a lowering life in restless pain.

The Queen's presence has restored the Lady to happiness; and the latter concludes her speech with the lines:

> And as my love to Arthur did appear,
> So shall't to you, in earnest and in sport,
> Pass on, Madame, you need no longer stand –
> The Lake, the Lodge, the Lord, are yours for to command.

The Queen smiled. She said: 'We had thought the lake had been ours, and do you call it yours, now? Well, we will herein commune more with you hereafter.' Another item for the Queen's amusement was the singing before her of *King*

Ryence's Challenge, a rhyming version of the story told by Geoffrey of Monmouth, of the insolent message sent to Arthur by King Ryence of Northgalis, demanding Arthur's beard to complete the trimming of a mantle furred with the beards of subjugated kings. Arthur refuses 'this villainous and lewd demand' and takes vengeance on Ryence. Robert Laneham, describing the festivities, puts down six verses of this song, then says: 'More is there, but I got it not.' That the song should have been sung was the interesting fact; as may be seen from its complete version in Percy's *Reliques*, the rest of it was no great loss.

Whatever vague if luminous ideas of Arthur the Queen may have entertained, a strong claim as his descendant, not to England only but to wide foreign domains, was put forward on her behalf by Blanche Parry's cousin, Dr John Dee. A man of exceptional gifts, historian, antiquarian, mathematician, scientist, Dee's reputation for intellect, which is now being restored,[30] has suffered from the fact that he was also a clairvoyant and a believer in spiritualism. It was Dee whom Elizabeth had asked to forecast a fortunate date for her coronation, and judging by her reign's success, the Doctor's choice of January 15, 1559, seems to have justified his reputation. Dee's clients who visited him at his house at Mortlake, a village beside Richmond, included Lord Leicester, Sir Francis Walsingham and Sir Philip Sidney, and he was more than once called upon to 'scrye' for the Queen in his speculum, a ball of some glassy substance. (This globe was once in Horace Walpole's possession; it was sold among his effects at his death, and is now at Renishaw, the seat of Mr Reresby Sitwell.)

Dee was convinced that Elizabeth was the lineal descendant of Arthur, and as, among his many projects, was the ardent wish that the British should gain an Empire, he urged that the Queen should take possession by force of arms of some of the lands which Arthur was reputed to have won. Even Dee, sanguine as he was, did not see a possibility of Elizabeth's mounting a full-scale war to regain possession of France, but he advised her, very strenuously, to acquire, as of right, the whole of Scandinavia and parts of Russia.

In October 1580, Elizabeth, who was then at Richmond Palace, sent for Dee after dinner, received him in the Privy Chamber and made him repeat his views in the presence of Lord Burlegh, that she might hear what the Lord Treasurer thought of them. Some days afterwards the Queen rode over to Mortlake and told Dee that the Lord Treasurer had 'greatly commended' Dee's doings for her title, but, it seemed, he had not felt able to advise that they should be acted on.

The mere idea of acquiring territory by military force was utterly foreign to the Queen's guiding principle. She once in the early years of her reign had made an abortive invasion of Boulogne, so important did the English then think it to gain a substitute for Calais, which had been lost under Mary Tudor; in 1586 she, with great reluctance and infinite caution, sent some help to the United Provinces, which were being ferociously attacked by a Spanish army under the Prince of Parma, because she had been persuaded that, once Spain had subjugated the Netherlands, England's turn would come next; but she refused the sovereignty

The death-throes of the dragon slain by the
Red Cross Knight

of the Provinces which their leaders attempted to force on her. Her determination
to avoid war as long as she possibly could and so allow the nation's energies to be
used for building prosperity, not only satisfied her own deep-seated instincts, it
was the cause of people's going down on their knees as she passed through the
streets. The contemplation of her descent from Arthur, with the notion of acquiring
Scandinavia and part of Russia (Dee had also some idea that she had claims to
America which she ought to prosecute), may have given the Queen amusement in
the realms of fancy, but the project was not going to find expression in any other
sphere; yet it must be admitted that though his schemes were totally impracticable
at the time, in succeeding centuries the British fulfilled Dee's ambition that they
should gain an empire.

Neither Chaucer nor Shakespeare showed any interest in Arthur as a leading figure; but one Elizabethan poet gave him an important role in a *chef d'œuvre*. Edmund Spenser, a bookish, inexperienced young man, was a protégé of Lord Leicester, and had the entrée to Leicester House on the Strand, the palace whose garden ran down to the Thames shore where fleets of swans floated by. The most celebrated of the Leicester House circle was the Earl's nephew Philip Sidney, who, with his grave beauty, his charming nature and his poetic gift, made a deep impression on most of the people who met him. In his *Defence of Poesy* he says that poetry creates pictures which convey a moral lesson. 'Whatsoever the philosopher saith should be done, [the poet] giveth a perfect picture of it, in some one by whom he pre-supposeth it was done.' Spenser fully adopted this view. Sidney himself wrote a very long, elaborately contrived prose romance, *Arcadia*; and Ben Jonson told Drummond of Hawthornden that Sidney had meant to make the work over into a set of stories connected with King Arthur. This he never did, but Spenser, using the method of conveying spiritual truth which Sidney had said was one of poetry's functions, composed an epic in which Arthur as a Prince had a part that, though it was small, was of great lustre. The first three books of *The Faerie Queene* were published in 1589, and three more, with a fragment, in 1596.

Spenser prefaced the first three with an explanatory letter to Sir Walter Raleigh, giving him a plan of the whole undertaking, which was to have occupied twelve books. He had chosen King Arthur 'as most fit for the excellency of his person, being made famous by many men's former works'. He means to show Arthur, before he was King, as the image of a brave knight, perfected in the twelve private moral virtues, as described by Aristotle. (If the work succeeded with the public, Spenser said, he would write twelve more books illustrating the public virtues.) Meanwhile he intended to make each of Arthur's twelve private virtues the subject of a book, in which a knight, distinguished by his pursuit of that virtue, should have Arthur's assistance in his adventures. In the first three books, the Red Cross knight stands for Holiness, Sir Guyon for Temperance and the armed girl Belphoebe for Chastity.

The framework is borrowed from the traditional convention of Arthur as the patron of a circle of knights, but Spenser was passionately eager to be promoted in the court circle, not from mere ambition or materialism, but because, to his longing eyes, its life appeared brilliant, exciting and glorious; instead of making Arthur an eponymous hero, he calls the work *The Faerie Queene*, and dedicates it to Elizabeth, that it may live 'with the eternity of her fame'. He explains in the dedicatory letter that Arthur's own quest of adventure is inspired by his having seen in a dream the Faerie Queene, 'with whose excellent beauty ravished, he was resolved to seek her out'. Spenser makes clear the identification with Elizabeth. 'In that Faerie Queene I mean Glory in my general intention, but in my particular I conceive the most excellent and glorious person of our sovereign the Queen and her kingdom in Faeryland.'

Spenser's allegories are sometimes threefold: Elizabeth is represented as the

From Spenser's *Faerie Queene*, Arthur killing
a giant to rescue a captive maiden;
OPPOSITE Spenser's patron, the Earl of
Leicester

Queen of Faerie, at whose great feast the knights have their adventures appointed
to them; as Belphoebe the warlike maid armoured in chastity; and as Mercilla,
the wise and merciful queen. Arthur too has several aspects; the most interesting
is the one in which he appears to represent Spenser's patron Lord Leicester. The
Queen gave Leicester the command of the English expeditionary force in the
Netherlands in 1586, and the identification is made certain when Arthur takes a
force to aid the 'Belge', the spirit of the persecuted Netherlanders. Spenser said:
'In the person of Arthur I set forth Magnificence.' It has been argued that he must
have meant 'Magnanimity', as this was one of Aristotle's private virtues, whereas

Magnificence, even if it could be regarded as a virtue, he does not mention, but if Spenser may be credited with having meant what he said, the association of Leicester with magnificence is as appropriate as the shadowing forth of his pursuit of Queen Elizabeth under the show of Arthur's devotion to the Faerie Queene. To trace the relation between the imagined splendours of the poem and the actual splendours of Leicester House is something of great interest. Leicester's tastes in furniture and decoration were not only sumptuous; it can be seen from the inventories of Kenilworth Castle and Leicester House that a fairy-like quality was imparted to them by his use of crystal and glass and the coloured lamé that

The 'Faerie Queene' Elizabeth I, to whom
Spenser dedicated his poem, inspired by the
legend of Arthur

was made by weaving a gold or silver thread one way and a coloured silk thread
the other. Spenser several times gives the impression, when describing palaces in
The Faerie Queene, that he is recording *choses vues*, of which the most striking
example is the green-gold hangings in the House of Pride:

> Woven of silk and gold so close and near
> That the rich metal lurked privily,
> Like a discoloured snake, whose hidden snares
> Through the green grass his long bright burnished back declares.[31]

A greater contrast to Malory's work than *The Faerie Queene* could not be
imagined. Malory writes with vivid, sometimes even clumsy, straightforwardness.
He writes of magical happenings, impossible happenings, but he writes of them

in the medium and the language of his own time, and reading his final books with their passion and pain is part of a life's experience. Spenser, a conscious literary artist with a profound admiration for Chaucer, used with deliberate archaism words that with Chaucer had been current coin. His pace is meandering, the action retarded by the elaborate eight-lined verse with the ninth line of twelve syllables. The endless repetition of this form induces a half-hypnotic state; the figures are beautiful or stately or horrible, but they pass before the mind at a remove, in the landscape of a dream. The figure of Arthur is clothed in glittering armour, his shield is cut from a solid diamond, his helmet is crested by the gold dragon. He looks indeed like one of the knights who jousted before Elizabeth in the tiltyard at Whitehall, in suits of richly enamelled, gold-ornamented armour, which would have had to be laid aside if a genuine battle had been the occasion instead of the highly trained activity of a tournament: such a scene as Philip Sidney described in Book III of his *Arcadia*. 'Phalantus' horse, young, and feeling the youth of his master, stood curvetting, which, being well governed by Phalantus, gave such a glittering grace as when the sun in a clear day shines upon waving water.' But although Arthur's victories are entirely predictable, and the story cannot there- fore exert a narrative interest, the picture of him has other attractions. He accom- panies Sir Guyon to the House of Temperance, where Alma, its lady, allows them to look over her precious books:

> Whereat they, burning both with fervent fire
> Their country's ancestry to understand,

Guyon seizes upon one with the fashionable title of *Antiquity of Fairyland*, in which he reads of Queen Elizabeth's fairy lineage, while Arthur eagerly opens a volume with the equally modish one of *Briton Monuments*. Spenser breaks off the narrative in which Arthur and Queen Elizabeth are already figuring as contemporary characters, and exclaims:

> Thy name, oh sovereign Queen, thy realm and race
> From this renowned Prince derived are,

thus emphasizing the claims of Henry VII and giving hearty support to those put forward on the Queen's behalf by Dr Dee. He then returns to the chronology of the poem, and Arthur reads the story, taken from Geoffrey of Monmouth, of his land of Britain, with an expression of that intense love of country that we have so recently lost:

> Dear country, oh how dearly dear,
> How brutish is it, not to understand
> How much to her we owe, that all us gave
> That gave unto us all, whatever good we have . . .

Arthur follows the story as far as the appearance on the scene of Uther Pendragon; from there onwards, the time-scheme would have been too difficult to manipulate, and Spenser says that the book ended at that point, as if a hand had torn out the

King Arthur as one of the Nine Worthies:
the statue designed by Dürer for the Royal
Chapel at Innsbruck

remaining pages. Arthur does not show surprise or indignation at this; he is left in a trance of interest and wonder.

In 1596, the year in which Spenser published the remaining three books of *The Faerie Queene*, through which Arthur continued to wind his scintillating track, the London goldsmith Christopher Wace made a set of twelve silver-gilt spoons. The finials are little figures, representing Jesus Christ, St Peter, Queen Elizabeth and the Nine Worthies of the World: Hector of Troy, Alexander the Great, Julius Caesar, Joshua, David, Judas Maccabaeus, Charlemagne, Godfrey of Bouillon and King Arthur. The set was sold in June 1974, for £70,000.

15 Stuart Interest

Mary Queen of Scots had been obsessed by a devouring eagerness to take possession of the English crown. She had announced that she was Queen of England immediately upon the death of Mary Tudor in 1558. Her complicity in three major conspiracies, which included arranging for the assassination of Queen Elizabeth, had at last driven the English people wild with panic, and she was put to death on account of the final one in 1587. Her son James knew that, since Elizabeth was beyond the age of child-bearing, the English crown must almost certainly come to him, and by the time the great Queen died in 1603, he was avid for the power, the wealth, the grandeur upon which he was about to enter. His wife Anne of Denmark was similarly agog. When she had been told of the wardrobe the late Queen had left, she had said scornfully that she would not wear any old clothes. When she actually saw the dresses of Queen Elizabeth, she changed her tune, and the Venetian Ambassador reported that Whitehall Palace was full of dressmakers working day and night to adapt the late Queen's clothes to her present Majesty.

James, the 'wisest fool in Christendom', had not inherited his mother's charm, but he had some of her other qualities in good measure. Von Raumer has said: 'Mary combined a lust for power with the utmost incapacity for rule', and much the same could be said for all her descendants on the English throne except Charles II, Mary and Anne. James, after his mother's death, had been in close touch with Elizabeth, who treated him unofficially as her heir. He had had the benefit of letters of advice from this highly accomplished *politique*, but he had been too bumptious and too touchy about his own dignity to take much advantage of them. Now, with all restraints taken off, he acted not only without statecraft but without even rudimentary common sense.

The Wars of the Roses had lasted for thirty years, and Shakespeare's plays *Richard II*, *Henry IV*, *Henry VI* and *Richard III*, whether true or untrue to historical fact, do at least show how the populace, as represented by the theatre-going public, felt about civil war, their horror of sickening slaughter, their crying out for peace. Elizabeth's great reign had given them forty-five years of domestic quiet, and the general relief that James should succeed without a contest to a united England, Scotland and Wales, caused a wave of enthusiasm in his favour. Henry VII had declared that he was restoring the kingdom of Arthur, and the association was spontaneously made in James's favour; he was hailed in masques and pageants as the heir of Arthur or, as the climax to centuries of expectation, as Arthur's self returned.

168

The fact that, from his accession, England, Scotland and Wales were thenceforward called Great Britain was another reason for hailing James as Arthur. In April 1603, the Venetian Ambassador wrote that the King's naming the kingdoms 'Britain' was like the decision of 'the famous and ancient King Arthur, to embrace under one name the entire kingdom'. These references to Arthur, wholly without foundation as they were, could but increase the baneful excitement of James's already disastrous state of mind.

In Elizabeth's last speech to a Parliamentary deputation, she had said that she thanked God, not that He had made her a Queen, but that He had made her Queen over so thankful a people. She had nothing to wish, she said, 'except to content the subject, which is the duty that I owe'. James, on the other hand, asserted that the Coronation Oath was not a contract between the King and people: 'I deny any such contract to be made.' Unlike Elizabeth's, his conception of kingship was the one inherited from his fatal mother. The Queen of Scots had refused to answer questions about the murder of her husband, because, she said, she was not of the same order of being as her subjects, and, as she assured Elizabeth, 'I would sooner die than by any act of mine behave as if I were.' Within a few months of his accession, James issued a work showing how completely he had reproduced his mother's attitudes, and how much at variance his ideas were with those of the Parliament with which he had to deal. It was called *The True Law of Free Monarchies* and contained this statement: 'The wickedness, therefor, of the King can never make them that are ordained to be judged by him, to become his judges.' In June of 1603, the Venetian Ambassador wrote: 'The King declares that there are no ministers, and no laws, of which he is not master.'

This profoundly jarring impact of opposing views was felt very early in the reign while the King was still being hailed as Arthur in the festivities of the accession. This resulted in a natural alignment: those who supported the Divine Right of Kings upheld the historicity of Arthur; those who asserted the final authority of the English Common Law saw that they, too, must look for supporting arguments to a far-distant era. The Anglo-Saxon monarchy had been an elective one; the Coronation Oath of Alfred had limited the power of the King to the execution of laws made by the people; they turned for their authority, to the laws and customs of the Anglo-Saxons. The dispositions of the parties had completely altered, the values were reversed, but some of the bitterness of the old struggle infused itself into the new one.

The Parliamentary party were not the first to show an interest in the Anglo-Saxons. Matthew Parker, Queen Elizabeth's Archbishop of Canterbury, had taken a keen interest in the study of Anglo-Saxon writings. Strype[32] says: 'He was desirious to inquire everywhere for Saxon and British Antiquities, for the better knowledge of the history of the church and the nation.' The Archbishop sent to Dr Davies, Bishop of St David's, a manuscript of very great antiquity, 'which seemed to have been in the old British tongue, but the letters were not known, praying him to try to read it, and to show it to Mr Salisbury'. The latter had published a dictionary in English and Welsh; he had translated the New Testament into Welsh and several Welsh works into English, but though he and the bishop laid their heads together over the manuscript 'they despaired to do anything therein'. However, Dr Davies sent the Archbishop a *Giraldus Cambrensis* and a *Galfridus Monemutensis*. The Archbishop wrote to Dr Storey, the Bishop of Hereford, saying he should be glad to have any antique books or manuscripts that might be found in the diocese. Dr Storey discovered that the Dean had three

Anglo-Saxon books in his possession; he took these away and sent them to the Archbishop, 'but what they were, doth not appear'. Dr Parker had the good fortune to be very early in the field, and he made a fine collection of books and manuscripts. In 1572, he founded the Society of Antiquaries.

This body was formed for the study of the antiquities of Britain, and the Anglo-Saxon language and law was one of its leading interests. In the first decades of the seventeenth century its most distinguished members were Camden the historian, Spelman the historian and antiquary, who founded a readership in Anglo-Saxon at Cambridge, Cotton the collector of manuscripts, and Selden the jurist and legal antiquary. Their associate was Sir Edward Coke, the great upholder of the authority of the Common Law. As the Common Law goes by precedent, of what was decided last time a similar case came up, it was of the greatest importance to have the precedents recorded, and Coke began his famous compilation of Law Reports in 1604. He resisted the claim of the Anglican Church to be exempt from the authority of the Common Law, whereas James supported it, and he repudiated James's claim that the King could make laws by proclamation. To reduce the prestige of the Common Law, James asserted that it originated only with William the Conqueror. If he could have proved this, it would have gone some way to deprive the Common Law of its special value as the legacy of the Saxons, a people whose kings were not said to be divinely appointed but were elected by themselves. Selden, however, demonstrated that William the Conqueror had not only allowed the Anglo-Saxon law to stand, wherever practicable; he produced the document

Designs for a masque by Inigo Jones: a cave
palace and the Oberon costume worn by
Prince Henry, son of James I

STUART INTEREST

171

in which the Conqueror's legislation was enrolled, which bore the heading 'Laws
of the good King Edward, which William the Bastard afterwards confirmed'.

Since the Society of Antiquaries was devoted to the study of Anglo-Saxon,
which tended to uphold the supremacy of the Common Law, it was naturally
offensive to the King. He ordered its dissolution.

Meanwhile James's supporters did not spare their pains. On June 4, 1610, the
King's charming elder son Prince Henry, who, like Henry VII's Arthur, was to die
while still a boy, was created Prince of Wales, and Ben Jonson wrote two masques
for the occasion. These were put on at Whitehall, and mounted by Inigo Jones with
his imaginative and beautiful décor and his triumphs of moving scenery. The first
was *The Masque of Oberon*, in which Prince Henry himself took the part of the
Fairy Prince. It opened almost in darkness, showing dimly a massive rock with
trees beyond it 'till at one corner of the cliff, above the horizon the moon began to
show, and rising, a Satyr was seen to put forth his head and call'. The dialogue of
two satyrs shows that they are eagerly awaiting the arrival of Prince Oberon. Then
the rock opened, 'disclosing the frontspiece of a bright and glorious palace, whose
gates and walls were transparent'. After the singing and dancing of the satyrs 'the
whole palace opened and was seen to be full of fairies, some with instruments,
some bearing lights, others singing.' The producer had recruited some very small
girls as fairies, and the audience were astonished that the 'little ladies' performed
their intricate dance so well, 'considering the tenderness of their years'. The King's
second son Charles, the ten-year-old Duke of York, took part in the dance, and
however the changes went, 'the little Duke was still found to be in the midst of
these little dancers.' Then Oberon appeared in a chariot which, 'to a loud,
triumphant music, began to move forward'. As the Prince's chariot drew near to
where the King was sitting, the company sang:

> Melt earth to sea, sea flow to air,
> And air fly into fire,
> Whilst we in tunes to Arthur's chair
> Bear Oberon's desire;
> Than which there's nothing can be higher
> Save James, to whom it flies;
> But he the wonder is, of tongues, of ears, of eyes.

James, undignified but not unimpressive, with a fatherly fondness for children in
general and devoted to his own, must have presided very happily over this scene
of light and colour, music and grace, while he was eulogized in a final song:

> Every virtue of a king
> And of all, in him we sing . . .

The masque for the second day was planned as the introduction to a joust in which
Prince Henry and six companions were to form a team. The masque was therefore
called *The Speeches at Prince Henry's Barriers*, but it opened in a scene of romantic
beauty, and interpreted the mystery and the fairy elements in the Arthurian legend.

172 The set disclosed a lake between a cave's entrance and the leaning, tumbled fragments of ruins. From the water the Lady of the Lake arose, saying:

> A silence, calm as are my waters, meet
> Your raised attentions, while my silver feet
> Touch on the richer shore . . .

She indicates the ruins of ancient Britain and mourns its vanishing; whereupon Arthur appears above, as a star. A tinted drawing remains of the costume Inigo Jones designed for 'a Star Masquer' in *The Lords' Masque* three years later. It shows a young man in the seventeenth-century idea of Roman armour, a silver breastplate and greaves, with the glittering effect of cloth of silver cut into tongues like rays. Arthur announces himself as

> Arcturus, once thy King and now thy star . . .

The time has come, he says, that Merlin's prophecies are to be fulfilled:

> In Britain's name, the union of this Isle . . .
> Fair fall his virtue that doth fill that throne,
> In which I joy to find myself outshone.

To lightning and thunder, Merlin rises out of his tomb and commands the Lady of the Lake to bring forth Meliadus, the name devised by Prince Henry for himself from his motto *Miles a Deo*, 'God's Soldier'. She calls:

> The heavens, the fates and thy peculiar stars
> Meliadus, show thee! And conclude all jars.

At this point, Prince Henry and his party were 'discovered', ready to joust. Merlin delivers a very long recital, celebrating the deeds of English sovereigns from Edward I to Queen Elizabeth, concluding with an apostrophe to 'royal and mighty James', to which the Lady adds:

> Aye, this is he, Meliadus, whom you
> Must only serve and give yourself unto,
> And by your diligent practice to obey
> So wise a master, learn the art of sway.

Within the cave, the goddess of Chivalry now awakes from a death-like sleep, exclaiming that Meliadus has brought her back to life, and the joust begins.

However the court party might believe that James was the direct descendant of Arthur, or at least endure to sit through lavish, beautiful entertainments which maintained that he was, the party of critical investigators, headed by Selden, continued to find in their researches evidence to show that an English king had no powers superior to those of Parliament. James was determined not to yield an inch. When a sermon that had been preached at Oxford was published, saying 'If Kings grow unruly and tyrannical they may be corrected and brought into order by their subjects', James had copies of it burnt publicly by the hangman. He ordered Coke

Inigo Jones's design for a Star Masquer
in the 'Lords' Masque'

to expunge from his Law Reports all opinions unfavourable to the King's Prerogative. When in 1621 the House of Commons received a message from the King, 'that they should not presume to meddle with anything concerning Our Government or deep Matters of State', they replied that the King was attempting to abridge their ancient and undoubted rights, inherited from their ancestors. The King with his own hands tore the page recording this from the Journal of the House of Commons and dissolved Parliament.

Meanwhile Coke, Spelman and Selden were convinced that one of the important weapons in their struggle was the knowledge of Anglo-Saxon. When charters and other documents were studied in their original form, it was sometimes found that a Latin translation had misconstrued the sense. To find out what the documents really said it was essential to be able to read them in the language in which they had been written. Camden, whom Selden called 'that most learned nourice of antiquity, my instructing friend Mr Camden', agreed with them. They all had the benefit of Robert Cotton's great manuscript collection, but like Archbishop Parker they were anxious to form their own. Coke had a thirteenth-century copy of a register of Anglo-Saxon laws which had belonged to Parker himself.

The possession of these documents and the power to read them had an importance which James had recognized when he disbanded the Society of Antiquaries. In Roberta Brinkley's words, 'Upon the ancient laws of the nation depended the right of the people to revolt against and depose their king.'[30]

16 Decline

Coke and Selden were the great leaders in the movement against the Divine Right of Kings, and therefore they were ranged against the party which had attached the idea of Arthur to itself, as a symbol and ornament, but in 1613 Selden showed that as an antiquary he was not entirely unsympathetic on the subject of Arthurian lore. In this year his friend Michael Drayton published the first eighteen books of his long poetical work, *Poly-Olbion*, 'The Land of Many Blessings', and Selden supplied various passages with notes, which he called 'Illustrations'.

There had grown, under the Tudors, as an offshoot of the intense love of the English for their country, an enthusiasm for chorography: a description of the land, its physical features, its monuments and associations. Leland's *Itinerary* was an early example, though it was not published till the eighteenth century; Camden's *Britannia* was another, and so was Lambarde's *Topographical Discourse of Kent*. In 1572 Queen Elizabeth was on progress in Kent and was of course to be received in state at Canterbury. Archbishop Parker had known her since she was two years old, for he had been her mother's chaplain, and he knew how all-embracing her interest was in the districts of her realm through which she passed. She was to be escorted by Lord Burlegh, who was the Archbishop's great friend, and Dr Parker thought it would be a convenient thing for the Lord Treasurer to have at his finger-tips all the local information for some of which the Queen was almost certain to ask. Before the progress began he sent Lord Burlegh a copy of Lambarde's *Topographical Discourse of Kent* and a book on *British Antiquities*; but the Archbishop, in his kindness, was carrying coals to Newcastle. Lord Burlegh read the works, and returned them with a few errors and omissions corrected in his own hand.

The thirty books of *Poly-Olbion* form another chorographical work. They take the reader on a journey beginning in the Channel Islands, continuing to Chester, coming down to London, returning north-east to Lincoln, going on to Lancashire, Yorkshire, Northumberland and Westmorland. Though its length was too great for Drayton to keep the life in it and some of the passages are ineffective and dull, the work as a whole is lovely to read. Drayton, like Gildas, was responsive to the part water plays in English landscape; he celebrates brooks and rills, the great rivers streaming across the land and the seas into which they fall. Lamb said: 'He associated hills and streams with life and passion, beyond the dreams of old mythology.'

When he comes to the south-west regions haunted by Arthur's name, Drayton relates a whole body of Arthurian tradition. He makes the River Teste claim Winchester as Arthur's seat, 'whose old Round Table yet she vaunteth to be hers'. He speaks of Glastonbury, devastated by order of Henry VIII, whose ruins in the seventeenth century made an impression on him such as they make upon us now:

> Oh, who thy ruin sees, whom wonder doth not fill,
> With our great fathers' pomp, devotion and their skill? . . .
> When not great Arthur's tomb nor holy Joseph's grave
> From sacrilege had power their sacred bones to save.
> He, who that God-in-Man to his sepulchre brought
> Or he, which, for the faith, twelve famous battles fought.

Speaking of the River Brue which winds through the water meadows (he calls it Bry), Drayton says it claims to be

> The nearest neighbouring flood to Arthur's ancient seat
> Which made the Briton's name through all the world so great
> Like Camelot, what place was ever so renowned,
> When, as at Caerleon oft, he kept the Table Round?

The Ocean calls the rivers to a singing contest, and they pour, singing, into the Bristol Channel. Their object is to have it decided whether the Isle of Lundy, set in the Bristol Channel rather nearer to the Devonshire coast than to that of Pembrokeshire, shall belong to England or to Wales. The Welsh rivers sing the glories of Arthur, the English rivers sing of their Saxon history. The River Severn is to give the verdict. She is attired in watchet – a pale blue – 'with many a curious wave'; her skirts are fringed with coral. She sounds as though she had been dressed by Inigo Jones. The year before, in 1612, *The Masque of Tethys* had been presented at court, and Inigo Jones had dressed the twelve young ladies representing twelve English rivers, in sky-blue taffeta covered with waving silver lines and silver fish; they were crowned with shells and coral.

Before announcing her verdict, Severn recalls the prophecies of Merlin which have been fulfilled in James's accession; then she says that Lundy is to be allied equally to Wales and England.

Selden's Illustrations were made while he and his colleagues were concentrating on the translation of Anglo-Saxon documents. The legends of King Arthur were not only, in his opinion, largely without foundation, they were cited in support of a cause which he opposed with moral and professional earnestness, but in writing his Illustrations to the work of a poet who was his friend, he preserved a cool, humorous, courteous attitude. He says in his Introduction: 'I will insert, out of the British story, what I importune you not to credit.' He wishes 'that the poetical monks, in celebration of him, Arthur, and other such worthies, had contained themselves' within what he called 'the bounds of likelihood', because, 'from their intermixed and absurd fauxeties, hath proceeded doubt, and, in some, even denial of what was truth'. Speaking apropos Arthur's conquests, of which Drayton has made the usual recital (Iceland, Norway, Denmark, France), Selden says this is 'too hyperbolical'. As to the seal of red wax which Leland saw in Westminster Abbey, which called Arthur Emperor of Britain, Gaul, Germany and Denmark, surely this was 'counterfeited' and 'applied' to Arthur. From his examination of charters, Selden was able to say: 'No King of this land, except the Confessor, before the Conquest, ever signed their charters with anything but a name and cross.' This process of legendary aggrandization of Arthur, so far as sensible people are concerned, 'has defeated its own object'. The bards have, 'with this kind of unlimited attribute so loaden him, you can hardly guess what is true of him'.

His most interesting comment is the one on Leland's *Assertion of Arthur*. He accepts Leland's identification of Cadbury with Camelot, in words now famous: 'By South Cadbury is that Camelot, a hill of a mile's compass at the top, four trenches circling it and betwixt every one of them an earthen wall. The content of it, within about twenty acres, full of ruins and relics of old buildings.' Among Roman coins found there and other works of antiquity, Stow speaks of a silver horseshoe there, 'digged up in the memory of our fathers'.

Selden says: 'Being not very prodigal of my historical faith, after explanation I oft adventure an examination and censure.' Drayton, in speaking of the first conquest of these islands, follows Geoffrey of Monmouth in ascribing the foundation of the British kingdom to the Trojan prince, Brute. Touching this, Selden says: 'I have but as an advocate for the Muse, argued; disclaiming in it if alleged for my own opinion.'

With this nice discrimination, Selden courteously consecrates 'to gentlewomen and their lovers' all the passages about wooing and embracing, 'feigned by the Muse among the hills and rivers', while the descriptions of battles and antique monuments, and anything about the law of the kingdom, which, as he says, has been his own particular study – all this he devotes 'to the more Severe Reader'. The passages concerning Arthur are found only in the first four of Drayton's books, and therefore within the division of the eighteen books first published. When the remaining twelve were published in 1622, Selden did not 'illustrate' them. It is very fortunate, in the context of what he called his 'particular study', that we have his comments on the Arthurian Matter.

Chaucer and Shakespeare had made no use of the national myth; a third supremely great English poet considered such a project; but the idea of Arthur had now become one of such political significance, he discarded it for what may well have been political reasons.

Milton was born in 1608; his father, a prosperous scrivener, understood that his son was a genius and allowed him, after a university career at Cambridge, to spend his youth in teaching himself to be a poet without working for a living. Milton travelled in Italy between 1637 and 1639, and there he was introduced to Giovanni Battista Manso, a patron of writers. Milton addressed a Latin poem to him; how much he wished, he said, that he had so kind a friend, so generous a patron of poets, as Manso! If he had such a supporter, he would give his energies to writing about Arthur, who had carried his wars to regions of the Otherworld. This sounds as if Milton had read some version of *The Spoils of Annwyn*. Or, he says, he would write of the unconquered fellowship of the Round Table and, in his verse, crush the Saxons beneath warlike cohorts. In the year of his return from Italy, when they were both thirty-one, Milton lost by death his friend Charles Diodati. The latter's father, an Anglicized Italian, had been physician to the children of James I, and Charles himself was a doctor; he and Milton had been at St Paul's School together and had remained lifelong friends. Milton wrote a most admired Latin poem on his death; he called it *Epitaphium Damonis*, addressing his friend in the classical convention as the shepherd Damon. In this poem he

Cadbury Hill, like a fortified place
descending in steps to the farmlands of
the plain

says he means to write an epic, telling of the Britons' colonization of Armorica, the birth of Arthur and leading to scenes where the Britons shout their war-cries on the field of battle.

After a prolonged youth in which, as it seemed, his only concern had been poetry, the turn of events acted as a catalyst and Milton developed into an active revolutionary. The Civil War broke out in 1642; he had already published, in 1641, three pamphlets denying the authority of bishops; in 1643 he produced *The Doctrine and Discipline of Divorce*; in 1644, his tremendous *Areopagitica, the Freedom of the Press*; in 1649, after the execution of Charles I, *The Tenure of Kings and Magistrates*, in which he defended the act of putting the King to death, citing 'our ancient books of law', to prove that the people had a right to judge him and to carry out sentence on him.

Diplomatic correspondence was conducted in Latin, and in 1649 Milton was appointed Latin Secretary to Cromwell's Council of State, a post he held till the Restoration, though as blindness overtook him in the 1650s, he had to dictate his dispatches to amanuenses, one of whom was another poet, Andrew Marvell. In 1660, when the surviving Regicides, those who had actually signed the death warrant of Charles I, were executed, it was asked whether Milton also should not be put to death. Charles II, who combined his extreme good nature with a total want of respect, said: 'He's old and blind and full of fleas, so let him be.' The decision secured *Paradise Lost* for us.

Milton had already begun his epic; he finished it after five years' work, in 1663, but it was not about Arthur. *Paradise Lost* deals with the expulsion of Adam and Eve from Heaven; as Andrew Marvell said in his prefatory poem:

> Messiah crown'd, God's reconciled decree,
> Rebelling angels, the forbidden tree,
> Heaven, Hell, Satan, Chaos, all . . .

The stupendous theme is so drastic a change from the idea of an epic with Arthur as the hero, the change is in itself 'an image of the time, its form and pressure'. In 1655, three years before he was said to have begun *Paradise Lost*, Milton had written a *History of Britain*, from legendary times to the Norman Conquest. Its date makes it very interesting in the context of the abandoned epic. The work shows that Milton had become not only sceptical on the subject of Arthur but contemptuous of those who were not: 'Who Arthur was, and whether ever any such reigned in Britain, hath been doubted heretofore, and may again with good reason. For the monk of Malmesbury and others whose credit hath swayed most with the learneder sort, we may well perceive to have known no more of Arthur, five hundred years past, nor of his doings, than we now living.' It was hard that the forgers had exposed William of Malmesbury to Milton's slighting comments, but the latter's strictures on Geoffrey of Monmouth were deserved and inevitable; he observes how strange it must appear that the book in the ancient British tongue 'should be utterly unknown to the world till more than six hundred years after the day of Arthur'. So far from wanting to celebrate the martial triumphs of the British, he is now quite disenchanted with them; they are 'progenitors not to be gloried in'. His researches led him, in a style typical of revolutionaries, to despise those 'who take pleasure to be all their lifetime raking in the foundations of old Abbeys and Cathedrals'; the later writers on Arthur have bolstered their case by 'old legends and Cathedral regests', but, as he says, 'He who can accept of legends for good story may quickly swell a volume with trash.'

When he came to write *Paradise Lost*, he spoke in depreciation of the theme he had put aside. When, in Book I, Satan reviews his massed armies, Milton says their numbers exceeded any ever heard of, whether of those giants whom the gods overcame and buried in the Plain of Phlegrea, or the army brought against Thebes or to the Siege of Troy,

> and what resounds
> In fable or romance of Uther's son
> Begirt with British and Armoric knights . . .

He does not want, he says in Book IX, to write about wars, which up till now have been thought the only subject suitable for heroic verse, in which it has been reckoned the poet's chief accomplishment

> to dissect
> With long and tedious havoc, fabled knights
> In battles feigned.

or to describe

> tilting furniture, emblazoned shields
> Impresses quaint, caparisons and steeds,
> Bases and tinsel trappings, gorgeous knights
> At joust or tournament.

The whole trend of his mind on this subject had altered since he wrote the *Epitaphium Damonis*. The great upheaval, the awful beheading of the King, the establishing of the Republic and then its being overthrown, even these events were not in themselves of greater magnitude than the victories of the real Arthur; but he had been lost in time; the myth had replaced him; the myth was all that Milton could see, with its values of monarchy, warfare and false romanticism. The historical claims of the myth were dispelled by the researches of the historian and its figurehead was rejected as a fit subject for a *chef d'œuvre* by the Republican, the Regicide.

17 Revival

It was the middle of the seventeenth century when Milton, high-minded and austere, repudiated the idea of making Arthur the subject of an epic. The gist of late seventeenth-century learned opinion was expressed by Bishop Stillingfleet, cultivated, urbane, a popular preacher, chaplain to Charles II and also a very learned historian. The Bishop said of those who took sides on the matter of Arthur, 'I think both sides are to blame about him; I mean those who tell Incredible Tales of him, such as are utterly inconsistent with the circumstances of the British at that time, and those who deny that there was any such person, or of any considerable power, among the Britons.'

In the realms of popular entertainment, the subject had shown an alacrity in sinking. During the Civil War, William Lilly, an astrologer of genuine powers, had brought out an almanack, with the title *Merlinus Anglicanus Junior, the English Merlin Revived*, which prophesied that the present discontents would not be relieved till 1666, which, though six years out, was a not discreditable prophecy for one made in 1644. Numerous books of prophecies were brought out during the Civil War and under the Protectorate, with Merlin's name attached as a kind of trademark. That the idea of the British kings' descent from Arthur was still not extinguished in the mind of the people was demonstrated by the appearance in 1658 of *British and Outlandish Prophecies*, by Thomas Pugh, which said that the return of Charles II, which was already looked forward to, was a pattern of the long-expected return of Arthur. It contained a genealogy, 'His Highness' Lineal Descent from the ancient Princes of Britain, clearly manifesting that he is the Conqueror they so long prophesied of'.

The seventeenth and eighteenth centuries were not an era when the Matter of Arthur inspired any great work. Dryden, in the preface to his translation of the first six books of Juvenal's *Satires*, spoke of the kingdom's being under the protection of guardian angels, and mentioned that he might use this idea presently in a work about Arthur's repulse of the Saxons.

Before Dryden could set this in hand, William III's physician Sir Richard Blackmore had seized upon it and decided to write the epic that Milton had neglected. Sir Richard conceded that the epic was a difficult form, for in seventeen hundred years only Homer and Virgil had really succeeded in it; he would make a triumvirate with them, 'for the entertainment of my idle hours'. His friends in some alarm begged him, if he must write, to choose a medical subject; but Sir

Richard explained that this would not do; he wanted a theme which did not require him to have books about him – one that he could compose in his head, 'in Coffee Houses and in passing up and down the streets'. This was sympathetic enough, if only he had left out any reference to Homer and Virgil, the successful employers of the genre, and to Ariosto, Tasso and Spenser, whom he considered the failures. Blackmore produced his work in two parts, *Prince Arthur* in 1695 and *King Arthur* in 1700. The unfolding of Arthur's career before he was King was supposed to point gracefully to William of Orange, the model on whom the hero of the epic was based. Much of the narrative is taken from Geoffrey of Monmouth, and Blackmore also borrowed largely from *The Faerie Queene* and *Paradise Lost*; but it was the addition that he made out of his own head which caused, naturally, violent reaction among those who were Roman Catholics and supporters of the Stuarts. Blackmore identified Arthur, the Christian champion, with Protestantism, and Satan with Catholicism. The restoring of the Protestant form of worship by William III, after the attempt of James II to re-establish Catholic supremacy, is shown allegorically in the arrival of Arthur on English shores:

> His arms the lowering tempest shall dispel
> That, threatening Albion, rolls from Rome and Hell.

The doctor's friends had been nervous in case his literary début might be a failure with the public; on that score at least their anxieties had been needless. Blackmore's success was prodigious, and since, as Dr Johnson said, 'his head still teemed with heroic poetry', he went on to write more epics, and more again. He seems to have been one of those writers who are extremely popular with the readers of their own age and unreadable by those of any other. Nonetheless he aroused bitter animosity in those of his contemporaries whose religious and political beliefs he had insulted, and among these were, unfortunately, the two greatest poets of the time. Dryden and Pope were Catholics and resented Blackmore's handling of the religious issue, while Dryden was also indignant that Blackmore should have filched his idea of an Arthurian work: 'It was not for this noble knight that I drew the plan of an epic.' Pope was incontestably spiteful, and Blackmore's undeserved success cannot have softened his critical judgment, but in the last resort, that judgment was unassailable. He put Blackmore into Book II of the *Dunciad*, the poem that celebrates 'The Triumph of Dulness':

> All hail him victor, in both gifts of song.
> Who sings so loudly and who sings so long,

and a note explains that the lines refer to Sir Richard Blackmore, 'who wrote no less than six epic poems: Prince and King Arthur, twenty books, Eliza, ten, Alfred, twelve, The Redeemer, six, besides Job, in folio, the whole Book of Psalms, The Creation, seven books. In this sense he is styled the Everlasting Blackmore.'

Dryden said: 'Nothing ill is to be spoken of the dead, and therefor, peace be to the Manes of his Arthurs.'

The use which Dryden ultimately made of the Arthurian theme was, for him, no great achievement. His opera *King Arthur*, for which Purcell wrote the music, had been in his mind for several years: he kept postponing it, since he knew he could make money by writing plays and hesitated to risk his time on an opera. It was at last produced in 1691. The year before, Purcell had written his ravishing music for Nahum Tate's *Dido and Aeneas*, and the music for *King Arthur* seems insipid by comparison, while Dryden's libretto has the lowering effect of most things written about Arthur in later centuries which are conscious invention; entirely fresh elements worked into the story break the old spell without creating a new one. This King Arthur and the blind Princess Emmeline might as well be part of some entirely different legend; they add nothing to the existing story and gain no lustre from it themselves. Dryden, however, had the keen sensitiveness to public response of the man who makes his living in the theatre; the fact that he thought it worth while to write an opera on King Arthur is more interesting than the work.

In the eighteenth century, the Arthurian theme maintained its interest but not so much with the public as among scholars and critics. Two of these were exceptionally distinguished and laid the foundations of our future studies. The outstanding development of historical research during the past two hundred years might perhaps be called the interest attached to the conditions of ordinary life. Social histories and collections of pictures illustrating daily existence in past centuries explain and bring home to us the great forces of economic development, as charters and acts of parliament by themselves can scarcely do for the reader who is not a trained historian.

Thomas Warton, who was Poet Laureate from 1785 to 1790, was the instigator of this method. In his *Observations on The Faerie Queene* and his *History of English Poetry*, Warton illustrated the passages he cited with quotations from contemporary accounts of social life. His wide reading and his tenacious memory were all he had to guide him, for the compilations a writer uses now were not then written. Warton quoted the Wardrobe Rolls of Edward III, relating details of 'costly stuffs delivered for his tournaments, standards, pennons, tunics, caparisons'. He described the adornment of ships, of Henry v's galley with gilded masts and purple sails; he put together descriptions of gardens bright with roses from Gawain Douglas, William Dunbar, Alexander Lyndsay. He quoted Thomas Tusser to show the food eaten at the time; he said of tapestry: 'In the fourteenth and fifteenth century, the very walls of their apartments were clothed with romantic history', and he printed extracts from the catalogue of the tapestries in the palaces of Henry VIII; in the palace of The More, in Hertfordshire, he said, there were tapestries of Hercules, Astyages, Cyrus and King Arthur. He printed the works of minor poets, neglected since their own time, because, he said, a study of their work threw light on the work of their greater contemporaries. 'The antiquaries of former times rejected these valuable remains, which they despised as false and frivolous . . . but in the present age . . . the curiosity of the antiquarian is connected with taste and genius and his researches tend to display the progress of human manners and to illustrate the history of society.'

This point was at once taken by Dr Johnson. When Warton sent him a copy of his *Observations on The Faerie Queene*, Johnson said in his letter of thanks, of July 1758: 'You have shown to all, who shall hereafter attempt the study of our ancient authors, the way to success, by directing them to the perusal of the books which those authors had read. . . . The reason why the authors which are yet read, of the sixteenth century, are so little understood, is that they are read alone, and no help is borrowed from those who lived with them or before them.' Warton combined the emotional response of a lover of romance and poetry with the mind of a scholar. Dr Johnson said: 'A mere antiquarian is a rugged being' – a definition which might be used of Warton's great contemporary.

Arthur Johnston[33] has said of Joseph Ritson's *Life of King Arthur*, finished in 1803 though not published till 1825, that 'the chapters dealing with the birth, death and place of burial of Arthur, contain the first thoroughly documented discussion of most of the problems of Arthurian scholarship.' Ritson established that Cornwall and Somerset are the regions traditionally associated with Arthur, he detected the interpolations in William of Malmesbury's *De Antiquitate Glastoniensis Ecclesiae*, and he was the first to state that Geoffrey of Monmouth was responsible for making Arthur the son of Uther Pendragon, and to differentiate Ambrosius Aurelianus from Myrddin, with whom Geoffrey had confounded him.

He combined the most exacting standards of scholarship with an alarming truculence directed against his fellow antiquarians. To look into Bishop Percy's *Reliques of English Poetry* was, he said, 'to be fatally misled'. The Bishop had said that he possessed a manuscript collection from which he had taken many of the ballads he had printed. Where was it, then? Ritson demanded. When, unlike Geoffrey of Monmouth, the Bishop was able to produce his source, Ritson discovered, to his own satisfaction at least, that the Bishop's transcriptions from it had been not only unscholarly, but positively dishonest. Warton, in the flow of his recollected readings, sometimes made a small error. When he said that Marlowe died of a wound in the chest instead of being stabbed through the eye, Ritson wrote to him: 'Your propensity to corruption and falsehood seems so natural, I have been sometimes tempted to believe, you often substituted a lie in place of a fact, without knowing it.' The work of both these scholars, the one so kind and charming, the other so ferocious, was invaluable.

Of original works dealing with Arthur, the eighteenth century produced none that are remembered, except Fielding's hilarious, enchanting trifle *The Tragedy of Tragedies, or the Life and Death of Tom Thumb the Great*, acted in 1730. This uses a nursery story which says that Tom Thumb was the child of a ploughman in the days of Arthur. Fielding's Dramatis Personae says more about Arthur than the latter is given to say for himself in the text:

> *King Arthur*, a passionate sort of King, husband to Queen Dollalolla, of whom he stands a little in fear, father to Huncamunca, whom he is very fond of, and in love with Glumdalca. (Mr Mullart)
>
> *Merlin*, a conjuror, and in some sort, father to Tom Thumb. (Mr Hallam)
>
> *Queen Dollalolla*, wife to King Arthur and mother to Huncamunca, a woman entirely faultless, saving that she is a little given to drink, a little too much a virago towards her husband, and in love with Tom Thumb. (Mrs Mullart)
>
> *The Princess Huncamunca*, daughter to their Majesties, King Arthur and Queen Dollalolla, of a very sweet, gentle and amorous disposition, equally in love with Lord Grizzle and Tom Thumb and desirous to be married to them both. (Mrs Jones)

Swift told Laetitia Pilkington he had only laughed twice in his life; once was at a performance of *Tom Thumb*.

This is the sharp, sparkling era of the eighteenth century; the last decades, in the oncoming of the Romantic Revival, revert in a surprisingly beautiful manner to the imaginative values of the Celtic myth.

Coleridge, speaking of his love for the Arthurian romances, said that, through them, his mind had been 'habituated to the Vast'. In 1830 Wordsworth wrote a vapid poem, *The Egyptian Maid*, in which a fairy ship, coming from Egypt, is wrecked by Merlin's arts on the Cornish coast; a beautiful girl is washed ashore, senseless, and Arthur causes a procession of knights to file past her; the one whose touch awakens her is to have her for his bride. Galahad proves to be the fortunate assayer. The poem is scarcely recognizable as Wordsworth's; his contribution to the feelings aroused by Arthurian romance was made thirty years before, at the height of his powers, in Number 4 of *Poems on the Naming of Places*. Here he says how he, his sister Dorothy and Coleridge walked along the edge of Grasmere on a rough, natural stone causeway that lined the eastern shore; it had been altered even in his day to a public road for tourist traffic, but on that calm September morning, before the sun had altogether dispersed the mist, they made their way along the difficult path, stopping to look at the dried jetsam, water weeds and ferns, especially the tall Osmunda fern:

> Plant lovelier in its own retired abode
> On Grasmere's beach, than Naiad by the side
> Of Grecian brooks or Lady of the Mere
> Sole-sitting by the shores of old Romance . . .

Warton's interest in historical research was shared by Scott, the inaugurator of the modern historical novel. However cavalier his handling of historical fact, Scott's *mise-en-scène* was the result of wide reading and investigation. *Ivanhoe*, of 1819, and *The Talisman*, of 1825, are set in the reign of Richard 1, and these are the only two of his novels in which he enters a period when Arthur might have been viewed as a living reality; but once, in verse, he treated a theme in which Arthur himself was a leading character.

The Bridal of Triermain was published in 1813, and the opening is that of a romance of the Regency. The heiress Lucy cannot be interested in any of the fashionable and worthless men who fill her castle for a house-party. In the early mornings before these degenerate creatures are up and about, she steals out, to walk in the exquisite scenery of woods and streams with her humble but strong-minded admirer, whose name happens to be Arthur. He tells her a story of King Arthur, who, having ridden out for adventures, finds himself before a castle built on an outcrop of rock that rises in a narrow valley.

Scott bases the tale on the site of a famous optical illusion, noted by the topographer William Hutchinson in his *Excursion to the Lakes*. A group of shattered rocks in Cumberland are known as the Castle Rocks of St John, because in certain lights they present an uncannily convincing appearance of a castle. The state of mind produced by the impression, first that the castle is there, in all its solid masonry, and then that, under the influence of sun and wind, it has not only disappeared but has never been, is seized on by the poet and romancer. Scott makes the castle a reality; Arthur is welcomed there and enjoys a liaison with the enchantress Guendolen. When he leaves her he promises that their child, if a daughter, shall be bestowed in marriage on the victor in a great tournament. Fifteen years later the beautiful but implacable girl Gyneth appears at his court and demands the tribute of being competed for. A tournament is proclaimed, and when havoc and injury have been wreaked, Arthur begs her to release him from his promise, to save his knights from further pain and death. She refuses to forgo her rights, and with the effect of an earthquake, Merlin rises from the ground and declares she shall remain in her castle in an enchanted sleep, until the spell be broken. Six hundred years later Sir Ronald De Vaux, Baron of Triermain, comes to the castle, awakes her and marries her. The last stanzas reveal also that her lover has rescued Lucy from the high-born fortune-hunters. The pair are on their honeymoon, treading a mountain path while servants, horses and carriage wait for them on the lower slopes.

The story is, of course, Scott's own, but his vigour is such that it almost escapes the chilling effect of modern inventions about Arthur. Some passages are like those illustrations of historical figures which, whatever the date of the person they represent, and however correct the details of costume, have obviously been drawn in the first decades of the nineteenth century; but Scott had read so much and visited so many historical remains, his descriptions sometimes come as a revelation, as in the scene of Arthur's entering the castle:

> Yet the silence of that ancient place
> Sunk on his heart and he paused a space,
> Ere yet his horn he blew.
> But, instant as its 'larum rung
> The castle gate was open flung;
> Portcullis rose with crashing groan
> Full harshly up its groove of stone;
> The balance-beams obeyed the blast
> And down the trembling draw-bridge cast.
> The vaulted arch before him lay
> With naught to bar the gloomy way.

When De Vaux arrives on his quest he sees the vision of the castle emerge from what he had thought was a pile of rocks. He gains access to it by heroic determination, and as he kisses the enchanted girl, a terrific tempest wrecks walls, towers and keep; the magic halls melt away but

> In the arms of bold De Vaux
> Safe the Princess lay.

The poet says no one will find entrance to the castle again; it remains for ever 'a vain, illusive show' appearing and disappearing between sun and cloud; but he gives the sense of the deep attraction felt by man towards landscape he has peopled with history and legend:

> and we will love them yet,
> The mountain's misty coronet
> The greenwood and the wold,
> And love the more, that of their maze
> Adventure high of other days
> By ancient bards is told.

The Bridal of Triermain is not wholly serious except in the lines about the associations with scenery; *The Misfortunes of Elphin*, by Peacock, published in 1829, is wholly farcical, but with elements of descriptive power that are surprising in the context. Elphin, King of Caredigion, finds that his kingdom is threatened by the sea, because the tipsy Prince Seithenyn has neglected his duty of keeping the ramparts in repair. When reproached, Seithenyn exclaims with a fine display of drunken dignity: 'I do not know what right the wind has to blow upon me here, nor what business the sea has to show itself here, nor what business you have here . . . but terrible shall be the vengeance of Seithenyn ap Seithyn.' Peacock's description of the walls' collapsing and the moonlit waves tumbling in, is a *tour de force*. King Elphin is imprisoned by a neighbour, and his foster-son, the bard Taliesin, obtains Arthur's help to free him, in recompense for Taliesin's having rescued Guinevere from Melvas. Peacock clearly knew a great deal about the Welsh Arthurian Matter. The sixth-century Welsh Triads were arrangements in threes of various subjects: *The Three Mighty Swineherds, The Three Unfortunate Disclosures, The Three Fortunate Concealments of the Island of Britain*, and he parodies these when a dispute arises at Arthur's court between Guinevere and Gwenvach, the wife of Modred, which leads to *One of the Three Fatal Slaps of the Island of Britain.*

The reader is continually surprised to find a farce so vivid. One of the songs, 'Brilliance of Winter', reminds us of those intense effects of rich light in the descriptions of Chrétien de Troyes:

> Bright the torch light of the hall,
> When the wintry night winds blow,
> Brightest when its splendours fall
> On the mead-cup's sparkling flow,
> While the maiden's smile of light
> Makes the brightness trebly bright.

Like Fielding, Peacock had taken the Arthurian Matter in a comical aspect. The year 1829 was still the reign of George IV; the enormous pressure of the Industrial Revolution with its weight of material prosperity, its overcrowding of cities, its contrasts of wealth and starvation, of brilliance and gloom, had not yet deeply tinged the mental climate.

Arthur's knights in armour coursing a
wild animal, from an illustration by
Gustav Doré to Tennyson's *The Idylls of
the King*

18 The Pre-Raphaelites, Tennyson, Ourselves

In the great renaissance of the Arthurian Matter in the Victorian era, the serious treatment of the myth was, for the first time in all its history, consciously and deliberately artificial.

Malory had said in his colophon to the history of the Graal: 'The Tale of the Sankgreal . . . which is a tale chronicled for one of the truest and one of the holiest that is in this world.' Spenser's readers had found in *The Faerie Queene* descriptions of armed knights, the like of which they could see if they were spectators in the tiltyard at Whitehall. Peele in his *Polyhymnia* described the knights as they appeared in the great tournament of 1591: where, among contestants in white and sky-blue, green and silver, gold and red, the Earl of Essex rode into the lists on a coal-black horse, in black armour, his helmet shaded with black plumage:

> That from his armour borrowed such a light
> As boughs of yew receive from shady stream.

The imaginative use of colour was familiar to the readers of Malory, who described the Knight of the Red Launds, in red armour with his horse trapped in red. The Elizabethan Age was, like the Victorian, one of great national energy and immensely rapid progress, but the armour people saw in the tiltyard was of a kind that had been in use for the last three hundred years.

Milton, who had not had access to modern research, had not only banished Arthur as a subject worthy of an epic, but had barely allowed him historical reality; but, in Milton's lifetime, a civil war had been won by a general who was pre-eminently a cavalry commander. Cromwell had seen that though the King's supporters, who rode their own horses, were splendidly mounted, lack of discipline prevented them from driving home an advantage when they had won it. His own mounted troops were trained never to advance beyond a trot, until he, riding ahead, gave the signal to charge. A thousand years separated them, but Arthur and Cromwell had used the same military means. Arthur's mounted soldiers were armed with swords and spears, and Cromwell's carried swords and pistols, but each commander had gained his victories by superior forces of men on horseback.

Arthur's was still a name worth using to arouse attention through the second half of the seventeenth century; in the eighteenth century, he was the preserve of antiquaries and not seriously written of for the general reader. When he became once more a subject for serious literary interest, we had undergone the illimitable change in the texture of daily life, in the idiom of thought, brought about by the development of the Industrial Revolution. This, with its increasing rapidity and power, separated us once for all, it seemed, from the long history of our past; we belong, irrevocably, to the short section of it contained in the past hundred and fifty years. The beautiful furniture of the Regency with its Roman shapes, that we cherish and use, does not belong to our world as Victorian furniture belongs to it, clumsy, over-elaborate and unacceptable as we may feel that to be. The Regency treasury of furniture and ornament belongs to the era when the combined population of England and Wales was less than ten million, and man, though he had invented the machine, was still in control of it; the machine was an extra hand to man, instead of his being a cog in the machine. The increasing congestion of a rapidly developing population, and a rapidly expanding range of manufactured goods to buy, use and enjoy, are reflected in the Illustrated Catalogue of the International Exhibition of 1862. Its preface says: 'We may not be more moral, more imaginative nor better educated than our ancestors, but we have steam, gas, railways and power looms, while there are more of us and we have more money to spend.' Industrial development outstripped the social conscience; the shocking conditions of employment in mines, factories and mills were paralleled by the slums, which were infernos of vice and suffering, and the lack of sanitation which, in London, led to the raging outbreaks of cholera, typhoid and diphtheria of the 1850s.

The impressive programme of social reform initiated by Victorian philanthropists, scientists and statesmen had got the abuses more or less under control by the last decades of Victoria's reign, but the impression on the minds of young poets and painters of the mid-nineteenth century was that the heroic past, as represented by the Middle Ages, was a lost, ideal world to which they tried to return in imagination. They were not interested in the Middle Ages as social historians, or they might have found even more to shock them in the fourteenth century than in the nineteenth; their attention was focused on the tangible remains of medieval art: the pointed, aspiring architecture of cathedrals, the brilliant beauty of medieval stained glass, the illuminated manuscripts, the gold and silver church plate, so precious now that it cannot be used and remains locked up in banks. They were naturally led to reading Malory's *Morte D'Arthur*.

The last edition of this work, before the nineteenth century, had been published in 1634. Scott had meant to produce an edition, and in *Marmion*, published in 1808, he speaks, in the Introduction to the First Canto, of Lancelot the Champion of the Lake, adventuring into the Chapel Perilous, and of his being granted a vision of the Graal in a dream, as he was not worthy to see it with waking eyes.

In the notes to this introduction, Scott quotes two long passages from Malory, illustrating his allusions. The wide success of *Marmion* may, by publicizing these extracts, have aroused the interest which resulted in the publication of two editions of the *Morte D'Arthur* in 1816, one in two volumes and one in three,

and in yet another the following year, to which Southey, then Poet Laureate, wrote the preface.

The 1816 edition, which was in his father's library, came into the hands of a young man who was to be the last of the great writers on the Matter of Arthur, whose contribution was to earn him a place in the public mind beside Geoffrey of Monmouth and Thomas Malory.

In 1832, Alfred Tennyson was twenty-three, a powerful, gaunt young man with dark hair always rough and wild dark eyes; shy, sincere, subject to morbid melancholy and emerging from a youth of misfortune and misery. He had issued his second book of poems, in which one of them was based on Malory's story of Elaine; he called it *The Lady of Shalott*. Malory himself called Astolat 'Ascalot', and 'Shalott' seems to have been Tennyson's softening of that form. Tennyson's tale had almost none of the original narrative in it, but it is an extremely interesting psychological version of the story, of the girl who has lived safely at home until the sudden birth of a passion destroys her. It is significant that the first treatment of an Arthurian story by a great poet, after the Industrial Revolution, has lifted the story right out of its original mould and put it into one which might have been based on a psycho-analyst's case-book, projected though it is with Tennyson's powers of description, emotion and beautiful sound. In another poem in the same collection, *The Palace of Art*, he describes pictures of the past which were painted on the walls. Of one of them –

> That deep-wounded child of Pendragon
> Mid misty woods on sloping greens
> Dozed in a valley of Avilion,
> Tended by crowned queens –

Kathleen Tillotson [34] says: 'Thus early Tennyson's imagination was caught by the closing scene of the King's life.'

The collection of poems he published in 1842 contained the *Morte d'Arthur*, the most magical of any work written about Arthur after Malory. It also contained *Sir Galahad*, which, again, reproduces not only the elements of the Graal story as given by Malory but actually enlarges the magic sphere:

> Ah, blessed vision, blood of God,
> My spirit beats her mortal bars,
> As down dark tides the glory glides
> And, star-like, mingles with the stars . . .
> I leave the plain, I climb the height,
> No branchy thicket shelter yields,
> But blessed forms in whistling storms
> Fly o'er waste fens and windy fields.

There seems to have been a touch of the supernatural in Tennyson's faculties, and in some of the circumstances of his life. In *Locksley Hall*, published in 1842, he prophesied air-traffic and aerial warfare, and seeing that one of his *chefs-d'œuvre*

Arthur, dying from a blow by Modred,
whom he slew, carried with three queens
on his last voyage to Avalon

was to be a collection of poems on the Matter of Arthur, a theme on which his
mind was at work as early as 1830, it is strange that one of the most important
events of his life, the annihilating loss of his friend Arthur Hallam, in 1833, should
bear a reflection of it. Hallam had become Tennyson's friend at Trinity; his
genial, confident temperament and his warm affection had given Tennyson the
support that he so sorely needed. Hallam died in his sleep from breaking a blood
vessel while he was on a holiday in Vienna; his body was brought to England and
he was buried at Clevedon. Tennyson began to write *In Memoriam* in that year,
and published it seventeen years later in 1850. Some of the verses describe the
ship's drawing near the shores of England with the coffin:

> Fair ship that from the Italian shore
> Sailest the placid ocean plains,
> With my lost Arthur's loved remains
> Spread thy full wings and waft him o'er.

The longing to be reunited with the lost, for the vanished to return, fills one of the
most remarkable feats of sustained emotion ever written. The unexpressed parallel
is plain: the two heroes, each called Arthur, were carried, dying or dead, in a ship,
and in each case the followers were left yearning for him and trying to convince
themselves that he was alive.

> 'Speak to me from the stormy sky!'

The line would have been understood by a Celtic poet of the sixth century.

Tennyson's fame with the general public was established by the publication of
In Memoriam, but his earlier poems, including *The Lady of Shalott*, *Sir Galahad*
and the *Morte d'Arthur*, had gained an interesting following.

To believe that the Mid- and Late-Victorian Age was one of bigotry and self-
complacency, is to receive a series of shocks when one comes to read what some of
the most distinguished Victorians actually thought and said. In 1844, Matthew
Arnold wrote to his friend Arthur Hugh Clough on his sufferings from physical
and mental congestion: 'These are damned times – everything is against one . . .
the spread of luxury, the height to which knowledge has come . . . newspapers,
cities, the sickening consciousness of our difficulties.'

In 1853, he produced *The Scholar Gipsy*, where he speaks to the spirit of the
seventeenth-century student, who was said still to haunt the environs of Oxford:

> O born in days when wits were fresh and clear
> And life ran gaily as the sparkling Thames,
> Before this strange disease of modern life.

In the Oxford water meadows, the Thames was still sparkling; in London in the
1850s, it had inspired *Punch*'s cartoon 'Father Thames introducing his offspring
to the Fair City of London', where the monster rises out of his filthy flood, supporting dying scarecrows labelled Diphtheria, Scrofula, Cholera; while in 1854
was published the most powerful indictment of London ever penned: in *Bleak*

Paintings by Dante Gabriel Rossetti that inspired *The Idylls of the King*: The last meeting of Lancelot and Guinevere, and BELOW Sir Galahad pensive at the Ruined Castle

THE PRE-RAPHAELITES, TENNYSON, OURSELVES

197

House Dickens described the massive, smothering gloom of the London fog, the cholera-infested slum he calls Tom All-Alone's, and the putrefaction of the paupers' burial ground off Chancery Lane.

The group of young painters and poets working in the early 1850s were shocked by the threatening ugliness of much of the contemporary scene. They looked back to the Middle Ages for a source of inspiration which they could bring to bear on the present.

Loosely called the Pre-Raphaelites, they were in revolt against the nineteenth-century method of painting which imitated those of Italian artists of the sixteenth and seventeenth centuries; they felt that massed effects and sombre colours should give way to simplicity, exactitude and colours that were pure and vivid. They were supported in their beliefs by Ruskin, who said that the scientific age should lead the painter to copy what he saw with absolute fidelity to nature.

These views were put into practice by Millais, Holman Hunt, Rossetti, William Morris and Burne-Jones. The two latter, aged twenty and nineteen, met at Exeter College in 1853. Besides sharing opinions on painting, they joined in a passionate admiration of Tennyson. In his first year at Oxford, Burne-Jones wrote to a friend who was still at school: 'Learn *Sir Galahad* by heart; he is to be the patron of our order.'

The Pre-Raphaelites' idea of painting, taken from Italian painters of the fourteenth and early fifteenth centuries, led them naturally to a study of medieval literature. Burne-Jones discovered a copy of Southey's edition of Malory in a bookshop; it was beyond his means but Morris, who was well-to-do, bought it and the work became their Bible. In 1854, Rossetti painted a water-colour of Lancelot and Guinevere meeting above Arthur's tomb. It is entitled: 'How Sir Lancelot parted from Queen Guinevere at King Arthur's tomb and would have kissed her, but she would not'. It is executed with a savage intensity. Guinevere in the habit of a nun has a face gnarled with suffering, while Lancelot leans towards her, crouching over the tomb with a fierce and sinister eagerness. The effigy of Arthur, lying between them, is of a cadaverous, ancient man.

In 1857, Rossetti, Burne-Jones, Morris, with Arthur Hughes and three companions, were allowed to paint the upper reaches of the walls of the Oxford Union Debating Chamber. A gallery runs round the oval room, the walls above it pierced with windows that form ten bays. The friends filled seven of these before the enterprise was brought to a standstill by temperament and misunderstanding. William Morris painted a picture of *Tristram and La Belle Isoude*, whose foreground was filled with sunflowers; Rossetti illustrated the passage quoted from Malory by Scott, with Sir Lancelot dreaming of the Graal, his head leaning against a wall.

Morris, the child of a wealthy father, lived the first years of his life at Woodford Hall on the edge of Epping Forest. When he was eight, he was given a toy suit of armour and rode about the glades in it on his Shetland pony. Unfortunately there is no account of it, where his parents had it made or how they came by it; but while he was painting the walls of the Union, he felt the need of armour to copy and he

had a helmet and a coat of ringed mail forged for him, Burne-Jones said, 'by a stout little smith who had a forge near the castle'. Geoffrey of Monmouth had been a member of a learned community housed in Oxford Castle; seven hundred years later, in that very neighbourhood, mail such as he had seen worn was forged for a painter who was making pictures of the knights of Arthur. Burne-Jones said the mail was very heavy to lift, but once one had put it on, the weight was balanced and not uncomfortable.

When Coventry Patmore saw the paintings in the bays, he wrote in *The Saturday Review* that the colour was 'so brilliant, as to make the walls look like the margins of an illuminated manuscript'. It reads like some dire allegory that the paintings rapidly crumbled and all but disappeared. The walls were unplastered brick and the young men, with a lack of craftsmanship of which Morris, for one, would have been incapable in after years, had not prepared the surface to take the paint; they had only whitewashed it. Today faint ghosts of Arthurian legend glimmer, almost indecipherable on a background murky and dim; but Morris's absorbing interest in the craft of the Middle Ages, and in the Matter of Arthur, took a more enduring form.

In 1858 when he was twenty-four he produced *The Defence of Guinevere and Other Poems*. Of these, the most valuable are perhaps those which give the reader the benefit of Morris's visual imagination; applied in a medieval idiom, which found immortal expression in his wallpapers with designs of sunflowers and pomegranates, his spare, beautiful furniture, the swatches of silk dyed by himself, scarlet, amethyst and gold with red lights in it. One of the narrative poems, *Golden Wings*, describes a group of knights and ladies in a castle, 'midways of a walled garden, In the happy poplar land'.

> Many scarlet bricks were there
> In its walls and old grey stone
> Over which red apples shone
> At the right time of the year.
>
> Deep green water filled the moat.
> Each side had a red brick lip
> Green and mossy with the drip
> Of dew and rain. There was a boat
>
> Of carven wood with hangings green . . .

Five swans lived on the moat and never ate the water-weeds because the knights and ladies fed them every day with bread and cakes. The story is one of those long-drawn miserable ones of an abandoned girl, such as Christina Rossetti told with harrowing force. Morris's tragedy the reader takes as a story, merely. The desertion of Jehane du Castel Beau by the knight, Golden Wings, results in her suicide, the knights' riding out to avenge her in a civil war and the forlorn ladies left weeping and shivering in a castle falling to decay.

Gawaine, who might not see the Holy Grail
'because his eyes were blinded by
thoughts of the deeds of kings', from a
stained-glass window by Edward Burne-Jones

> The draggled swans most eagerly eat
> The green weeds trailing in the moat;
> Inside the rotting, leaky boat
> You see a slain man's stiffened feet.

One of his inspired pieces of re-creation is the poem *In Prison*, about a knight enduring an imprisonment more dolorous than Malory's.

> Wearily, drearily,
> Half the day long
> Flap the great banners
> High over the stone.
> Strangely and eerily
> Sounds the wind's song
> Bending the banner poles.
>
> While all alone
> Watching the loop-hole's spark
> Lie I, with life all dark . . .
> Still strain the banner poles
> Through the wind's song
> Westward the banner rolls
> Over my wrong.

The poem which gives its title to the book is not interesting as a medieval picture; there is very little distinctive detail in it. It is largely a monologue in which Guinevere makes a defence of her conduct before a company of knights headed by Gawaine. The Queen, ashamed to admit the charge, and indignant with her accusers for having made it, pleads her own beauty as an excuse for the love affair, and the fact that she had been bought

> By Arthur's great name and his little love.

Seeing that the reader is expected to be entirely on her side, the poem is extraordinarily modern in its attitude to adultery. Her refrain is:

> Nevertheless you, O Sir Gawaine, lie,
> Whatever may have happened these long years,
> God knows I speak the truth, saying that you lie.

But did he? Gawaine does not speak in the poem; it is implied that he has been harsh and merciless; but how can he be said to have lied? Only by the standards of some truth which is superior to mere factual truth. The attitude is not surprising to us, but it is very surprising in a poem of 1858. In the next piece, *Arthur's Tomb*, inspired by Rossetti's painting, Morris adopts a more conventional attitude; Guinevere in despair reviles Lancelot with his treachery to Arthur and causes him to faint over the tomb. Malory's work had been their origin, but there could hardly be a greater contrast than between these feverish, overwrought passages and his unselfconscious beauty and power.

how gawaine sought the sangreal and might not see it
because his eyes were blinded by thoughts of the deeds of kings

A portent of greatness: the youthful
Arthur shown Excalibur by the Lady of
the Lake

But Tennyson was working in a different key and on a far wider scale. His melancholy might showed itself in his conception of the Round Table, a society where primitive strength, loyalty and chivalry were brought to destruction by the weakness of human nature, by the sensual overcoming the spiritual. He saw an annihilation of the good, redeemed from utter hopelessness only by the faint intimation of dawn:

> God fulfils Himself in many ways
> Lest one good custom should corrupt the world.

Though he was working on other poems almost all the time, the map of his travels for the next fifteen years reads like a chart of his preoccupation with the Matter of Arthur. In 1848 he went to Cornwall, and a fortunate chance introduced him to the Reverend Stephen Hawker, the Vicar of Morwenstowe, a village in a combe above rocks so perilous that ships were continually wrecked on them, and Hawker had to bury the drowned seamen in his churchyard. Scholarly and brave, and also imaginative and wild, he had been known to sit on the rocks at Bude pretending to be a merman, naked except for an oilskin tail and a wig of seaweed. He was deeply interested in Arthurian lore; he was also an intense admirer of Tennyson's poetry, and when he met 'a tall, swarthy man with an eye like a sword' and found him to be the poet, their rapprochement was complete. They wandered on the shore together talking of Arthur, and he lent Tennyson an armful of books and manuscripts, which, as he said, he did not entirely depend on seeing again. In 1863, Hawker himself published part of an Arthurian poem, *The Quest of the Sangreal*; it is passionate and interesting, but no one else's verse on this subject, in this era, abides the touch of Tennyson's.

In the two years from 1855 to 1857, Tennyson made visits of exploration to Glastonbury, Amesbury and Salisbury. He read Nennius, Geoffrey of Monmouth, the Mabinogion, Wace, Layamon, the stanzaic *Morte d'Arthur* and Malory. The Tennyson Research Centre at Lincoln has a collection of some of the books he used. It sounds as if he must also have come upon some version of the legend of the Fisher King. In *Gareth and Lynette*, he describes the carving on the main gate of Camelot of the Lady of the Lake:

> all her dress
> Wept from her sides as water flowing away . . .
> And o'er her breast floated the sacred fish.

In 1856 he went to Wales, where he made a point of talking to the inhabitants of Welsh villages, schoolmasters and cobblers and old men who could still play the harp.

In 1859, he published the first four of what he called *Idylls of the King*: *Merlin and Vivien*, *Geraint and Enid*, *Lancelot and Elaine* and *Guinevere*.

The Victorian Age was the age of great novel-writing, and the first four *Idylls* have some of the attractions of a psychological novel. Somerset Maugham's

saying 'a novel is a story about people who are emotionally connected with each other' defines them to admiration. Tennyson is hampered, as the great novelists are not, by having to focus the past from the viewpoint of the present; the picture of Arthur as 'a modern gentleman of stateliest port' is not only unlike anything that Arthur could conceivably have been, it is unlike anyone at all. But the prejudices and even the justifiable criticisms which the reader entertains when the book is shut, are banished, for stretches of time, outside time, when one is reading some, at least, of the work of a great poet. Tennyson might be claimed as

The magic charms of Nimue beguiling
Merlin to his death, in a painting by
Burne-Jones

204

the easiest to read of all the great poets. In each of the first four *Idylls*, the situation between the two central characters is absorbing, and it is mounted with Tennyson's uncanny force of description. In *Merlin and Vivien*, two passages give almost the whole picture:

> Bellowed the tempest and the rotten branch
> Snapt in the rushing of the river rain
> Above them; and in change of glare and gloom
> Her eyes and neck glittering went and came;

until she has extracted his secret –

> And shrieking out, O fool! the harlot leapt
> Adown the forest, and the thicket closed
> Behind her, and the forest echoed: Fool!

The whole episode derives from a few lines of Malory's; Tennyson alters it from the pursuit by Merlin of an unwilling lady, to the seduction of the reluctant Merlin by Vivien. He altered the name from Nimue to Vivien, which is an alternative said to be owing to scribal miscopying, because Burne-Jones said that Nimue, the Lady of the Lake, was too gracious a character to have this story fastened upon her.

Geraint and Enid, one of the stories of love, misunderstanding and reconciliation, is left very much as it was found; but in *Lancelot and Elaine* Tennyson makes a very drastic change, in the character of Elaine. Malory says that when Lancelot rejected her offer of herself, 'she shrieked shrilly and fell down in a swoon, and then women bore her into her chamber'; Tennyson says:

> Then as a little helpless innocent bird
> That has but one plain message of few notes
>   . . . so this simple maid
> Went half the night, repeating: Must I die? . . .
> And, him or death, she muttered, death or him,
> Again and like a burden: him or death.

The whole version is pathetic rather than tragic; but after the appearance of her corpse in the barge, which, again, Tennyson makes much gentler than Malory's, putting a lily in her hand, the King says to Lancelot:

>   Now I would to God,
> Seeing the homeless trouble in thine eyes
> Thou couldst have loved this maiden . . .
> Who might have brought thee, now a lonely man,
> Wifeless and heirless, noble issue, sons
> Born to the glory of thy name and fame,
> My knight, the great Sir Lancelot of the Lake.

The readers who were devoted to great novels would find here a similar attraction.

The parting of Lancelot and Guinevere:
an illustration by Doré to *The Idylls of
the King*

The *Idyll* presenting the greatest problem in appreciation is *Guinevere*; it is the most powerful and it is the one which in our time has the scales most heavily weighted against it. The modern tendency to sympathize with the adulterers rather than with their victim means that most readers are against Arthur before they so much as hear what he has to say, and even in 1859 Arthur's reproaching his wife with the ruin of his life's work as she lies prostrate on the floor, was felt by some people to be disagreeable. Meredith said that Arthur lectured his Queen as if he were a curate. If he did, curates in Meredith's day must have had an amazing eloquence; but the task Tennyson had set himself was a formidable one: to enlist sympathy for Arthur, after he had so brilliantly gained it for the lovers. Guinevere (in *Lancelot and Elaine*) says to Lancelot:

> The low sun makes the colour; I am yours,
> Not Arthur's.

In her eulogy of Arthur she can only say:

> I thought I could not breathe in that fine air,
> That pure severity of perfect light.

It would not be impossible to make a convincing character of whom this could be said; the lines could represent an unusual and chilling but not unrecognizable man; but to say of him

> Who wast, as is the conscience of a saint
> Among his warring senses, to thy knights,

is to make the King an abstraction, instead of an injured and suffering human being. It is of course much easier to gain sympathy for some one in agonies of remorse than for some one who speaks in a morally superior and censorious role, and Guinevere's lines are the success of the poem; but Tennyson's powers are such, that there are some piercing effects even with Arthur's. When the King says of the ruinous effect of the adultery

> The children born of thee are sword and fire,
> Red ruin and the breaking-up of laws,

a man whose wife has deserted him for another man, and who has then been deprived of his children because the court thinks it better they should be with their mother, is likely to see some valid comment in the lines.

Arthur's best words are those in which he makes a plea for their union in another world; their stamp of deep emotion has made a separate, self-contained quotation of

> Not Lancelot, nor another.

When he has departed in the shrouding mist to meet his death in the last battle, Guinevere exclaims:

> The years will roll into the centuries
> And mine will ever be a name of scorn –

a prophecy strangely fulfilled when, in West of England villages even today, a flighty woman is called 'a regular Guinevere'. But she says:

> I must not dwell on that defeat of fame,

and after three years of repentance and devoted work for the community which has sheltered her, she passes

> To where, beyond these voices, there is peace.

If some of the passages strike a jarring note, the end is faultless. But it is arresting, as a contrast of the two centuries, to put Tennyson's version and Malory's side by

Guinevere, painted by William Morris
from Jane Burden, who soon afterwards
became his wife

side. The latter makes it overwhelmingly clear that it was the love of Lancelot and Guinevere which wrecked the society of the Round Table, and makes Guinevere condemn herself as responsible for Arthur's death, in words that have never been bettered; but he nevertheless says of her, in his apostrophe to the month of May: 'Therefore all ye that be lovers, call unto your remembrance the month of May, as did Queen Guinevere, for whom I make here a little mention, that while she lived, she was a true lover, and therefore she had a good end.' In 1469, a queen convicted of adultery would have been judged guilty of high treason, and could, legally, have been burned alive, as Guinevere was in danger of being. In 1859, such a penalty would have been completely unthinkable, but the moral severity of the two ages seems in inverse proportion to the severity of their sentences.

Tennyson's steeping of his mind in the sources of Arthurian legend sometimes produced the following-out of an intimation in a piece of fascinating description. Layamon said that, at Arthur's birth, fairies – 'alven' – were present. In *Guinevere*, the novice who does not recognize the Queen tells her that before Guinevere's wicked influence dispelled them, the land was full of fairies. The novice's father

> Himself beheld three spirits, mad with joy,
> Come dashing down on a tall wayside flower
> That shook beneath them,

and when he arrived at Camelot,

> A wreath of airy dancers, hand in hand,
> Swung round the lighted lantern of the hall.

Malory says that, at the Christmas after the death of Elaine, 'there was jousts made for a diamond; who that jousted best, should have a diamond.' Tennyson transfers the diamond prize backwards to the Winchester jousts, and makes it not a single diamond but the ninth and last awarded in a series, and says from where they had been brought. Arthur, he says, had come upon the ancient skeletons of two fratricides, lying in a distant, rocky glen. One had been a king and still wore a diamond crown. His skeleton being almost invisible, 'lichened into colour with the crags', Arthur had trodden on its neck,

> and from the skull, the crown
> Rolled into light, and turning on its rims
> Fled like a glittering rivulet to the tarn.

Ruskin said of the 1859 publication, that the *Idylls* contained 'word-painting such as never was, for concentration', and he felt that such great powers 'ought not to be spent on visions of things past, but on the living present'. But he, and the reviewer in *Bentley's Quarterly Miscellany* for October 1859, were at variance with what the public felt. The latter had said: 'Say what people like, the world in general cares uncommonly little about King Arthur.' This was proved wrong by an eager readership.

Tennyson continued to trace the Arthurian map. In 1860 he went to Tintagel,

in 1864 to Brittany. In 1869, he published four more *Idylls*: *The Coming of Arthur*, *The Holy Grail*, *Pelleas and Ettard*, and *The Passing of Arthur*, his original *Morte d'Arthur* of 1842, with new lines preceding it. The visit to Tintagel had produced the invention of Arthur's birth, a combination of Geoffrey of Monmouth's siting his conception at Tintagel, and of the tale of Modred's being washed ashore as a baby. The description is terrific, of a night of storm in which Merlin descends 'from the castle gate-way by the chasm', down to the cove where a tremendous sea is pounding in, until the great ninth wave

> slowly rose and plunged
> Roaring, and all the wave was in a flame
> And down the wave and in the flame was borne
> A naked babe, and rode to Merlin's feet.

The Holy Grail, of which the story is narrated by Percival, who has become a monk, has not the magic of *Sir Galahad*, written nearly thirty years before, but the descriptions of the Chalice, of which the vision was vouchsafed to Percival's sister, a nun, has Tennyson's brilliant visual imagery:

> Rose red, with beatings in it, as if alive.

When Sir Bors describes it as

> In colour like the fingers of a hand
> Before a burning taper,

one is reminded of a Pre-Raphaelite reaction to colour produced by flesh with light through it. Holman Hunt said to Mr Justice Lushington, who had noticed the ears of a witness bright crimson against the light, that he had painted the foremost sheep in his picture *Strayed Sheep* with the sun shining through its ears, 'making them so rosy, the prosaic and unobservant spectator has often said that the colour must be unwarranted'.

The King says at the end of the poem that he cannot go on the Quest himself because his duties as a king tie him to one spot, as if he were a ploughing serf, but that visions sometimes come to him:

> Until this earth he walks on, seems not earth,
> This air that smites his forehead, is not air
> But vision – yea, his very hand and foot
> In moments when he feels he cannot die
> And knows himself no vision to himself.

Tennyson once said to some friends to whom he read this passage: 'You may tell me this hand and foot are not mine, that they may be only an imaginative symbol of my existence, and I could believe you, but you can't convince me that *I* am not an Eternal Reality.' The mystical strain in himself was another element in his reinterpretation of the figure, behind whom lay a past in which men had raised Stonehenge.

BELOW Arthur of England: a living model
photographed by J. Margaret Cameron in the
time of Tennyson to illustrate scenes from
The Idylls of the King

210   In Malory's *Pelleas and Ettarre*, Pelleas wins the gold circlet at a tournament
where it is offered as a prize to whatever knight can prove his lady the fairest by
force of arms. This tribute does not mollify Ettarre's scorn of him, and the Lady
of the Lake on his behalf works a cruel revenge on her; she disenchants Pelleas so
that he no longer cares a straw about Ettarre, and lays Ettarre under the spell of a
hopeless passion for him. Though brought about by magic in the story, the situation
is one not unknown in real life, where it is called 'bad timing'. Tennyson, however,

alters it to make a prophecy of the tragedy coming on. Pelleas, finding Ettarre
sleeping with Gawaine, runs demented; his appearance in Arthur's hall as the
raving victim of betrayed love strikes a chill on many who are present:

> And all talk died, as in a grove all song
> Beneath the shadow of some bird of prey.

The fame and success of the 1869 volume made it impossible for anyone now to
hold the view that 'the world in general cares uncommonly little about King

Arthur.' In 1853, Charlotte Yonge in *The Heir of Redclyffe* made Guy Morville, when asked to name his favourite hero of fiction, say, 'Sir Galahad.' His cousin Charles exclaims, 'Sir how much?' Guy tells him about Malory's *Morte d'Arthur*, of which Charles has never heard, and says its two fat volumes were his boating book during three summers. As Kathleen Tillotson says, 'By 1870, there can have been no one left to say Sir how much?'

Not only had Tennyson his own immense public, he had opened the vein for other writers which has been mined ever since, and in the forms of history, archaeology, theatre, film and fiction is continuously successful today, fulfilling the prediction of Arthur in Geoffrey of Monmouth's *Prophecies of Merlin*, 'Renowned shall he be in the mouth of the peoples, and his deeds shall be as meat unto them that tell thereof.' In 1870, the *Dublin Review* said that gentlemen were calling their racehorses after the knights of the Round Table, though the writer does not mention any of the horses' names.

Tennyson rounded off his great enterprise with three more sections: *The Last Tournament*, which he wrote in 1871, *Gareth and Lynette* in 1872, and *Balin and Balan* in 1873. This made the collection up to twelve books. Up till now the pieces had been published out of chronological order; now it was possible to arrange them, from *The Coming of Arthur*, through the story of the rise and success of the Round Table, to the poisoning of the society by the example of Lancelot's amour with the Queen, to its final destruction and Arthur's passing, as consecutive parts of a complete whole, a whole which had employed the poet's mind for over thirty years.

Tennyson's great reputation does not now rest on *The Idylls of the King*, and, with one exception, it is impossible to read them without feeling that some passages are contrived and ineffective and beneath his own level. That exception is the *Morte d'Arthur*, renamed in the 1869 volume *The Passing of Arthur*. Though numerous Victorian writers made verses on some part or other of the Arthurian theme, only one other poet produced anything to equal it; Swinburne's *Tristram of Lyonesse*, published in 1882, is not about Arthur, but in his description of the sea off the Cornish coast and of Tintagel,

> And on the mighty-moulded stairs that clomb
> Sheer from the fierce lip of the lapping foam . . .
> Stair based on stair, between the rocks unhewn
> To those strange halls, where through the tidal tune
> Rang loud or lower, from soft or strengthening sea
> Tower shouldering tower . . .

the lines are a link in the chain of inspired writing about the Arthurian scene which stretches back into our past. Swinburne's passion for the sea made him evoke it as a third entity in the story of *Tristram and Iseult*. Tennyson divined the significance of water in the myth that had been made out of the real figure of Arthur. His line, uttered by Merlin in *The Coming of Arthur*,

The release of the Sword: Excalibur cast
over the water by Sir Bedivere and grasped
by the Lady of the Lake

From the great deep to the great deep he goes,

is a contribution to the store of great utterances about Arthur, made at a time when it might have been thought we had outlived the power to make them.

As a rule, when Tennyson alters Malory's material or departs from it altogether, we dislike the change. It is significant that, in *The Passing of Arthur*, the description of eerie, intense beauty is firmly based on Malory; the details of the original are very small but all the brilliant features have been taken from points mentioned by Malory, taken and enlarged and made more magical.

Malory says the final battle was fought 'upon a down by Salisbury, not far from the sea-side', which shows that he did not know Salisbury himself. Southampton Water would be the nearest sea-coast to Salisbury, separated from it by part of Wiltshire and part of Hampshire. Sir Lucan and Sir Bedivere carry Arthur to 'a little chapel not far from the sea-side'. When Sir Lucan went off to reconnoitre the battlefield, 'he saw and hearkened by moonlight, how the pillers and robbers were come into the field.' Tennyson says:

> The bold Sir Bedivere uplifted him . . .
> And bore him to a chapel nigh the field,
> A broken chancel and a broken cross
> That stood on a dark strait of barren land.
> On one side lay the ocean, and on one
> Lay a great water, and the moon was full.

Malory says that Bedivere, having received Arthur's command to take the sword Excalibur and throw it 'in that water', Sir Bedivere 'beheld that noble sword, that the pommel and the haft was all of precious stones, and then he said to himself, if I throw this rich sword in the water, thereof shall never come good, but harm and loss'.

With Tennyson, this has become

> The winter moon . . .
> . . . sparkled keen with frost against the hilt,
> For all the haft twinkled with diamond sparks,
> Myriads of topaz-lights and jacinth work
> Of subtlest jewellery.

When Sir Bedivere finally obeys the King, Malory says he took the sword 'and went to the water side, and there he bound the girdle about the hilts and threw the sword as far into the water as he might'. Tennyson sees it happening:

> . . . The great brand
> Made lightnings in the splendour of the moon,
> And flashing round and round, whirled in an arch,
> Shot like a streamer of the northern morn.

When Bedivere has carried the King on his back to the water's edge, he finds a

214

barge floating there, with black-stoled ladies in it who wept and shrieked. Tennyson makes the brief statement into a picture of the sound:

> And from them rose
> A cry that shivered to the tingling stars . . .
> A lamentation like a wind that shrills
> All night in a waste land where no one comes
> Or hath come, since the making of the world.

Malory says that Bedivere followed the departing barge with his eyes as long as he could. 'And as soon as Sir Bedivere had lost sight of the barge, he wept and wailed, and so took to the forest.' Tennyson says he climbed as high as he could and saw,

> Straining his eyes beneath an arch of hand,
> Or thought he saw, the speck that bore the king
> Down that long water opening on the deep,
> Somewhere far off, pass on and on, and go
> From less to less and vanish into light.

These are the last great lines written about Arthur in our literature.

The development of the myth, the pertinacity with which people have held to it, been eager to repeat and add to it, and see in it a reflection of their own interests and needs is like nothing else in our history.

Men will not now, as they once did, knock other men down for disagreeing with their views on the historicity of Arthur, but interest in Arthur has never been stronger than it is today. The story is treated in fiction for a host of readers, and captivates them in all the other media, but the most exciting aspect of this modern interest is the research and insight of historians and archaeologists. These have stripped away the surrounding legends, the ornaments, the very name of king, but what they have left is incomparably more valuable than the rich incrustations of a thousand years.

Some extraordinary charisma rested on this soldier. The people who told and listened to tales about him made him a king, to put him into the most glorious shape they could imagine. The influence of his name carried his story to France, and from France back again to us. Dr A. L. Rowse[35] has said: 'It was the hero of the losing side, King Arthur, who imposed himself on the imagination, the chief and lasting contribution of the Celts to the mind and literature of Europe.'

So far as an explanation may be found, it lies perhaps in the unforgotten effect made on a courageous, desperate people, whom a leader of exceptional powers delivered, for his own lifetime, from a cruel and abominable enemy.

We find ourselves threatened today; our sick condition is imaged in the pollution of our rivers and of the sea around our shores, and the long-term outlook seems to forecast

> The darkness of that battle in the West
> Where all of high and holy dies away.

This makes us look with heightened interest on the two entries in the Easter
Annals:

> 518. Battle of Badon, in which Arthur carried the
> cross of our Lord Jesus Christ on his shoulders for
> three days and three nights and the Britons were
> victors.

> 539. The strife of Camlann, in which Arthur and
> Modred perished.

They are all we have of fact, but of what an edifice they made the foundation! –
not of stories only but of belief, that

> An Arthur should yet come to help the English.

Literary References

1 Hawkins, Gerald S., and White, John B. *Stonehenge Decoded*. New York, Doubleday, 1965; London, Souvenir Press, 1966.

2 Loomis, Roger Sherman. 'The Legend of Arthur's Survival' in *Arthurian Literature in the Middle Ages: A Collaborative History*, edited by R. S. Loomis. Oxford, Clarendon Press, 1959.

3 Saklatvala, Beram. *Arthur, Roman Britain's Last Champion*. Newton Abbot, David & Charles, 1971.

4 Alcock, Leslie. *Arthur's Britain: History and Archeology, A.D. 367–634*. London, Allen Lane, Penguin Press, 1971.

5 Jackson, Kenneth Hurlstone. 'The Arthur of History' in *Arthurian Literature in the Middle Ages*. Oxford, Clarendon Press, 1959.

6 Wildman, S. G. *The Black Horses, English Inns and King Arthur*. London, John Baker, 1971.

7 Dent, A. A., and Goodall, D. M. *The Foals of Epona: A History of British Ponies from the Bronze Age to Yesterday*. London, Gallery Press, 1962.

8 Alcock, Leslie. *By South Cadbury is That Camelot: Excavations at Cadbury Castle, 1966–70*. London, Thames & Hudson, 1972.

9 Morris, John. '*The Age of Arthur: A History of the British Isles from 350 to 650*. London, Weidenfeld &

Nicolson, 1973.

10 Barber, Richard. *Arthur of Albion: An Introduction to the Arthurian Literature and Legends of England*. London, Boydell Press, 1961.

11 Parry, John H., and Caldwell, Robert A. 'Geoffrey of Monmouth' in *Arthurian Literature in the Middle Ages*. Oxford, Clarendon Press, 1959.

12 Loomis, Roger Sherman. *The Development of Arthurian Romance*. London, Hutchinson University Library, 1963.

13 Chambers, E. K. *Arthur of Britain: The Story of King Arthur in History and Legend*. London, Sidgwick & Jackson, 1966.

14 Weston, Jessie L. *From Ritual to Romance*. Cambridge University Press, 1920.

15 Frappier, Jean. 'The Vulgate Cycle' in *Arthurian Literature in the Middle Ages*. Oxford, Clarendon Press, 1959.

16 Evans, Sebastian (translator). Geoffrey of Monmouth's *History of the Kings of Britain*. London, Dent, Everyman Series, 1963.

17 Evans, Sebastian (translator). *The High History of the Holy Grail*. London, Dent, 1899.

18 Nitze, William Albert. 'Perlesvaus' in *Arthurian Literature in the Middle Ages*. Oxford, Clarendon Press, 1959.

19 Radford, C. A. Ralegh. *Glastonbury Abbey: The Pictorial History*. London, Pitkin, 1970.

20 Maltwood, K. E. *A Guide to

Glastonbury's Temple of the Stars*. London, James Clarke, 1964.

21 Shakespeare. *Henry IV, Part I*, Act IV, Scene 1, lines 104–10.

22 Thomas Malory. *Morte D'Arthur*, Book XXI, Chapter 1.

23 Ibid., XIX, 13.

24 Ibid., VI, 10.

25 Ibid, II, 16.

26 Ibid., I, 16.

27 Ibid., XVI, 12.

28 Ibid., VII, 6.

29 Greenlaw, E. A. 'Studies in Spenser's Historical Allegory' in *John Hopkins Monographs in Literary History*, Vol. 2. Baltimore and London, 1932.

30 French, Peter J. *John Dee*. London, Routledge & Kegan Paul, 1972.

31 Smith, J. C., and de Selincourt, E. (editors). *The Poetical Works of Edmund Spenser*. Henry Frowde, Oxford University Press, 1912.

32 Strype, John. *The Life and Acts of Matthew Parker, Archbishop of Canterbury*. London, 1711.

33 Johnston, Arthur. *Enchanted Ground: A Study of Mediaeval Romance in the Eighteenth Century*. Athlone Press of the University of London, 1964.

34 Tillotson, Kathleen. 'Tennyson's Serial Poem' in *Mid-Victorian Studies* by Geoffrey and Kathleen Tillotson. Athlone Press of the University of London, 1965.

35 Rowse, A. L. *The Spirit of English History*. London, Cape, 1943.

Bibliography of Other Sources Used

Ashe, Geoffrey (editor). *The Quest for Arthur's Britain*. London, Granada Publishers, 1968.

Ashe, Geoffrey. *Camelot and the Vision of Albion*. London, Heinemann, 1971.

Barber, Richard. *The Knight in Chivalry*. New York, Scribner, 1970.

Barber, Richard. *King Arthur in Legend and History*. London, Sphere Books, 1973.

Brinkley, Roberta Florence. *Arthurian Legend in the Seventeenth Century*. Oxford University Press, 1932.

Comfort, W. W. (translator). *Arthurian Romances : Chrétien de Troyes*. London, Dent, 'Everyman' Series, 1967.

Finlayson, John (editor). *Morte Arthure*. London, Edward Arnold, 1967.

Gaunt, William. *The Pre-Raphaelite Tragedy*. Paperback. London, Cape, 1965.

Mason, Eugene (translator). *Arthurian Chronicles : Wace, Layamon*. London, Dent, 'Everyman' Series, 1966.

Matarasso, Pauline M. *The Quest of the Holy Grail*. Harmondsworth, Penguin, 1969.

Richmond, Ian A. *Roman Britain*. Harmondsworth, Penguin, 1967.

Saxtorph, Niels M. *Warriors and Weapons of Early Times*. London, Blandford Press, 1972.

Stone, Brian. *Sir Gawaine and the Green Knight*. Harmondsworth, Penguin, 1971.

Taylor, A. J. 'Military Architecture' in *Mediaeval England*, edited by Austin Lane Poole, Vol. 1. Oxford University Press, 1958.

Vinaver, Eugène (editor). *The Works of Sir Thomas Malory*. Oxford University Press, 1954.

Whitelock, Dorothy. *The Beginnings of English Society*. Harmondsworth, Penguin, 1966.

Wilkinson, Frederick. *Arms and Armour*. London, Hamlyn, 1971.

Illustrations Acknowledgments

The producers of this book wish to express their thanks to all those indicated by the list below, who have kindly given permission for items from their collections to be reproduced here.

Abbreviations used are:

AGB City Museums and Art Gallery, Birmingham

BL Reproduced by permission of the British Library Board, London

BM The Trustees of the British Museum, London

BN La Bibliothèque Nationale, Paris

BR Bibliothèque Royale Albert Ier, Brussels

Bodleian The Curators of the Bodleian Library, Oxford

Mansèll The Mansell Collection, London

NPG National Portrait Gallery, London

PM Pierpont Morgan Library, New York

RTH Radio Times Hulton Picture Library, London

V&A By courtesy of the Victoria and Albert Museum, London

A number in **bold** type indicates the page facing a colour plate.

Reverse of frontispiece MS. Fr. Carpentras 403 f. 7v. BELOW MS. Fr. Carpentras 403 f. 151. Both Bib. Inguimbertine, Paris. Photos: Giraudon.

Frontispiece Beardsley illustration to Malory's *Morte D'Arthur*, 1909. BL.

8 Photo: Edwin Smith.

11 Photo: Aerofilms.

13 Photo: Edwin Smith.

15 Photo: W. F. Meadows; Barnaby's Picture Library.

17 Photo: Edwin Smith.

18 Graffito, after M. A. R. Colledge, *The Parthians*.

23 MS. Douce 178 f. 156v. Italian *c.* 1300–25. Bodleian.

25 From the *Chronicle of England* by Peter Langtoft, MS. Royal 20 AII f. 3. *c.* 1307–27. BL.

26 MS. Harley 3859 f. 190a. 11th c. BL.

29 From the *Chronicles of St Albans*, MS. 6 f. 43v. *c.* 1470. The Archbishop of Canterbury and the Trustees of the Lambeth Palace Library, London.

31 *Historia Britonum*, MS. Harley 3859 f. 187. 11th c. RIGHT MS. Add 17006 f. 8. Both photos: BL.

32 MS. 10294 f. 93. 13th c. BL.

33 Photo: Robert Estall.

35 Photo: Bryan Campbell; copyright Camera Press.

36–7 MS. XX f. 163v. Dutch early 14th c. Koninklijke Nederlandse Akademie van Wetenschappen, Amsterdam, on loan to the Koninklijke Bib., The Hague.

38 Archivolt at Modena Cathedral, *c.* 1100–10. Photo: Orlandini. BELOW Mosaic at Otranto Cathedral, *c.* 1165. Photo: Mansell.

43 Map by Tom Stalker-Miller.

46 MS. Egerton 3028 f. 49. 13th c. BL.

48 MS. Egerton 3028 f. 51. 13th c. BL.

49 MS. Royal 14 EIII f. 89. French *c.* 1316. BL.

52 From the *Chronicle of England* by Peter Langtoft, MS. Royal 20 AII f. 3v. *c.* 1307–27. BL.

55 Photo: Aerofilms.

57 From *Les chroniques de Hainaut*,

MS. 9243 f. 42, 1468. BR.

59 MS. Douce 199 f. 252v. French mid-14th c. Bodleian.

61 From *Liber Merlini Ambrosii* edited by Galfridus, MS. Cotton Claudius BVII Art. 15 f. 224, 1250–70. BL.

67 Wace's *Chronicles*, MS. Egerton 3028 f. 48. RIGHT MS. Egerton 3028 f. 37. Both photos: BL.

70 Chertsey Abbey tile. BM.

72 From *Le recueil des poesies françaises*, MS. Fr. 3142 f. 256, *c.* 1280–90. Bib. Arsenal, Paris. Photo: Giraudon. Sicilian quilt, *c.* 1295. V&A. Photo: Sally Chapel.

76–7 MS. 805 f. 39. 1300–25. PM.

78 MS. Fr. 3479 f. 1. 15th c. Bib. Arsenal, Paris. Photo: Giraudon. BELOW MS. Douce 199 f. 221v. French 14th c. Bodleian.

80 MS. Fr. 3479 f. 550. Early 15th c. Bib. Arsenal, Paris. Photo: Giraudon.

81 MS. 805 ff. 119v., 158, 166. 1300–25. PM.

82 MS. Fr. 118 f. 219v. French *c.* 1405. BN. Photo: Giraudon. OPPOSITE MS. Fr. 343 f. 4. Italian *c.* 1370–80. BN.

85 Photo: Derek Bayes; Aspect Pictures.

89 MS. Fr. 12577 f. 18v. French *c.* 1330. BN.

91 Miniature from a 12th-c. Syriac codex. MS. Add. 7169 f. 11r. BL. BELOW MS. Fr. 343 f. 3. Italian *c.* 1370–80. BN.

94 MS. Fr. 112 Vol. 3 f. 193v. *c.* 1470. BN.

96 MS. Fr. 112 f. 5. *c.* 1470. BN.

97 *Les chroniques de Hainaut*, MS. 9243 f. 45, 1468. BR.

98 Edward the Black Prince

(1330–76). Mary Evans Picture Library.
103 From the *Chronicle of England* by Peter Langtoft, MS. Royal 20 AII f. 4r. 14th c. BL.
104 MS. Fr. 3479 f. 516, *c.* 1450. Bib. Arsenal, Paris. Photo: Giraudon.
106 From Froissart's *Chroniques*, MS. Harley 4379 f. 43. 15th c. BL.
108 MS. Fr. 112 Vol. 3 f. 15v. *c.* 1470. BN. Photo: Giraudon.
111 MS. 805 f. 109, 14th c. PM.
112–13 MS. 805 f. 262, 14th c. PM.
114 Photo: J. Allan Cash.
118 MS. Fr. Carpentras 403 f. 7v. 14th c. Bib. Inguimbertine. Photo: Giraudon.
121 Tomb of Edward the Black Prince, Dean and Chapter of Canterbury Cathedral. Photo: Edwin Smith.
124 MS. Cotton Nero AX f. 129. English poem *c.* 1400. BL.
126 Dean and Chapter of Lincoln Cathedral. *c.* 1350. Photo: Edwin Smith.
128 *Sir Gawaine and the Green Knight*, MS. Cotton Nero AX f. 94. English poem *c.* 1400. BL.
129 MS. Fr. 343 f. 8v. Italian *c.* 1370–80. BN.
131 Richard Neville (1428–71). BL: Weidenfeld Archives.
134 Winchester Castle. Photo: J. Allan Cash.
136 Woodcut to Malory's *Morte D'Arthur*, Wynkyn de Worde edition, 1529. BL. Photo: Freeman.
138 MS. 38117 f. 97v. BL. OPPOSITE MS. Fr. 95 f. 159v. Flemish written in French *c.* 1290. BN.
142 MS. Douce 199 f. 44v. Mid-

14th c. Bodleian.
143 MS. Douce 199 f. 70bv. Mid-14th c. Bodleian.
144 MS. Add. Meladius 12228 f. 202v. *c.* 1352. BL.
145 Tapestry. 1490. Historisches Museum, Basle.
149 MS. Douce 199 f. 157v. Mid-14th c. Bodleian.
151 MS. Add. 10294 f. 94. French *c.* 1316. BL.
154 Woodcut to first edition, Edmund Spenser's *The Faerie Queene*, 1590. Photo: RTH.
160 Illustration by C. M. B. Morrell for 19th-c. edition of *The Faerie Queene*. Photo: RTH.
162 Illustration after C. M. B. Morrell for 19th-c. edition of *The Faerie Queene*. Photo: RTH. OPPOSITE Robert Dudley, oil by Van der Muellen, *c.* 1565–70. NPG.
164 Elizabeth I by Nicholas Hilliard, *c.* 1480. Photo: RTH.
166 In the Royal Chapel, Innsbruck. *c.* 1480. Photo: RTH.
168 Oil by Daniel Mytens, 1621. NPG.
170 Stage set for the *Barrier Masque*; RIGHT costume for the *Masque of Oberon*. Both by Inigo Jones. Devonshire Collection, Chatsworth. Reproduced by permission of the Trustees of the Chatsworth Settlement. Photo: Courtauld Inst.
173 Costume by Inigo Jones for the *Lords Masque*. Devonshire Collection, Chatsworth. Reproduced by permission of the Trustees of the Chatsworth Settlement. Photo: Courtauld Inst.
176 18th-c. engraving. Mary Evans Picture Library.
179 Photo: Ron Startup/Observer;

copyright Camera Press.
184 Engraving from *Old England*, Book II. Photo: RTH.
190 From the original engraving by Gustave Doré to the 1867 edition of *The Idylls of the King*. Lent by Pauline Harrison.
192 *Morgan le Fee* by Arthur Sandys. 1864. AGB. Photo: Cecil Reilly Assoc.
193 Detail of *The Lady of Shalott* by J. W. Waterhouse, 1888. Tate Gallery. Photo: Witty.
194 Illustration by Daniel Maclise to Tennyson's *Morte D'Arthur*, 1893 edition. London Library.
196 Paintings by D. G. Rossetti. 1860. Tate Gallery. BELOW AGB.
198 Detail of tapestry by Edward Burne-Jones and William Morris. AGB. Photo: Cecil Reilly Assoc.
201 One of four windows in the series *The Queste for the Sangreal*. V&A. Photo: Carltograph.
203 Illustration by Daniel Maclise to Tennyson's *Morte D'Arthur*, 1893 edition. London Library.
205 *The Beguiling of Merlin* by Edward Burne-Jones, 1874. Lady Lever Art Gallery, Port Sunlight.
207 From the original engraving by Gustave Doré to the 1867 edition of *The Idylls of the King*. Lent by Pauline Harrison.
208 *Guinevere* by William Morris, 1858. Tate Gallery. Photo: Witty.
209 *Arthur in Avalon*, detail from tapestry designed by Edward Burne-Jones, 1881–98. Museo de Arte de Ponce, Puerto Rico.
210 Photograph by J. Margaret Cameron for *The Idylls of the King*, 1874. Photo: Royal Photographic Society.
212 Drawing by Aubrey Beardsley for 1909 edition of Malory's *Morte D'Arthur*. BL.

Index

A number in **bold** type refers to the page facing a colour plate;
a page number in *italics*, to a black-and-white illustration.